Weather and Climate

PRENTICE HALL Science Explorer

PEARSON

Boston, Massachusetts
Glenview, Illinois
Shoreview, Minnesota
Upper Saddle River, New Jersey

Weather and Climate

Book-Specific Resources

Student Edition
StudentExpress™ CD-ROM
Interactive Textbook Online
Teacher's Edition
All-in-One Teaching Resources
Color Transparencies
Guided Reading and Study Workbook
Student Edition in MP3 Audio
Discovery Channel School® Video
Consumable and Nonconsumable Materials Kits

Program Print Resources

Integrated Science Laboratory Manual
Computer Microscope Lab Manual
Inquiry Skills Activity Books
Progress Monitoring Assessments
Test Preparation Workbook
Test-Taking Tips With Transparencies
Teacher's ELL Handbook
Reading Strategies for Science Content

Differentiated Instruction Resources

Adapted Reading and Study Workbook
Adapted Tests
Differentiated Instruction Guide for Labs and Activities

Program Technology Resources

TeacherExpress™ CD-ROM
Interactive Textbooks Online
PresentationExpress™ CD-ROM
ExamView®, Test Generator CD-ROM
Lab zone™ Easy Planner CD-ROM
Probeware Lab Manual With CD-ROM
Computer Microscope and Lab Manual
Materials Ordering CD-ROM
Discovery Channel School® DVD Library
Lab Activity Video Library—DVD and VHS
Web Site at PearsonSchool.com

Spanish Print Resources

Spanish Student Edition
Spanish Guided Reading and Study Workbook
Spanish Teaching Guide With Tests

Acknowledgments appear on page 182, which constitutes an extension of this copyright page.

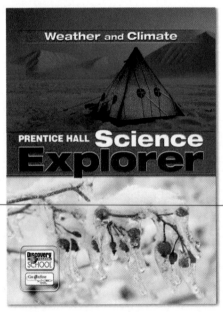

Cover
The "midnight sun" of the Arctic illuminates a tent on Spitsbergen (top). Ice covers rose hips in Rock Bridge State Park, Missouri (bottom).

13-digit ISBN 978-0-13-365109-6
10-digit ISBN 0-13-365109-6
6 7 8 9 10   V063   12 11 10

PEARSON

Program Authors

Michael J. Padilla, Ph.D.
Associate Dean and Director
Eugene T. Moore School of Education
Clemson University
Clemson, South Carolina

Michael Padilla is a leader in middle school science education. He has served as an author and elected officer for the National Science Teachers Association and as a writer of the National Science Education Standards. As lead author of Science Explorer, Mike has inspired the team in developing a program that meets the needs of middle grades students, promotes science inquiry, and is aligned with the National Science Education Standards.

Ioannis Miaoulis, Ph.D.
President
Museum of Science
Boston, Massachusetts

Originally trained as a mechanical engineer, Ioannis Miaoulis is in the forefront of the national movement to increase technological literacy. As dean of the Tufts University School of Engineering, Dr. Miaoulis spearheaded the introduction of engineering into the Massachusetts curriculum. Currently he is working with school systems across the country to engage students in engineering activities and to foster discussions on the impact of science and technology on society.

Martha Cyr, Ph.D.
Director of K–12 Outreach
Worcester Polytechnic Institute
Worcester, Massachusetts

Martha Cyr is a noted expert in engineering outreach. She has over nine years of experience with programs and activities that emphasize the use of engineering principles, through hands-on projects, to excite and motivate students and teachers of mathematics and science in grades K–12. Her goal is to stimulate a continued interest in science and mathematics through engineering.

Book Author

Barbara Brooks Simons
Science Writer
Boston, Massachusetts

Contributing Writers

Emery Pineo
Science Teacher
Barrington Middle School
Barrington, Rhode Island

Karen Riley Sievers
Science Teacher
Callanan Middle School
Des Moines, Iowa

Sharon M. Stroud
Science Teacher
Widefield High School
Colorado Springs, Colorado

Consultants

Reading Consultant

Nancy Romance, Ph.D.
Professor of Science
    Education
Florida Atlantic University
Fort Lauderdale, Florida

Mathematics Consultant

William Tate, Ph.D.
Professor of Education and
    Applied Statistics and
    Computation
Washington University
St. Louis, Missouri

Reviewers

Tufts University Content Reviewers

Faculty from Tufts University in Medford, Massachusetts, developed *Science Explorer* chapter projects and reviewed the student books.

Astier M. Almedom, Ph.D.
Department of Biology

Wayne Chudyk, Ph.D.
Department of Civil and Environmental Engineering

John L. Durant, Ph.D.
Department of Civil and Environmental Engineering

George S. Ellmore, Ph.D.
Department of Biology

David Kaplan, Ph.D.
Department of Biomedical Engineering

Samuel Kounaves, Ph.D.
Department of Chemistry

David H. Lee, Ph.D.
Department of Chemistry

Douglas Matson, Ph.D.
Department of Mechanical Engineering

Karen Panetta, Ph.D.
Department of Electrical Engineering and Computer Science

Jan A. Pechenik, Ph.D.
Department of Biology

John C. Ridge, Ph.D.
Department of Geology

William Waller, Ph.D.
Department of Astronomy

Content Reviewers

Paul Beale, Ph.D.
Department of Physics
University of Colorado
Boulder, Colorado

Jeff Bodart, Ph.D.
Chipola Junior College
Marianna, Florida

Michael Castellani, Ph.D.
Department of Chemistry
Marshall University
Huntington, West Virginia

Eugene Chiang, Ph.D.
Department of Astronomy
University of California – Berkeley
Berkeley, California

Charles C. Curtis, Ph.D.
Department of Physics
University of Arizona
Tucson, Arizona

Daniel Kirk-Davidoff, Ph.D.
Department of Meteorology
University of Maryland
College Park, Maryland

Diane T. Doser, Ph.D.
Department of Geological Sciences
University of Texas at El Paso
El Paso, Texas

R. E. Duhrkopf, Ph.D.
Department of Biology
Baylor University
Waco, Texas

Michael Hacker
Co-director, Center for Technological Literacy
Hofstra University
Hempstead, New York

Michael W. Hamburger, Ph.D.
Department of Geological Sciences
Indiana University
Bloomington, Indiana

Alice K. Hankla, Ph.D.
The Galloway School
Atlanta, Georgia

Donald C. Jackson, Ph.D.
Department of Molecular Pharmacology, Physiology, & Biotechnology
Brown University
Providence, Rhode Island

Jeremiah N. Jarrett, Ph.D.
Department of Biological Sciences
Central Connecticut State University
New Britain, Connecticut

David Lederman, Ph.D.
Department of Physics
West Virginia University
Morgantown, West Virginia

Becky Mansfield, Ph.D.
Department of Geography
Ohio State University
Columbus, Ohio

Elizabeth M. Martin, M.S.
Department of Chemistry and Biochemistry
College of Charleston
Charleston, South Carolina

Joe McCullough, Ph.D.
Department of Natural and Applied Sciences
Cabrillo College
Aptos, California

Robert J. Mellors, Ph.D.
Department of Geological Sciences
San Diego State University
San Diego, California

Joseph M. Moran, Ph.D.
American Meteorological Society
Washington, D.C.

David J. Morrissey, Ph.D.
Department of Chemistry
Michigan State University
East Lansing, Michigan

Philip A. Reed, Ph.D.
Department of Occupational & Technical Studies
Old Dominion University
Norfolk, Virginia

Scott M. Rochette, Ph.D.
Department of the Earth Sciences
State University of New York, College at Brockport
Brockport, New York

Laurence D. Rosenhein, Ph.D.
Department of Chemistry
Indiana State University
Terre Haute, Indiana

Ronald Sass, Ph.D.
Department of Biology and Chemistry
Rice University
Houston, Texas

George Schatz, Ph.D.
Department of Chemistry
Northwestern University
Evanston, Illinois

Sara Seager, Ph.D.
Carnegie Institution of Washington
Washington, D.C.

Robert M. Thornton, Ph.D.
Section of Plant Biology
University of California
Davis, California

John R. Villarreal, Ph.D.
College of Science and Engineering
The University of Texas – Pan American
Edinburg, Texas

Kenneth Welty, Ph.D.
School of Education
University of Wisconsin–Stout
Menomonie, Wisconsin

Edward J. Zalisko, Ph.D.
Department of Biology
Blackburn College
Carlinville, Illinois

Teacher Reviewers

David R. Blakely
Arlington High School
Arlington, Massachusetts

Jane E. Callery
Two Rivers Magnet Middle
    School
East Hartford, Connecticut

Melissa Lynn Cook
Oakland Mills High School
Columbia, Maryland

James Fattic
Southside Middle School
Anderson, Indiana

Dan Gabel
Hoover Middle School
Rockville, Maryland

Wayne Goates
Eisenhower Middle School
Goddard, Kansas

Katherine Bobay Graser
Mint Hill Middle School
Charlotte, North Carolina

Darcy Hampton
Deal Junior High School
Washington, D.C.

Karen Kelly
Pierce Middle School
Waterford, Michigan

David Kelso
Manchester High School Central
Manchester, New Hampshire

Benigno Lopez, Jr.
Sleepy Hill Middle School
Lakeland, Florida

Angie L. Matamoros, Ph.D.
ALM Consulting, INC.
Weston, Florida

Tim McCollum
Charleston Middle School
Charleston, Illinois

Bruce A. Mellin
Brooks School
North Andover, Massachusetts

Ella Jay Parfitt
Southeast Middle School
Baltimore, Maryland

Evelyn A. Pizzarello
Louis M. Klein Middle School
Harrison, New York

Kathleen M. Poe
Fletcher Middle School
Jacksonville, Florida

Shirley Rose
Lewis and Clark Middle School
Tulsa, Oklahoma

Linda Sandersen
Greenfield Middle School
Greenfield, Wisconsin

Mary E. Solan
Southwest Middle School
Charlotte, North Carolina

Mary Stewart
University of Tulsa
Tulsa, Oklahoma

Paul Swenson
Billings West High School
Billings, Montana

Thomas Vaughn
Arlington High School
Arlington, Massachusetts

Susan C. Zibell
Central Elementary
Simsbury, Connecticut

Safety Reviewers

W. H. Breazeale, Ph.D.
Department of Chemistry
College of Charleston
Charleston, South Carolina

Ruth Hathaway, Ph.D.
Hathaway Consulting
Cape Girardeau, Missouri

Douglas Mandt, M.S.
Science Education Consultant
Edgewood, Washington

Activity Field Testers

Nicki Bibbo
Witchcraft Heights School
Salem, Massachusetts

Rose-Marie Botting
Broward County Schools
Fort Lauderdale, Florida

Colleen Campos
Laredo Middle School
Aurora, Colorado

Elizabeth Chait
W. L. Chenery Middle School
Belmont, Massachusetts

Holly Estes
Hale Middle School
Stow, Massachusetts

Laura Hapgood
Plymouth Community
    Intermediate School
Plymouth, Massachusetts

Mary F. Lavin
Plymouth Community
    Intermediate School
Plymouth, Massachusetts

James MacNeil, Ph.D.
Cambridge, Massachusetts

Lauren Magruder
St. Michael's Country
    Day School
Newport, Rhode Island

Jeanne Maurand
Austin Preparatory School
Reading, Massachusetts

Joanne Jackson-Pelletier
Winman Junior High School
Warwick, Rhode Island

Warren Phillips
Plymouth Public Schools
Plymouth, Massachusetts

Carol Pirtle
Hale Middle School
Stow, Massachusetts

Kathleen M. Poe
Fletcher Middle School
Jacksonville, Florida

Cynthia B. Pope
Norfolk Public Schools
Norfolk, Virginia

Anne Scammell
Geneva Middle School
Geneva, New York

Karen Riley Sievers
Callanan Middle School
Des Moines, Iowa

David M. Smith
Eyer Middle School
Allentown, Pennsylvania

Gene Vitale
Parkland School
McHenry, Illinois

Contents

Weather and Climate

Careers in Science **Eyes in the Sky** x

Chapter 1 | **The Atmosphere** **4**

Discovery SCHOOL VIDEO
The Atmosphere

1 The Air Around You 6
2 **Integrating Physics** Air Pressure 10
3 Layers of the Atmosphere 16
4 **Integrating Environmental Science** Air Quality 22

Chapter 2 | **Weather Factors** **34**

Discovery SCHOOL VIDEO
Weather Factors

1 Energy in Earth's Atmosphere 36
2 **Integrating Physics** Heat Transfer 42
3 Winds 46
4 Water in the Atmosphere 54
5 Precipitation 61

Chapter 3 | **Weather Patterns** **70**

Discovery SCHOOL VIDEO
Weather Patterns

1 Air Masses and Fronts 72
2 Storms 80
3 **Tech & Design** Predicting the Weather 92

Chapter 4 | **Climate and Climate Change** **106**

Discovery SCHOOL VIDEO
Climate and Climate Change

1 What Causes Climate? 108
2 Climate Regions 118
3 Long-Term Changes in Climate 130
4 **Integrating Environmental Science**
Global Changes in the Atmosphere 135

Interdisciplinary Exploration
Antarctica **146**

Reference Section

Skills Handbook 152
   Think Like a Scientist 152
   Making Measurements 154
   Conducting a Scientific Investigation 156
   Technology Design Skills 158
   Creating Data Tables and Graphs 160
   Math Review 163
   Reading Comprehension Skills 168

Appendix A Laboratory Safety 172
English and Spanish Glossary 174
Index 179
Acknowledgments 182

VIDEO

Enhance understanding through dynamic video.

Preview Get motivated with this introduction to the chapter content.

Field Trip Explore a real-world story related to the chapter content.

Assessment Review content and take an assessment.

Get connected to exciting Web resources in every lesson.

SC*LINKS* NSTA Find Web links on topics relating to every section.

Active Art Interact with selected visuals from every chapter online.

Planet Diary® Explore news and natural phenomena through weekly reports.

Science News® Keep up to date with the latest science discoveries.

Experience the complete textbook online and on CD-ROM.

Activities Practice skills and learn content.

Videos Explore content and learn important lab skills.

Audio Support Hear key terms spoken and defined.

Self-Assessment Use instant feedback to help you track your progress.

Activities

Lab zone™ Chapter **Project** — Opportunities for long-term inquiry

Watching the Weather 5
Design and Build Your Own
    Weather Station 35
The Weather Tomorrow 71
Investigating Microclimates 107

Lab zone Discover **Activity** — Exploration and inquiry before reading

How Long Will the Candle Burn? 6
Does Air Have Mass? 10
Is Air There? 16
What's on the Jar? 22
Does a Plastic Bag Trap Heat? 36
What Happens When Air Is Heated? 42
Does the Wind Turn? 46
How Does Fog Form? 54
How Can You Make Hail? 61
How Do Fluids of Different Densities
    Behave? 72
Can You Make a Tornado? 80
What's the Weather? 92
How Does Latitude Affect Climate? 108
How Do Climates Differ? 118
What Story Can Tree Rings Tell? 130
What Is the Greenhouse Effect? 135

Lab zone Try This **Activity** — Reinforcement of key concepts

Breathe In, Breathe Out 8
Soda-Bottle Barometer 12
Temperature and Height 44
Build a Wind Vane 47
Lightning Distances 81
Modeling a Climate 123
It's Your Skin! 140

Lab zone Skills **Activity** — Practice of specific science inquiry skills

Calculating 64
Calculating 75
Classifying 76
Interpreting Data .96
Inferring 111
Classifying 124

Lab zone — Labs — In-depth practice of inquiry skills and science concepts

Skills Lab Working Under Pressure 15

Design Your Own Lab How Clean Is
the Air? 26

Skills Lab Heating Earth's Surface 40

Technology Lab Measuring the Wind . . .53

Skills Lab Tracking a Hurricane 90

Skills Lab Reading a Weather Map 99

Skills Lab Sunny Rays and Angles 116

Consumer Lab Cool Climate Graphs . . .128

Lab zone — At-Home Activity — Quick, engaging activities for home and family

Model Air Pressure 14

Dust in the Air 25

Heating Your Home 39

Water in the Air 60

Storm Eyewitness 89

What's Your Climate? 127

Sun Protection 141

• Tech & Design • — Design, build, test, and communicate

Tech & Design in History Explorers of
the Atmosphere 18

Science and Society
Cars and Clean Air 28

Technology Chapter Project Design and
Build Your Own Weather Station 35

Technology Lab Measuring the Wind . . .53

Science and History Weather That
Changed History 84

Technology and Society
Doppler Radar 100

Math — Point-of-use math practice

Analyzing Data
Changing Temperatures 20

Determining Relative Humidity 56

Computer Weather Forecasting 95

Ice Ages and Temperature 133

Math Skills
Converting Units 43

Percentage 114

active art — Illustrations come alive online

Measuring Air Pressure 12

Global Winds 51

The Water Cycle 55

Types of Fronts 77

The Seasons 115

Continental Drift 134

Marshall Shepherd tracks powerful thunderstorms at the Goddard Visualization Studio (left). Marshall looks at satellite images like this one of Florida (above).

Eyes in the Sky

At the Kennedy Space Center on the east coast of Florida, a crew prepares to launch a satellite into space. The crew knows that a thunderstorm may be moving toward them. Should they launch the mission or delay it? Before deciding, the crew consults with meteorologists at the National Weather Service for the latest weather forecast.

More summer thunderstorms occur in central Florida than in any other area in the United States. Predicting when severe storms will develop and where they will move is one of the most demanding jobs for a meteorologist. One of the best people at this job is J. Marshall Shepherd.

Talking With
Dr. J. Marshall Shepherd

Starting Out in Science

Marshall Shepherd is an "old hand" at predicting the weather. He's been at it since sixth grade, when his teacher suggested that he enter a science fair. He constructed a weather station for his science project. The weather station contained an anemometer to measure wind speed, a wind vane to measure wind direction, a barometer to measure air pressure, a hair hygrometer to measure humidity, and a rain gauge. "From these basic instruments, I took weather observations around my neighborhood," he explains. Marshall won prizes for his instruments and scientific work on this project at local, district, and state science fairs.

By the time he graduated from high school, he had a definite goal. "One day, I planned to be a research scientist at NASA (National Aeronautics and Space Administration)," he stated.

Predicting Severe Storms

In graduate school, Marshall investigated the way powerful thunderstorms form and move, especially those in central Florida. The long, narrow shape of Florida is part of the reason that so many storms form there. "When you have land heating faster than water, you get something called sea-breeze circulation," he explains. "On a typical summer day, a sea-breeze forms on both the west coast and the east coast of Florida. They tend to move toward the center. When they collide, you get intense thunderstorm development."

Career Path

Marshall Shepherd, the son of two school principals, grew up in the small town of Canton, Georgia. He graduated from Florida State University, where he later received his Ph.D. in meteorology. Today he works for NASA as a research meteorologist at the Goddard Space Flight Center in Maryland. Below, Marshall acts as a NASA spokesperson to TV and radio reporters.

Lightning flashes in a thunderstorm over Tucson, Arizona.

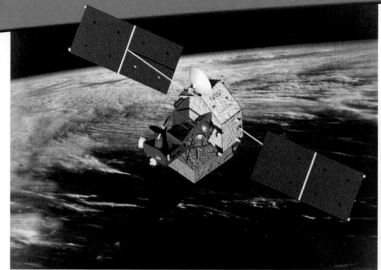

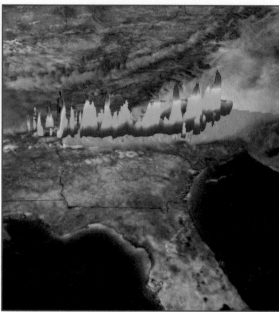

This TRMM satellite image shows an area of severe thunderstorms north of Florida.

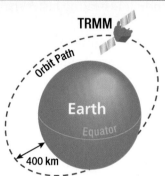

TRMM, a satellite that records weather conditions from space, contains two solar panels and instruments to collect weather data (above). TRMM orbits Earth at an altitude of about 400 kilometers. It flies over each position on Earth at a different time each day (right).

NASA's Earth Science Enterprise

In 1993, Marshall started working at NASA. His research there contributes to NASA's Earth Science Enterprise. This long-term program uses information from satellites, aircraft, and ground stations to understand Earth as a single system. NASA scientists track changes in the atmosphere, land, ocean, and ice. They investigate how those changes affect weather and climate.

Marshall's knowledge of hurricanes and thunderstorms is especially valuable in interpreting data from the Tropical Rainfall Measuring Mission (TRMM). The TRMM is a satellite with instruments that measure tropical and subtropical rainfall. Rainfall cycles located in tropical regions affect weather throughout the world.

Marshall's work involves both observation and calculation. The instruments that Marshall uses are some of the most advanced in the world. Marshall specializes in "remote sensing"—making observations of weather conditions, such as rainfall, from a distance. After collecting data, he uses a computer to analyze it.

Studying Global Rainfall

Recently, radar helped Marshall identify a relatively new factor in global climate—big cities. Modern cities have cars, roads, buildings, and large areas of concrete and asphalt surfaces. These surfaces hold heat, creating "urban heat islands." As a result, temperatures inside a city can be up to 5.6°C warmer than temperatures in the nearby suburbs.

But satellite pictures showed something more—"urban heat islands" may actually create local weather. Heated air rises over the city, producing clouds. As a result, summer rainfall is heavier over some cities. It is also heavier downwind, in the direction in which the wind is blowing, from the cities. Marshall and his colleagues mapped rainfall around several cities worldwide. Data showed a clear link between rainfall patterns and urban areas. This connection matters because world cities are growing quickly. As they grow, urban areas could have greater effects on the weather.

Looking Ahead

TRMM's mission will end in a few years. Meanwhile, Marshall is already working on a new project, the Global Precipitation Measurement mission. It is scheduled to launch sometime after 2010. Its satellites will carry the next generation of space-based instruments. In planning for this next project, Marshall meets with engineers to talk about the project's scientific goals and how to design spacecraft to meet those goals.

Marshall wears other hats at NASA, too. Sometimes he acts as spokesperson to TV, radio, and magazine reporters. He also talks to government policymakers.

What is it like to fulfill his dream of working at NASA? "I am like a kid in a candy store," Dr. Shepherd says. "I got into the field by doing a science project. Now I make a living doing 'really big' science projects. . . . The biggest difference is that I no longer have to make my own instruments. I can use the satellite, aircraft, and computer model technology at NASA."

Writing in Science

Career Link Marshall Shepherd credits his career success to having detailed goals. "I always write down goals, and check them off as they happen," he says. Think of a task that you would like to accomplish over the next year. In a paragraph, write the steps you will take to reach your goal. Explain how those steps help bring you closer to achieving your goal.

Go Online
PHSchool.com

For: More on this career
Visit: PHSchool.com
Web Code: cfb-4000

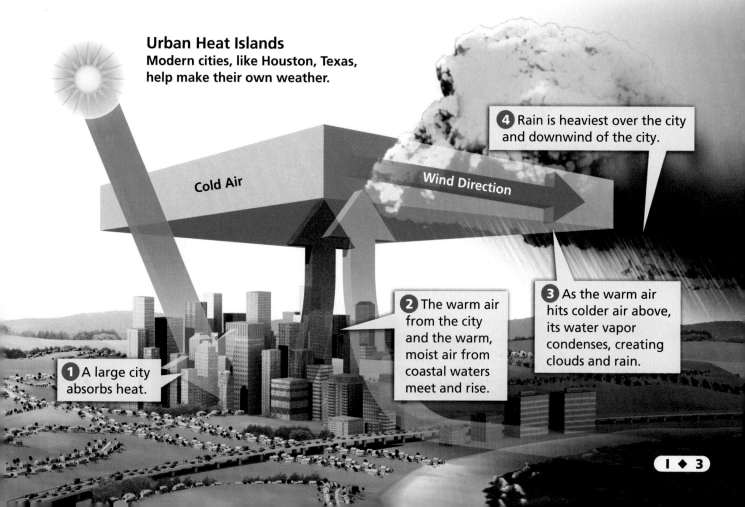

Urban Heat Islands
Modern cities, like Houston, Texas, help make their own weather.

Cold Air

Wind Direction

4 Rain is heaviest over the city and downwind of the city.

1 A large city absorbs heat.

2 The warm air from the city and the warm, moist air from coastal waters meet and rise.

3 As the warm air hits colder air above, its water vapor condenses, creating clouds and rain.

The Atmosphere

The **BIG** Idea

Structure of Earth's Atmosphere

 How do air pressure and temperature vary in the atmosphere?

Chapter Preview

❶ **The Air Around You**
Discover How Long Will the Candle Burn?
Try This Breathe In, Breathe Out

❷ **Air Pressure**
Discover Does Air Have Mass?
Try This Soda-Bottle Barometer
Active Art Measuring Air Pressure
At-Home Activity Model Air Pressure
Skills Lab Working Under Pressure

❸ **Layers of the Atmosphere**
Discover Is Air There?
Tech & Design in History Explorers of the Atmosphere
Analyzing Data Changing Temperatures

❹ **Air Quality**
Discover What's on the Jar?
At-Home Activity Dust in the Air
Design Your Own Lab How Clean Is the Air?
Science and Society Cars and Clean Air

Bubbles are pockets of air surrounded ▶ by a thin film of liquid.

◢Lab zone™ Chapter **Project**

Watching the Weather

The weather is always changing. If you pay close attention to weather patterns, you can learn to predict whether a storm is brewing or fair weather will continue. In this project, you will observe weather conditions without using instruments. Then you will look for hints about tomorrow's weather in the weather conditions today.

Your Goal Your project must

- include a plan for observing and describing a variety of weather conditions over a period of two to three weeks
- show your observations in a daily weather log
- display your findings about weather conditions

Plan It! Begin by discussing what weather conditions you can observe. Decide how, when, and where you will make your observations. Organize a notebook to record them. Think of ways to make comparisons from day to day. Then begin your observations. Look for patterns in your data. At the end of the chapter, you will display your weather observations to the class.

The Air Around You

1

Reading Preview

Key Concepts
- What is the composition of Earth's atmosphere?
- How is the atmosphere important to living things?

Key Terms
- weather
- atmosphere
- ozone
- water vapor

Target Reading Skill

Using Prior Knowledge Before you read, look at the section headings and visuals to see what this section is about. Then write what you know about the atmosphere in a graphic organizer like the one below. As you read, write what you learn.

What You Know
1. The atmosphere contains oxygen.
2.

What You Learned
1.
2.

Lab zone Discover **Activity**

How Long Will the Candle Burn?

1. Put on your goggles.
2. Stick a small piece of modeling clay onto an aluminum pie pan. Push a short candle into the clay. Carefully light the candle.
3. Hold a small glass jar by the bottom. Lower the mouth of the jar over the candle until the jar rests on the pie pan. As you do this, start a stopwatch or note where the second hand is on a clock.
4. Watch the candle carefully. How long does the flame burn?
5. Wearing an oven mitt, remove the jar. Relight the candle and then repeat Steps 3 and 4 with a larger jar.

Think It Over

Inferring How would you explain any differences between your results in Steps 4 and 5?

The sky is full of thick, dark clouds. In the distance you see a bright flash. Thirty seconds later, you hear a crack of thunder. You begin to run and reach your home just as the downpour begins. That was close! From your window you look out to watch the storm.

Does the weather where you live change often, or is it fairly constant from day to day? **Weather** is the condition of Earth's atmosphere at a particular time and place. But what is the atmosphere? Earth's **atmosphere** (AT muh sfeer) is the envelope of gases that surrounds the planet. To understand the relative size of the atmosphere, imagine that Earth is the size of an apple. If you breathe on the apple, a thin film of water droplets will form on its surface. Earth's atmosphere is like that water on the apple—a thin layer of gases on Earth's surface.

◄ From space, Earth's atmosphere appears as a thin layer near the horizon.

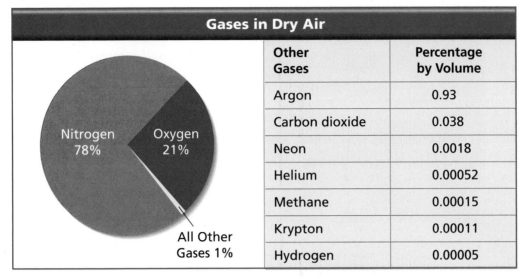

Gases in Dry Air		
	Other Gases	Percentage by Volume
	Argon	0.93
	Carbon dioxide	0.038
	Neon	0.0018
	Helium	0.00052
	Methane	0.00015
	Krypton	0.00011
	Hydrogen	0.00005

Nitrogen 78%
Oxygen 21%
All Other Gases 1%

FIGURE 1
Dry air in the lower atmosphere generally has about the same composition of gases.
Interpreting Data
What two gases make up most of the air?

Composition of the Atmosphere

The atmosphere is made up of a mixture of atoms and molecules of different kinds. An atom is the smallest unit of a chemical element that can exist by itself. Molecules are made up of two or more atoms. **Earth's atmosphere is made up of nitrogen, oxygen, carbon dioxide, water vapor, and many other gases, as well as particles of liquids and solids.**

Nitrogen As you can see in Figure 1, nitrogen is the most abundant gas in the atmosphere. It makes up a little more than three fourths of the air we breathe. Each nitrogen molecule consists of two nitrogen atoms.

Oxygen Even though oxygen is the second most abundant gas in the atmosphere, it makes up less than one fourth of the volume. Plants and animals take oxygen directly from the air and use it to release energy from their food.

Oxygen is also involved in many other important processes. Any fuel you can think of, from the gasoline in a car to the candles on a birthday cake, uses oxygen as it burns. Without oxygen, a fire will go out. Burning uses oxygen rapidly. During other processes, oxygen is used slowly. For example, steel in cars and other objects reacts slowly with oxygen to form iron oxide, or rust.

Most oxygen molecules have two oxygen atoms. **Ozone** is a form of oxygen that has three oxygen atoms in each molecule instead of the usual two. Have you ever noticed a pungent smell in the air after a thunderstorm? This is the odor of ozone, which forms when lightning interacts with oxygen in the air.

 Reading Checkpoint **What is ozone?**

FIGURE 2
Burning Uses Oxygen
Oxygen is necessary in order for the wood to burn.

FIGURE 3
Water Vapor in the Air
There is very little water vapor in the air over the desert where this lizard lives. In the tropical rain forest (right), where the frog lives, as much as four percent of the air may be water vapor.

Lab zone Try This **Activity**

Breathe In, Breathe Out

How can you detect carbon dioxide in the air you exhale?

1. Put on your goggles.
2. Fill a glass or beaker halfway with limewater.
3.  Using a straw, slowly blow air through the limewater for about a minute. **CAUTION:** *Do not suck on the straw or drink the limewater.*
4. What happens to the limewater?

Developing Hypotheses What do you think would happen if you did the same experiment after jogging for 10 minutes? What would your results tell you about exercise and carbon dioxide?

Carbon Dioxide Each molecule of carbon dioxide has one atom of carbon and two atoms of oxygen. Carbon dioxide is essential to life. Plants must have carbon dioxide to produce food. When the cells of plants and animals break down food to produce energy, they give off carbon dioxide as a waste product.

When fuels such as coal and gasoline are burned, they release carbon dioxide. Burning these fuels increases the amount of carbon dioxide in the atmosphere.

Other Gases Oxygen and nitrogen together make up 99 percent of dry air. Argon and carbon dioxide make up most of the other one percent. The remaining gases are called trace gases because only small amounts of them are present.

Water Vapor So far, we have discussed the composition of dry air. In reality, air is not dry because it contains water vapor. **Water vapor** is water in the form of a gas. Water vapor is invisible. It is not the same thing as steam, which is made up of tiny droplets of liquid water. Each water molecule contains two atoms of hydrogen and one atom of oxygen.

The amount of water vapor in the air varies greatly from place to place and from time to time. Water vapor plays an important role in Earth's weather. Clouds form when water vapor condenses out of the air to form tiny droplets of liquid water or crystals of ice. If these droplets or crystals become heavy enough, they can fall as rain or snow.

Particles Pure air contains only gases. But pure air exists only in laboratories. In the real world, air also contains tiny solid and liquid particles of dust, smoke, salt, and other chemicals. You can see some of these particles in the air around you, but most of them are too small to see.

Reading Checkpoint What is water vapor?

Importance of the Atmosphere

Earth's atmosphere makes conditions on Earth suitable for living things. The atmosphere contains oxygen and other gases that you and other living things need to survive. In turn, living things affect the atmosphere. The atmosphere is constantly changing, with gases moving in and out of living things, the land, and the water.

Living things need warmth and liquid water. By trapping energy from the sun, the atmosphere keeps most of Earth's surface warm enough for water to exist as a liquid. In addition, Earth's atmosphere protects living things from dangerous radiation from the sun. The atmosphere also prevents Earth's surface from being hit by most meteoroids, or rocks from outer space.

Go Online

SciLINKS NSTA

For: Links on atmosphere
Visit: www.SciLinks.org
Web Code: scn-0911

Section 1 Assessment

Target Reading Skill Using Prior Knowledge
Review your graphic organizer and revise it based on what you just learned in the section.

Reviewing Key Concepts

1. a. **Defining** What is the atmosphere?
   b. **Listing** What are the four most common gases in dry air?
   c. **Explaining** Why are the amounts of gases in the atmosphere usually shown as percentages of dry air?

2. a. **Describing** What are three ways in which the atmosphere is important to life on Earth?

   b. **Predicting** How would the amount of carbon dioxide in the atmosphere change if there were no plants?
   c. **Developing Hypotheses** How would Earth be different without the atmosphere?

Writing in Science

Summary Write a paragraph that summarizes in your own words how oxygen from the atmosphere is important. Include its importance to living things and in other processes.

Air Pressure

Reading Preview

Key Concepts
- What are some of the properties of air?
- What instruments are used to measure air pressure?
- How does increasing altitude affect air pressure and density?

Key Terms
- density
- pressure
- air pressure
- barometer
- mercury barometer
- aneroid barometer
- altitude

Target Reading Skill

Identifying Main Ideas As you read the Properties of Air section, write the main idea—the biggest or most important idea—in a graphic organizer like the one below. Then write two supporting details. The supporting details give examples of the main idea.

Main Idea

Because air has mass, it also . . .

Detail	**Detail**

Lab zone Discover Activity

Does Air Have Mass?

1. Use a balance to find the mass of a deflated balloon.
2. Blow up the balloon and tie the neck closed. Predict whether the mass of the balloon plus the air you have compressed into it will differ from the mass of the deflated balloon.
3. Find the mass of the inflated balloon. Compare this to the mass of the deflated balloon. Was your prediction correct?

Think It Over

Drawing Conclusions What can you conclude about whether air has mass? Explain your conclusion.

The air is cool and clear—just perfect for an overnight hiking trip. You've stuffed your backpack with your tent, sleeping bag, stove, and food. When you hoist your pack onto your back, its weight presses into your shoulders. That pack sure is heavy! By the end of the day, you'll be glad to take it off and get rid of all that weight.

But here's a surprise: Even when you take off your pack, your shoulders will still have pressure on them. The weight of the atmosphere itself is constantly pressing on your body.

Like a heavy backpack ▶ pressing on your shoulders, the weight of the atmosphere causes air pressure.

Properties of Air

It may seem to you that air has no mass. But in fact, air consists of atoms and molecules, which have mass. So air must have mass. **Because air has mass, it also has other properties, including density and pressure.**

Density The amount of mass in a given volume of air is its **density.** You can calculate the density of a substance by dividing its mass by its volume.

$$\text{Density} = \frac{\text{Mass}}{\text{Volume}}$$

If there are more molecules in a given volume, the density is greater. If there are fewer molecules, the density is less.

Pressure The force pushing on an area or surface is known as **pressure.** The weight of the atmosphere exerts a force on surfaces. **Air pressure** is the result of the weight of a column of air pushing down on an area. The column of air extends upward through the entire atmosphere, as shown in Figure 4.

The atmosphere is heavy. The weight of the column of air above your desk is about the same as the weight of a large schoolbus. So why doesn't air pressure crush your desk? The reason is that the molecules in air push in all directions—down, up, and sideways. The air pushing down on top of your desk is balanced by the air pushing up on the bottom of your desk.

Air pressure can change from day to day. A denser substance has more mass per unit volume than a less dense one. So denser air exerts more pressure than less dense air.

 **How does the density of air affect air pressure?**

FIGURE 4
Air Pressure
There is a column of air above you all the time. The weight of the air in the atmosphere causes air pressure.

Try This Activity

Soda-Bottle Barometer

Here's how to build a device that shows changes in air pressure.

1. Fill a 2-liter soda bottle one-half full with water.
2. Lower a long straw into the bottle so that the end of the straw is in the water. Seal the mouth of the bottle around the straw with modeling clay.
3. Squeeze the sides of the bottle. What happens to the level of the water in the straw?
4. Let go of the sides of the bottle. Watch the level of the water in the straw.

Inferring Explain your results in terms of air pressure.

Measuring Air Pressure

A **barometer** (buh RAHM uh tur) is an instrument that is used to measure air pressure. **Two common kinds of barometers are mercury barometers and aneroid barometers.**

Mercury Barometers Figure 5 shows the way a mercury barometer works. A **mercury barometer** consists of a glass tube open at the bottom end and partially filled with mercury. The space in the tube above the mercury is almost a vacuum—it contains very little air. The open end of the tube rests in a dish of mercury. The air pressure pushing down on the surface of the mercury in the dish is equal to the pressure exerted by the weight of the column of mercury in the tube. When the air pressure increases, it presses down more on the surface of the mercury. Greater air pressure forces the column of mercury higher. At sea level the mercury column is about 76 centimeters high, on average.

Aneroid Barometers If you have a barometer at home, it is probably an aneroid barometer. The word aneroid means "without liquid." An **aneroid barometer** (AN uh royd) has an airtight metal chamber, as shown in Figure 6. The metal chamber is sensitive to changes in air pressure. When air pressure increases, the thin walls of the chamber are pushed in. When the pressure drops, the walls bulge out. The chamber is connected to a dial by a series of springs and levers. As the shape of the chamber changes, the needle on the dial moves.

Go Online

active art

For: Measuring Air Pressure activity
Visit: PHSchool.com
Web Code: cfp-4012

FIGURE 5
Mercury Barometer
Air pressure pushes down on the surface of the mercury in the dish, causing the mercury in the tube to rise. The air pressure is greater on the barometer on the right, so the mercury is higher in the tube.
Predicting *What happens to the level of mercury in the tube when the air pressure decreases?*

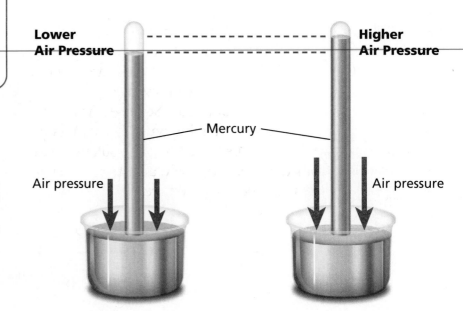

Lower Air Pressure · Higher Air Pressure · Mercury · Air pressure · Air pressure

FIGURE 6

Aneroid Barometer
This diagram shows an aneroid barometer. Changes in air pressure cause the walls of the airtight metal chamber to flex in and out. The needle on the dial indicates the air pressure.

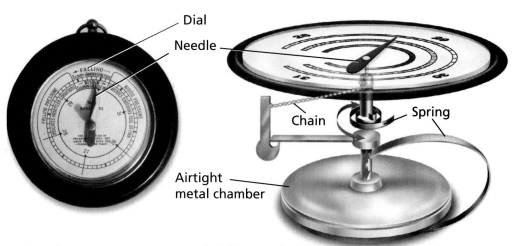

Dial

Needle

Chain

Spring

Airtight metal chamber

Units of Air Pressure Weather reports use several different units for air pressure. Most weather reports for the general public use inches of mercury. For example, if the column of mercury in a mercury barometer is 30 inches high, the air pressure is "30 inches of mercury" or just "30 inches."

National Weather Service maps indicate air pressure in millibars. One inch of mercury is approximately 33.87 millibars, so 30 inches of mercury is approximately equal to 1,016 millibars.

 **Reading Checkpoint** | **What are two common units that are used to measure air pressure?**

Altitude and the Properties of Air

At the top of a mountain, the air pressure is less than the air pressure at sea level. **Altitude,** or elevation, is the distance above sea level, the average level of the surface of the oceans. **Air pressure decreases as altitude increases. As air pressure decreases, so does density.**

Altitude Affects Air Pressure Imagine a stack of books. Which book has more weight on it, the second book from the top or the book at the bottom? The second book from the top has only the weight of one book on top of it. The book at the bottom of the stack has the weight of all the books pressing on it.

Air at sea level is like the bottom book. Sea-level air has the weight of the whole atmosphere pressing on it. So air pressure is greater at sea level. Air near the top of the atmosphere is like the second book from the top. There, the air has less weight pressing on it, and thus has lower air pressure.

FIGURE 7
Air Pressure and Altitude
Air pressure is greater at sea level and decreases as the altitude increases.

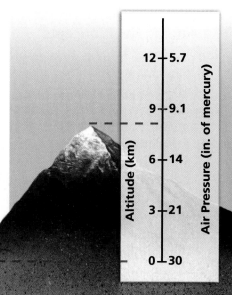

Altitude (km)

Air Pressure (in. of mercury)

12	5.7
9	9.1
6	14
3	21
0	30

Sea Level

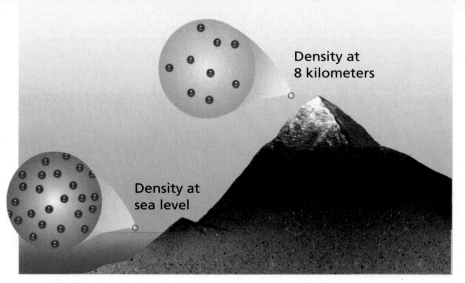

FIGURE 8
Altitude and Density
The density of air decreases as altitude increases. Air at sea level has more gas molecules in each cubic meter than air at the top of a mountain.

Density at 8 kilometers

Density at sea level

The Atmosphere

Video Preview
▶ Video Field Trip
Video Assessment

Altitude Also Affects Density As you go up through the atmosphere, the density of the air decreases. This means the gas molecules that make up the atmosphere are farther apart at high altitudes than they are at sea level. If you were near the top of a tall mountain and tried to run, you would quickly get out of breath. Why? The air contains 21 percent oxygen, whether you are at sea level or on top of a mountain. However, since the air is less dense at a high altitude, there are fewer oxygen molecules to breathe in each cubic meter of air than at sea level. So you would become short of breath quickly at high altitudes.

 **Reading Checkpoint** **Why is it hard to breathe at the top of a mountain?**

Section 2 Assessment

 Target Reading Skill Identifying Main Ideas Use your graphic organizer to help you answer Question 1 below.

Reviewing Key Concepts

1. **a. Defining** What is air pressure?
   b. Explaining How does increasing the density of a gas affect its pressure?
2. **a. Listing** What two instruments are commonly used to measure air pressure?
   b. Measuring What units are commonly used to measure air pressure?
   c. Calculating How many millibars are equal to 27.23 inches of mercury?
3. **a. Defining** What is altitude?
   b. Relating Cause and Effect As altitude increases, how does air pressure change? How does density change?
   c. Predicting What changes in air pressure would you expect if you carried a barometer down a mine shaft?

Lab zone **At-Home Activity**

Model Air Pressure Here's how you can show your family that air has pressure. Fill a glass with water. Place a piece of cardboard over the top of the glass. Hold the cardboard in place with one hand as you turn the glass upside down. **CAUTION:** *Be sure the cardboard does not bend.* Now remove your hand from the cardboard. What happens? Explain to your family that the cardboard doesn't fall because the air pressure pushing up on it is greater than the weight of the water pushing down.

Working Under Pressure

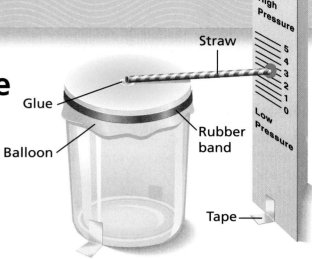

Problem

How can a barometer detect changes in air pressure?

Skills Focus

interpreting data, drawing conclusions

Materials

- modeling clay • scissors • white glue
- tape • pencil • wide-mouthed glass jar
- metric ruler • cardboard strip, 10 cm × 25 cm
- rubber band • large rubber balloon
- drinking straw, 12–15 cm long

Procedure

1. Cut off the narrow opening of the balloon.

2. Fold the edges of the balloon outward. Carefully stretch the balloon over the open end of the glass jar. Use a rubber band to hold the balloon on the rim of the glass jar.

3. Place a small amount of glue on the center of the balloon top. Attach one end of the straw to the glue. Allow the other end to extend several centimeters beyond the edge of the glass jar. This is your pointer.

4. While the glue dries, fold the cardboard strip lengthwise and draw a scale along the edge with marks 0.5 cm apart. Write "High pressure" at the top of your scale and "Low pressure" at the bottom.

5. After the glue dries, add a pea-sized piece of modeling clay to the end of the pointer. Place your barometer and its scale in a location that is as free from temperature changes as possible. Note that the pointer of the straw must just reach the cardboard strip, as shown in the diagram.

6. Tape both the scale and the barometer to a surface so they do not move during your experiment.

7. Make a data table like the one below in your notebook. Record the date and time. Note the level of the straw on the cardboard strip.

Data Table		
Date and Time	Air Pressure	Weather Conditions

8. Check the barometer twice a day. Record your observations in your data table.

9. Record the weather conditions for at least three days.

Analyze and Conclude

1. **Interpreting Data** What change in atmospheric conditions must occur to cause the free end of the straw to rise? What change must occur for it to fall?

2. **Drawing Conclusions** Based on your observations, what kind of weather is usually associated with high air pressure? With low air pressure?

3. **Communicating** Write a paragraph in which you discuss what effect, if any, a large temperature change might have on the accuracy of your barometer.

More to Explore

Compare your pressure readings with high and low pressure readings shown in newspaper weather maps for the same period. How do your readings compare with those in the newspaper?

3 Layers of the Atmosphere

Reading Preview

Key Concepts
- What are the four main layers of the atmosphere?
- What are the characteristics of each layer?

Key Terms
- troposphere • stratosphere
- mesosphere • thermosphere
- ionosphere • exosphere

Target Reading Skill

Previewing Visuals Before you read this section, preview Figure 9. Then write at least two questions that you have about the diagram in a graphic organizer like the one below. As you read, answer your questions.

Layers of the Atmosphere

Q. Where is the ozone layer?
A.
Q.

Lab zone Discover **Activity**

Is Air There?

1. Use a heavy rubber band to tightly secure a plastic bag over the top of a wide-mouthed jar.
2. Gently try to push the bag into the jar. What happens? Is the air pressure higher inside or outside the bag?
3. Remove the rubber band and line the inside of the jar with the plastic bag. Use the rubber band to tightly secure the edges of the bag over the rim of the jar.
4. Gently try to pull the bag out of the jar with your fingertips. What happens? Is the air pressure higher inside or outside the bag?

Think It Over

Predicting Explain your observations in terms of air pressure. How do you think differences in air pressure would affect a balloon as it traveled up through the atmosphere?

Imagine taking a trip upward into the atmosphere in a hot-air balloon. You begin on a warm beach near the ocean, at an altitude of 0 kilometers above sea level.

You hear a roar as the balloon's pilot turns up the burner to heat the air in the balloon. The balloon begins to rise, and Earth's surface gets farther and farther away. As the balloon rises to an altitude of 3 kilometers, you realize that the air is getting colder. As you continue to rise, the air gets colder still. At 6 kilometers you begin to have trouble breathing. The air is becoming less dense. It's time to go back down.

What if you could have continued your balloon ride up through the atmosphere? As you rose higher, the air pressure and temperature would change dramatically.

Scientists divide Earth's atmosphere into four main layers classified according to changes in temperature. These layers are the troposphere, the stratosphere, the mesosphere, and the thermosphere. The four main layers of the atmosphere are shown in Figure 9. Read on to learn more about each of these layers.

▲ **Hot-air balloon**

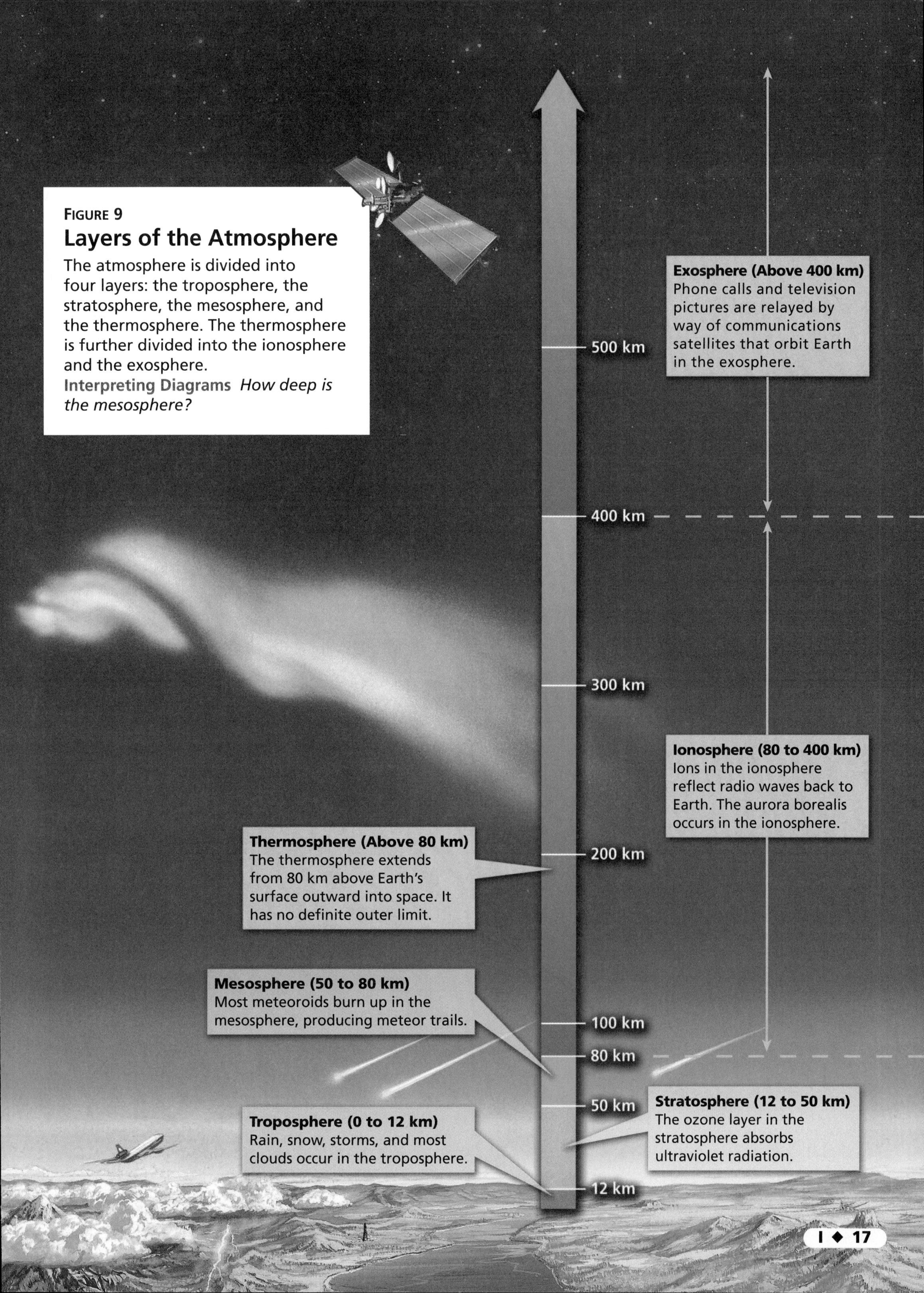

FIGURE 9

Layers of the Atmosphere

The atmosphere is divided into four layers: the troposphere, the stratosphere, the mesosphere, and the thermosphere. The thermosphere is further divided into the ionosphere and the exosphere.

Interpreting Diagrams *How deep is the mesosphere?*

Exosphere (Above 400 km)
Phone calls and television pictures are relayed by way of communications satellites that orbit Earth in the exosphere.

— 500 km

— 400 km

— 300 km

Ionosphere (80 to 400 km)
Ions in the ionosphere reflect radio waves back to Earth. The aurora borealis occurs in the ionosphere.

Thermosphere (Above 80 km)
The thermosphere extends from 80 km above Earth's surface outward into space. It has no definite outer limit.

— 200 km

Mesosphere (50 to 80 km)
Most meteoroids burn up in the mesosphere, producing meteor trails.

— 100 km

— 80 km

— 50 km

Stratosphere (12 to 50 km)
The ozone layer in the stratosphere absorbs ultraviolet radiation.

Troposphere (0 to 12 km)
Rain, snow, storms, and most clouds occur in the troposphere.

— 12 km

Go Online
PLANET DIARY

For: More on the ozone layer
Visit: PHSchool.com
Web Code: cfd-4013

The Troposphere

You live in the inner, or lowest, layer of Earth's atmosphere, the **troposphere** (TROH puh sfeer). *Tropo-* means "turning" or "changing." Conditions in the troposphere are more variable than in the other layers. **The troposphere is the layer of the atmosphere in which Earth's weather occurs.**

The depth of the troposphere varies from 16 kilometers above the equator to less than 9 kilometers above the North and South poles. Although it is the shallowest layer, the troposphere contains almost all of the mass of the atmosphere.

As altitude increases in the troposphere, the temperature decreases. On average, for every 1-kilometer increase in altitude, the air gets about 6.5 Celsius degrees cooler. At the top of the troposphere, the temperature stops decreasing and stays at about −60°C. Water here forms thin, feathery clouds of ice.

• Tech & Design in History •

Explorers of the Atmosphere
The atmosphere has been explored from the ground and from space.

**1643
Torricelli Invents
the Barometer**
Italian physicist and mathematician Evangelista Torricelli improved existing scientific instruments and invented some new ones. In 1643 he invented the mercury barometer.

**1746
Franklin Experiments
With Electricity**
American statesman and inventor Benjamin Franklin experimented with electricity in the atmosphere. To demonstrate that lightning is a form of electricity, Franklin flew a kite in a thunderstorm. However, Franklin did not hold the kite string in his hand, as this historical print shows.

**1804 Gay-Lussac
Studies the Upper
Troposphere**
French chemist Joseph-Louis Gay-Lussac ascended to a height of about 7 kilometers in a hydrogen balloon to study the upper troposphere. Gay-Lussac studied pressure, temperature, and humidity.

| 1600 | 1700 | 1800 |

The Stratosphere

The **stratosphere** extends from the top of the troposphere to about 50 kilometers above Earth's surface. *Strato-* means "layer" or "spread out." **The stratosphere is the second layer of the atmosphere and contains the ozone layer.**

The lower stratosphere is cold, about −60°C. Surprisingly, the upper stratosphere is warmer than the lower stratosphere. Why is this? The middle portion of the stratosphere contains a layer of air where there is much more ozone than in the rest of the atmosphere. (Recall that ozone is the three-atom form of oxygen.) When the ozone absorbs energy from the sun, the energy is converted into heat, warming the air. The ozone layer is also important because it protects Earth's living things from dangerous ultraviolet radiation from the sun.

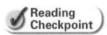 **Reading Checkpoint** Why is the upper stratosphere warmer than the lower stratosphere?

Writing in Science

Research and Write
Imagine you were one of the first people to travel into the atmosphere in a balloon. What would you need to take? Find out what the early explorers took with them in their balloons. Write at least two paragraphs about what you would take and why.

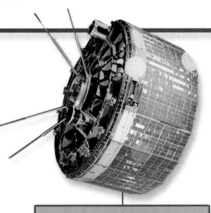

1931 Piccard Explores the Stratosphere

Swiss-Belgian physicist Auguste Piccard made the first ascent into the stratosphere. He reached a height of about 16 kilometers in an airtight cabin attached to a huge hydrogen balloon. Piccard is shown here with the cabin.

1960 First Weather Satellite Launched

TIROS-1, the first weather satellite equipped with a camera to send data back to Earth, was put into orbit by the United States. As later weather satellites circled Earth, they observed cloud cover and recorded temperatures and air pressures in the atmosphere.

1999 *Terra* Satellite Launched

The *Terra* satellite is equipped to study Earth's surface, atmosphere, and oceans from orbit. The data it gathers are used to help understand changes in Earth's climate.

| 1900 | 2000 | 2100 |

Changing Temperatures

The graph shows how temperatures in the atmosphere change with altitude. Use it to answer the questions below.

1. **Reading Graphs** What two variables are being graphed? In what unit is each measured?

2. **Reading Graphs** What is the temperature at the bottom of the stratosphere?

3. **Interpreting Data** Which layer of the atmosphere has the lowest temperature?

4. **Making Generalizations** Describe how temperature changes as altitude increases in the troposphere.

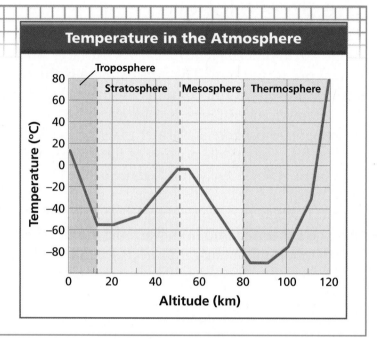

Temperature in the Atmosphere

The Mesosphere

Above the stratosphere, a drop in temperature marks the beginning of the next layer, the **mesosphere.** *Meso-* means "middle," so the mesosphere is the middle layer of the atmosphere. The mesosphere begins 50 kilometers above Earth's surface and ends at an altitude of 80 kilometers. In the outer mesosphere, temperatures approach −90°C.

The mesosphere is the layer of the atmosphere that protects Earth's surface from being hit by most meteoroids. Meteoroids are chunks of stone and metal from space. What you see as a shooting star, or meteor, is the trail of hot, glowing gases the meteoroid leaves behind in the mesosphere.

The Thermosphere

Near the top of the atmosphere, the air is very thin. At 80 kilometers above Earth's surface, the air is only about 0.001 percent as dense as the air at sea level. It's as though you took a cubic meter of air at sea level and expanded it into 100,000 cubic meters at the top of the mesosphere. **The outermost layer of Earth's atmosphere is the thermosphere.** The **thermosphere** extends from 80 kilometers above Earth's surface outward into space. It has no definite outer limit, but blends gradually with outer space.

The *thermo-* in thermosphere means "heat." Even though the air in the thermosphere is thin, it is very hot, up to 1,800°C. This is because sunlight strikes the thermosphere first. Nitrogen and oxygen molecules convert this energy into heat.

Despite the high temperature, you would not feel warm in the thermosphere. An ordinary thermometer would show a temperature well below 0°C. Why is that? Temperature is the average amount of energy of motion of each molecule of a substance. The gas molecules in the thermosphere move very rapidly, so the temperature is very high. However, the molecules are spaced far apart in the thin air. There are not enough of them to collide with a thermometer and warm it very much.

The thermosphere is divided into two layers. The lower layer, called the **ionosphere** (eye AHN uh sfeer), begins about 80 kilometers above the surface and extends to about 400 kilometers. Energy from the sun causes gas molecules in the ionosphere to become electrically charged particles called ions. Radio waves bounce off ions in the ionosphere back to Earth's surface. Brilliant light displays, such as those shown in Figure 10, also occur in the ionosphere. In the Northern Hemisphere, these displays are called the Northern Lights, or the aurora borealis. Auroras are caused by particles from the sun that enter the ionosphere near the poles. These particles strike atoms in the ionosphere, causing them to glow.

Exo- means "outer," so the **exosphere** is the outer portion of the thermosphere. The exosphere extends from about 400 kilometers outward for thousands of kilometers.

FIGURE 10
Aurora Borealis
The aurora borealis, seen from Fairbanks, Alaska, creates a spectacular display in the night sky.

 **Reading Checkpoint** **What is the ionosphere?**

Section 3 Assessment

⊙ **Target Reading Skill** Previewing Visuals
Refer to your graphic organizer about Figure 9 to help you answer the following questions.

Reviewing Key Concepts

1. a. Listing List the four main layers of the atmosphere, beginning with the layer closest to Earth's surface.
 b. Classifying What properties are used to distinguish the layers of the atmosphere?
 c. Interpreting Diagrams According to Figure 9, in which layer of the atmosphere do communications satellites orbit?
2. a. Identifying Give at least one important characteristic of each of the four main layers of Earth's atmosphere.

 b. Comparing and Contrasting How does temperature change as height increases in the troposphere? Compare this to how temperature changes with height in the stratosphere.
 c. Applying Concepts Why would you not feel warm in the thermosphere, even though temperatures can be up to 1,800°C?

Writing in Science

Cause and Effect Paragraph How do you think Earth's surface might be different if it had no atmosphere? Write a paragraph explaining your ideas.

4 Air Quality

Reading Preview

Key Concepts
- What are the major sources of air pollution?
- What causes smog and acid rain?
- What can be done to improve air quality?

Key Terms
- pollutants
- photochemical smog
- acid rain

Target Reading Skill

Outlining As you read, make an outline about air quality that you can use for review. Use the red headings for the main topics and the blue headings for the subtopics.

Air Quality
I. Sources of air pollution
A. Natural sources
B.
C.
II. Smog and acid rain
A.

Discover Activity

What's on the Jar?
1. Put on your goggles.
2. Put a small piece of modeling clay on a piece of aluminum foil. Push a candle into the clay. Light the candle.
3. Wearing an oven mitt, hold a glass jar by the rim so that the bottom of the jar is just above the flame.

Think It Over
Observing What do you see on the jar? Where did it come from?

As you are reading this page, you are breathing without even thinking about it. Breathing brings air into your lungs, where the oxygen you need is taken into your body. But not everything in the air is healthful. You may also breathe in tiny particles or even a small amount of harmful gases.

If you live in a large city, you may have noticed a brown haze in the air. Even if you live far from a city, the air around you may contain pollutants. **Pollutants** are harmful substances in the air, water, or soil. Air that contains harmful particles and gases is said to be polluted.

Air pollution can affect the health of humans and other living things. Figure 12 identifies the effects of some pollutants.

FIGURE 11
Air Pollution
Air pollution in large cities, such as Mexico City, can cause serious health problems.

Effects of Air Pollution on Human Health		
Pollutant	**Source**	**Health Effect**
Carbon monoxide	Burning of fossil fuels	Reduced ability of blood to deliver oxygen to cells
Nitrogen dioxide	Burning of fossil fuels	Breathing problems, lung damage
Ozone	Chemical reaction of certain carbon compounds	Breathing problems, asthma, eye irritation
Particles of dust, smoke, or soot	Burning of wood and fossil fuels, volcanic eruptions	Respiratory illnesses, nose and throat irritation
Sulfur dioxide	Burning of fossil fuels, volcanic eruptions	Breathing problems, lung damage

Dizziness and headaches

Eye, nose and throat irritation

Allergies

Cough

Lung diseases

Chest pains

FIGURE 12
Air pollution can cause many different problems. The table shows the health effects of air pollution. Pollen also can cause difficulties for people with allergies.

Sources of Pollution

Some air pollution occurs naturally. But many types of air pollution are the result of human activities.

Natural Sources Many natural processes add particles to the atmosphere. Forest fires, soil erosion, and dust storms release a great deal of smoke and dust into the air. The wind carries particles of molds and pollen. Erupting volcanoes spew out clouds of dust and ash along with poisonous gases.

Human Activities Human activities, such as farming and construction, can send soil and dust into the air. But most air pollution is the result of burning fossil fuels, such as coal, oil, gasoline, and diesel fuel. Almost half of this pollution comes from cars and other motor vehicles. Factories and power plants that burn coal and oil also release pollution.

When fossil fuels burn, they release both particles and gases. When people burn wood or coal, particles of soot enter the air. Soot gives smoke its dark color. All fossil fuels contain hydrocarbons, compounds made of hydrogen and carbon. As fossil fuels burn, some hydrocarbons do not burn completely and escape into the air. Burning fossil fuels produces a variety of pollutants, including carbon monoxide, nitrogen oxides, and sulfur oxides.

 **Reading Checkpoint** What are some air pollutants produced by burning fossil fuels?

Go Online
PHSchool.com

For: More on air pollution
Visit: PHSchool.com
Web Code: cfd-4014

Smog and Acid Rain

High levels of air pollution decrease the quality of the air. **The burning of fossil fuels can cause smog and acid rain.**

London-Type Smog One hundred years ago, the city of London, England, was dark and dirty. Factories burned coal, and most houses were heated by coal. The air was full of soot. In 1905, the term *smog* was created by combining the words *smoke* and *fog* to describe this type of air pollution. Typically, London-type smog forms when particles in coal smoke combine with water droplets in humid air. Today, people in London burn much less coal. As a result, the air in London now is much cleaner than it was 100 years ago.

Photochemical Smog Fortunately, London-type smog is no longer common in the United States. Instead, many cities today have another type of smog. The brown haze that develops in sunny cities is called **photochemical smog** (foh toh KEM ih kul). The *photo-* in photochemical means "light." Photochemical smog is formed by the action of sunlight on pollutants such as hydrocarbons and nitrogen oxides. These chemicals react to form a brownish mixture of ozone and other pollutants.

Recall that ozone in the stratosphere blocks ultraviolet radiation, thus protecting living things on Earth. But in the troposphere, ozone is a pollutant that can irritate the eyes, throat, and lungs. It can also harm plants and other living things and damage many materials.

FIGURE 13
Results of Acid Rain
This scientist is studying trees damaged by acid rain. Needle-leafed trees such as pines and spruce are especially sensitive to acid rain. Acid rain may make tree needles turn brown or fall off.

Acid Rain Another result of air pollution is acid rain. Rain is naturally slightly acidic, but rain that contains more acid than normal is known as **acid rain.**

How does acid rain form? The burning of coal that contains a lot of sulfur produces sulfur oxides, substances composed of oxygen and sulfur. Acid rain forms when nitrogen oxides and sulfur oxides combine with water in the air to form nitric acid and sulfuric acid. Rain, sleet, snow, fog, and even dry particles carry these two acids to trees and lakes.

Acid rain is sometimes strong enough to damage the surfaces of buildings and statues. It also harms lakes and ponds. Acid rain can make water so acidic that plants, amphibians, fish, and insects can no longer survive in it.

Reading Checkpoint What is the main pollutant in photochemical smog?

Improving Air Quality

In the United States, the federal and state governments have passed a number of laws and regulations to reduce air pollution. The Environmental Protection Agency (EPA) monitors air pollutants in the United States. Air quality in this country has generally improved over the past 30 years. The amounts of most major air pollutants have decreased. Many newer cars cause less pollution than older models. Recently built power plants are less polluting than power plants that have been in operation for many years.

However, there are now more cars on the road and more power plants burning fossil fuels than in the past. Unfortunately, the air in many American cities is still polluted. Voluntary measures, such as greater use of public transportation in place of driving, could reduce the total amount of air pollution produced. Many people think that stricter regulations are needed to control air pollution. Others argue that reducing air pollution can be very expensive and that the benefits of stricter regulations may not be worth the costs.

FIGURE 14
Public Transportation
Public transportation, like the light rail system above, can reduce air pollution.

Reading Checkpoint) **Explain one way that air quality could be improved.**

Section 4 Assessment

Target Reading Skill

Outlining Use the information in your outline about air quality to help you answer the questions below.

Reviewing Key Concepts

1. a. Defining What is a pollutant?
  b. Identifying Name three natural processes and three human activities that cause air pollution.
  c. Summarizing What is the major source of air pollution today?
2. a. Identifying What human activity is responsible for the formation of smog and acid rain?
  b. Explaining What kinds of harm does photochemical smog cause?
  c. Inferring Do you think that photochemical smog levels are higher during the winter or during the summer? Explain.

3. a. Identifying What government agency monitors air quality?
  b. Summarizing How and why has the air quality changed in the United States over the last 30 years?

 **At-Home Activity**

Dust in the Air It's easy to see particles in the air. Gather your family members in a dark room. Open a window shade or blind slightly, or turn on a flashlight. Can they see tiny particles suspended in the beam of light? Discuss where the particles came from. What might be some natural sources? What might be some human sources?

Design Your Own Lab

How Clean Is the Air?

Problem

How do weather and location affect the number of particles in the air?

Skills Focus

measuring, interpreting data

Materials

- rubber band
- coffee filters
- thermometer
- low-power microscope
- vacuum cleaner with intake hose (1 per class)

Procedure

PART 1 Particles and Weather

1. Predict what factors will affect the number of particles you collect. How might different weather conditions affect your results?

2. In your notebook, make a data table like the one on the next page.

3. Place a coffee filter over the nozzle of the vacuum cleaner hose. Fasten the coffee filter securely to the hose with a rubber band. Make sure the air passes through the coffee filter as it enters the vacuum cleaner.

4. You will take air samples in the same outdoor location for five days. If necessary, you can run the vacuum cleaner cord out of a classroom window. **CAUTION:** *Do not use the vacuum cleaner outdoors on wet or rainy days.* If it is wet or rainy, collect the sample on the next clear day.

5. Hold the vacuum nozzle at least one meter above the ground each time you use the vacuum. Turn on the vacuum. Run the vacuum for 30 minutes.

6. While the vacuum is running, observe the weather conditions. Measure the outdoor temperature. Estimate the amount of precipitation, if any, since the previous observation. Note the direction from which the wind, if any, is blowing. Also note whether the wind is strong, light, or calm. Record your observations.

7. Shut off the vacuum. Remove the coffee filter from the nozzle. Label the filter with the place, time, and date. Draw a circle on the filter to show the area that was over the vacuum nozzle.

8. Place the coffee filter on the stage of a microscope (40 power). Be sure that the part of the filter that was over the vacuum nozzle is directly under the microscope lens. Without moving the coffee filter, count all the particles you see. Record the number in your data table.

9. Repeat Steps 3–8 each clear day.

PART 2 Particles and Locations

10. Based on what you learned in Part 1, write a hypothesis for how the number of particles you collect can vary between two locations. The locations you choose should differ in some factor that might influence particle numbers.

Data Table					
Date and Time	Temperature	Amount of Precipitation	Wind Direction	Wind Speed	Number of Particles

11. Design an experiment to test your hypothesis. As you design your plan, consider the following:
- What factors might affect the number of particles collected?
- Which locations will you choose?
- What procedure will you follow?
- How will you control the variables in your experiment?
- How will you record your new data?

12. Obtain your teacher's approval before carrying out your experiment. Be sure to record all your observations.

Analyze and Conclude

1. **Measuring** In Part 1, was there a day of the week when you collected more particles?

2. **Interpreting Data** What factors changed during the week that could have caused changes in the particle count recorded in Part 1?

3. **Inferring** Did the weather have any effect on your day-to-day results? If so, which weather factor do you think was most important?

4. **Interpreting Data** Did your experiment in Part 2 prove or disprove your hypothesis?

5. **Controlling Variables** In your experiment in Part 2, which variables did you control? What was the manipulated variable? The responding variable?

6. **Classifying** Make a list of some possible sources of the particles you collected. Are these sources natural, or did the particles come from manufactured products?

Go Online
PHSchool.com

For: Data sharing
Visit: PHSchool.com
Web Code: cfd-4010

7. **Designing Experiments** How could you improve your method to obtain more particles out of the air?

8. **Communicating** Identify areas in or around your school where there may be high levels of dust and other airborne particles. Write a brochure that suggests what people should do to protect themselves in these areas. Include suggestions for improvements that might lower the levels of particles in the identified areas.

More to Explore

Do you think time of day will affect the number of particles you collect? Develop a hypothesis and a plan for testing it. Could you work with other classes to get data at different times of the day? Before carrying out your plan, get your teacher's approval.

Cars and Clean Air

New technology and strict laws have brought cleaner air to many American cities. But in some places the air is still polluted. Cars and trucks cause about half the air pollution in cities. And there are more motor vehicles on the road every year!

Worldwide, there are nearly 600 million cars. More cars will mean more traffic jams and more air pollution. What can people do to reduce air pollution by cars?

Number of Cars in Use Worldwide

The Issues

Can Cars Be Made to Pollute Less?

From 1975 until 1987, the fuel economy of new cars and light trucks improved significantly. However, since 1987, the average fuel economy of such vehicles has gotten slightly worse. Why? People are driving larger vehicles, such as trucks, vans, and SUVs. These vehicles have more power, but get fewer miles per gallon of gasoline. As a result, the total amount of pollution from motor vehicles has been increasing in recent years.

New technologies offer the promise of improved fuel economy in the future. Hybrid vehicles use a combination of gasoline and electricity to obtain much improved gas mileage. A few vehicles use fuels such as hydrogen or natural gas in place of gasoline. Vehicles using such fuels produce little pollution.

Battery-powered electric cars produce no air pollution. But the electricity to charge the batteries comes from power plants that may burn oil or coal. So electric cars produce some pollution indirectly.

A futuristic hybrid car ▼

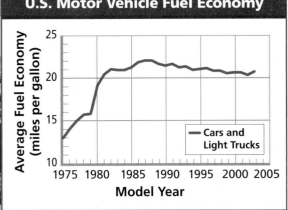

U.S. Motor Vehicle Fuel Economy

Average Fuel Economy (miles per gallon) vs. Model Year

— Cars and Light Trucks

Should People Drive Less?

Many car trips are shorter than a mile—an easy distance for most people to walk. People might also consider riding a bicycle sometimes instead of driving. Many cars on the road are occupied by just one person. People might consider riding with others in car pools or taking buses or trains instead of driving.

Are Stricter Standards or Taxes the Answer?

Some state governments have led efforts to reduce pollution. The state of California, for example, has strict anti-pollution laws. These laws set standards for gradually reducing pollutants released by cars. Stricter pollution laws might make new cars more expensive and old cars more costly to maintain.

Another approach is to make driving more expensive so that people use their cars less. That might mean higher gasoline taxes or fees for using the highways at busy times.

You Decide

1. Identify the Problem
In your own words, explain how trends in automobile use make it hard to improve air quality. What kinds of pollution are caused by automobiles?

2. Analyze the Options
What are some ways to reduce the pollution caused by cars? Should these actions be voluntary, or should governments require them?

3. Find a Solution
How would you encourage people to try to reduce the pollution from cars? Create a visual essay from newspaper and magazine clippings. Write captions to explain your solution.

For: More on cars and clean air
Visit: PHSchool.com
Web Code: cfh-4010

The BIG Idea

Structure of Earth's Atmosphere Air pressure and temperature vary with altitude, location, and time. Changes in temperature with altitude result in distinct atmospheric layers: the troposphere, stratosphere, mesosphere, and exosphere.

① The Air Around You

Key Concepts

- Earth's atmosphere is made up of nitrogen, oxygen, carbon dioxide, water vapor, and many other gases, as well as particles of liquids and solids.
- Earth's atmosphere makes conditions on Earth suitable for living things.

Key Terms

weather   ozone
atmosphere   water vapor

② Air Pressure

Key Concepts

- Because air has mass, it also has other properties, including density and pressure.
- Two common kinds of barometers are mercury barometers and aneroid barometers.
- Air pressure decreases as altitude increases. As air pressure decreases, so does density.

Key Terms

density
pressure
air pressure
barometer
mercury barometer
aneroid barometer
altitude

③ Layers of the Atmosphere

Key Concept

- Scientists divide Earth's atmosphere into four main layers classified according to changes in temperature. These layers are the troposphere, the stratosphere, the mesosphere, and the thermosphere.
- The troposphere is the layer of the atmosphere in which Earth's weather occurs.
- The stratosphere is the second layer of the atmosphere and contains the ozone layer.
- The mesosphere is the layer of the atmosphere that protects Earth's surface from being hit by most meteoroids.
- The outermost layer of Earth's atmosphere is the thermosphere.

Key Terms

troposphere
stratosphere
mesosphere
thermosphere
ionosphere
exosphere

④ Air Quality

Key Concepts

- Some air pollution occurs naturally. But many types of air pollution are the result of human activities.
- The burning of fossil fuels can cause smog and acid rain.
- In the United States, the federal and state governments have passed a number of laws and regulations to reduce air pollution.

Key Terms

pollutant
photochemical smog
acid rain

Review and Assessment

Organizing Information

Concept Mapping Copy the concept map about air pressure onto a separate sheet of paper. Then complete it and add a title. (For more on concept mapping, see the Skills Handbook.)

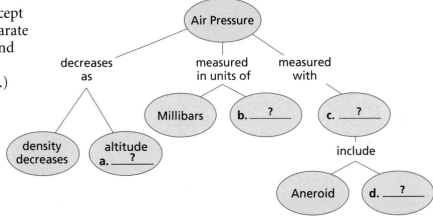

Reviewing Key Terms

Choose the letter of the best answer.

1. The most abundant gas in the atmosphere is
   a. ozone.
   b. water vapor.
   c. oxygen.
   d. nitrogen.

2. Air pressure is typically measured with a
   a. thermometer.
   b. satellite.
   c. barometer.
   d. hot-air balloon.

3. The layers of the atmosphere are classified according to changes in
   a. altitude.
   b. temperature.
   c. air pressure.
   d. pollutants.

4. The layer of the atmosphere that reflects radio waves is called the
   a. mesosphere.
   b. troposphere.
   c. ionosphere.
   d. stratosphere.

5. Most air pollution is caused by
   a. ozone.
   b. acid rain.
   c. photochemical smog.
   d. the burning of fossil fuels.

If the statement is true, write *true*. If it is false, change the underlined word or words to make the statement true.

6. <u>Weather</u> is the condition of Earth's atmosphere at a particular time and place.

7. The force pushing on an area or surface is known as <u>density</u>.

8. Earth's weather occurs in the <u>thermosphere</u>.

9. The ozone layer is found in the <u>exosphere</u>.

10. When sulfur and nitrogen oxides mix with water in the air, they form <u>photochemical smog</u>.

Writing in Science

Descriptive Paragraph Suppose you are on a hot air balloon flight to the upper levels of the troposphere. Describe how the properties of the atmosphere, such as air pressure and amount of oxygen, would change during your trip.

Discovery CHANNEL SCHOOL

The Atmosphere
Video Preview
Video Field Trip
▶ Video Assessment

Review and Assessment

Checking Concepts

11. Explain why it is difficult to include water vapor in a graph that shows the percentages of various gases in the atmosphere.

12. Name two ways in which carbon dioxide is added to the atmosphere.

13. List the following layers of the atmosphere in order, moving up from Earth's surface: thermosphere, stratosphere, troposphere, mesosphere.

14. Describe the temperature changes that occur as you move upward through the troposphere.

15. What is the difference between photochemical smog and London-type smog?

16. How does acid rain form and what kinds of problems can it cause?

Thinking Critically

17. **Applying Concepts** Why can an aneroid barometer be used to indicate changes in elevation as well as air pressure?

18. **Reading Graphs** According to the graph below, what is the air pressure at an altitude of 4 km? In general, how does air pressure change with altitude?

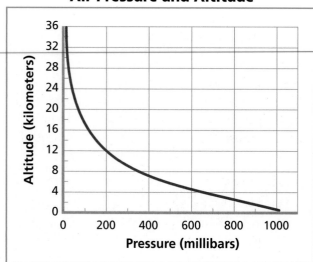

Air Pressure and Altitude

19. **Inferring** Why are clouds at the top of the troposphere made of ice crystals rather than drops of water?

20. **Comparing and Contrasting** Compare the effect of ozone in the troposphere with its effect in the stratosphere. Where is it harmful? Where is it helpful?

21. **Relating Cause and Effect** How could burning high-sulfur coal in a power plant harm a forest hundreds of kilometers away?

Applying Skills

Use the table below to answer the questions that follow.

The table shows the temperature at various altitudes above Omaha, Nebraska on a January day.

Altitude (kilometers)	0	1.6	3.2	4.8	6.4	7.2
Temperature (°C)	0	−4	−9	−21	−32	−40

22. **Graphing** Make a line graph of the data in the table. Put temperature on the horizontal axis and altitude on the vertical axis. Label your graph.

23. **Reading Graphs** At about what height above the ground was the temperature −15°C?

24. **Reading Graphs** What was the approximate temperature 2.4 kilometers over Omaha?

25. **Calculating** Suppose an airplane was about 6.8 kilometers above Omaha on this day. What was the approximate temperature at 6.8 kilometers? How much colder was the temperature at 6.8 kilometers above the ground than at ground level?

Lab zone Chapter **Project**

Performance Assessment For your class presentation, prepare a display of your weather observations. Include drawings, graphs, and tables that summarize the weather you observed. Practice presenting your project to your group.

Standardized Test Prep

Layers of the Atmosphere

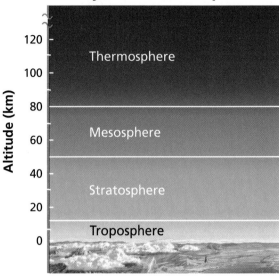

Use the the diagram above and your knowledge of science to answer Questions 3 and 4.

Choose the letter of the best answer.

1. What two gases make up approximately 99% of Earth's atmosphere?
   A nitrogen and carbon dioxide
   B oxygen and carbon dioxide
   C nitrogen and hydrogen
   D nitrogen and oxygen

2. In the troposphere, as altitude increases
   F air pressure decreases.
   G temperature decreases.
   H air density decreases.
   J all of the above

3. Use the diagram to estimate the depth of the stratosphere.
   A about 50 kilometers
   B about 40 kilometers
   C about 30 kilometers
   D about 20 kilometers

4. According to the diagram, where is a meteoroid when it is 75 kilometers above Earth's surface?
   F the mesosphere
   G the stratosphere
   H the thermosphere
   J the troposphere

5. The ozone layer is found in the
   A troposphere.
   B stratosphere.
   C mesosphere.
   D thermosphere.

Constructed Response

6. What is acid rain, and why is it considered an environmental problem? Describe how acid rain forms and how it affects living things. Include in your answer the specific substances that combine to form acid rain.

Chapter

2

Weather Factors

The BIG Idea
Transfer of Energy

 What factors interact to produce changes in weather?

Chapter Preview

❶ Energy in Earth's Atmosphere
Discover Does a Plastic Bag Trap Heat?
At-Home Activity Heating Your Home
Skills Lab Heating Earth's Surface

❷ Heat Transfer
Discover What Happens When Air Is Heated?
Math Skills Converting Units
Try This Temperature and Height

❸ Winds
Discover Does the Wind Turn?
Try This Build a Wind Vane
Active Art Global Winds
Technology Lab Measuring the Wind

❹ Water in the Atmosphere
Discover How Does Fog Form?
Active Art The Water Cycle
Analyzing Data Determining Relative Humidity
At-Home Activity Water in the Air

❺ Precipitation
Discover How Can You Make Hail?
Skills Activity Calculating

Rain is an important factor in helping these black-eyed Susans grow. ▶

Lab zone™ Chapter **Project**

Design and Build Your Own Weather Station

In this chapter, you will learn about a variety of weather factors—such as air pressure, precipitation, and wind speed. As you learn about these factors, you will build your own weather station. Your weather station will include simple instruments that you will use to monitor the weather.

Your Goal To design and build a weather station to monitor at least three weather factors and to look for patterns that can be used to predict the next day's weather

You must

- design and build instruments for your weather station
- use your instruments to collect and record data in a daily log
- display your data in a set of graphs
- use your data to try to predict the weather
- follow the safety guidelines in Appendix A

Plan It! Begin your project by deciding where your weather station will be located. Plan which instruments you will build and how you will make your measurements. Prepare a log to record your daily observations. Finally, graph the data and look for any patterns that you can use to predict the next day's weather.

Energy in Earth's Atmosphere

Reading Preview

Key Concepts
- In what forms does energy from the sun travel to Earth?
- What happens to the sun's energy when it reaches Earth?

Key Terms
- electromagnetic waves
- radiation
- infrared radiation
- ultraviolet radiation
- scattering
- greenhouse effect

Target Reading Skill

Sequencing As you read, make a flowchart that shows how the sun's energy reaches Earth's surface. Put each step of the process in a separate box in the order in which it occurs.

How Earth's Atmosphere Gets Energy

Sun gives off energy.

↓

Energy travels to Earth as electromagnetic radiation.

↓

Lab zone Discover **Activity**

Does a Plastic Bag Trap Heat?

1. Record the initial temperatures on two thermometers. (You should get the same readings.)
2. Place one of the thermometers in a plastic bag. Put a small piece of paper in the bag so that it shades the bulb of the thermometer. Seal the bag.
3. Place both thermometers on a sunny window ledge or near a light bulb. Cover the bulb of the second thermometer with a small piece of paper. Predict what you think will happen.
4. Wait five minutes. Then record the temperatures on the two thermometers.

Think It Over

Measuring Were the two temperatures the same? How could you explain any difference?

In the deserts of Arizona, summer nights can be chilly. In the morning, the sun is low in the sky and the air is cool. As the sun rises, the temperature increases. By noon it is quite hot. As you will learn in this chapter, heat is a major factor in the weather. The movement of heat in the atmosphere causes temperatures to change, winds to blow, and rain to fall.

Energy From the Sun

Where does this heat come from? Nearly all the energy in Earth's atmosphere comes from the sun. This energy travels to Earth as **electromagnetic waves,** a form of energy that can move through the vacuum of space. Electromagnetic waves are classified according to wavelength, or distance between waves. **Radiation** is the direct transfer of energy by electromagnetic waves.

What kinds of energy do we receive from the sun? Is all of the energy the same? **Most of the energy from the sun travels to Earth in the form of visible light and infrared radiation. A small amount arrives as ultraviolet radiation.**

As the sun rises, energy in the form of electromagnetic waves reaches Earth's surface.

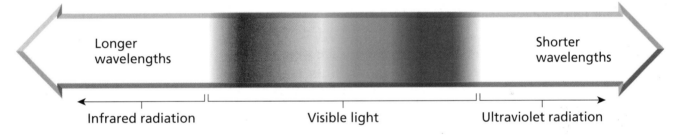

Longer wavelengths

Shorter wavelengths

Infrared radiation   Visible light   Ultraviolet radiation

Visible Light Visible light includes all of the colors that you see in a rainbow: red, orange, yellow, green, blue, and violet. The different colors are the result of different wavelengths. Red and orange light have the longest wavelengths, while blue and violet light have the shortest wavelengths, as shown in Figure 1.

Non-Visible Radiation One form of electromagnetic energy, **infrared radiation,** has wavelengths that are longer than red light. Infrared radiation is not visible, but can be felt as heat. The sun also gives off **ultraviolet radiation,** which is an invisible form of energy with wavelengths that are shorter than violet light. Ultraviolet radiation can cause sunburns. This radiation can also cause skin cancer and eye damage.

 **Reading Checkpoint** **Which color of visible light has the longest wavelengths?**

FIGURE 1
Radiation From the Sun
Energy from the sun travels to Earth as infrared radiation, visible light, and ultraviolet radiation.
Interpreting Diagrams *What type of radiation has wavelengths that are shorter than visible light?*

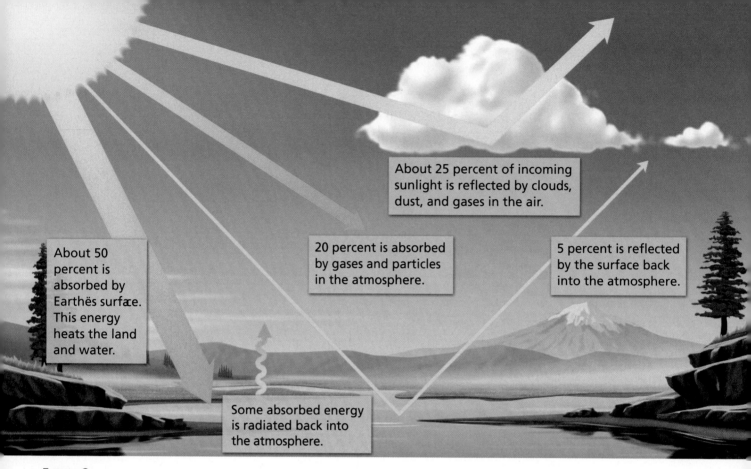

About 25 percent of incoming sunlight is reflected by clouds, dust, and gases in the air.

About 50 percent is absorbed by Earth's surface. This energy heats the land and water.

20 percent is absorbed by gases and particles in the atmosphere.

5 percent is reflected by the surface back into the atmosphere.

Some absorbed energy is radiated back into the atmosphere.

FIGURE 2

Energy in the Atmosphere
The sun's energy interacts with Earth's atmosphere and surface in several ways. About half is either reflected back into space or absorbed by the atmosphere. The rest reaches Earth's surface.

Energy in the Atmosphere

Before reaching Earth's surface, sunlight must pass through the atmosphere. The path of the sun's rays is shown in Figure 2. **Some sunlight is absorbed or reflected by the atmosphere before it can reach the surface. The rest passes through the atmosphere to the surface.**

Part of the sun's energy is absorbed by the atmosphere. The ozone layer in the stratosphere absorbs most of the ultraviolet radiation. Water vapor and carbon dioxide absorb some infrared radiation. Clouds, dust, and other gases also absorb energy.

Some sunlight is reflected. Clouds act like mirrors, reflecting sunlight back into space. Dust particles and gases in the atmosphere reflect light in all directions, a process called **scattering.** When you look at the sky, the light you see has been scattered by gas molecules in the atmosphere. Gas molecules scatter short wavelengths of visible light (blue and violet) more than long wavelengths (red and orange). Scattered light therefore looks bluer than ordinary sunlight. This is why the daytime sky looks blue.

When the sun is rising or setting, its light passes through a greater thickness of the atmosphere than when the sun is higher in the sky. More light from the blue end of the spectrum is removed by scattering before it reaches your eyes. The remaining light contains mostly red and orange light. The sun looks red, and clouds around it become very colorful.

Go Online
scinks NSTA

For: Links on energy in Earth's atmosphere
Visit: www.SciLinks.org
Web Code: scn-0921

Energy at Earth's Surface

Some of the sun's energy reaches Earth's surface and is reflected back into the atmosphere. About half of the sun's energy, however, is absorbed by the land and water and changed into heat.

When Earth's surface is heated, it radiates most of the energy back into the atmosphere as infrared radiation. As shown in Figure 3, much of this infrared radiation cannot travel all the way through the atmosphere back into space. Instead, it is absorbed by water vapor, carbon dioxide, methane, and other gases in the air. The energy from the absorbed radiation heats the gases in the air. These gases form a "blanket" around Earth that holds heat in the atmosphere. The process by which gases hold heat in the air is called the **greenhouse effect.**

The greenhouse effect is a natural process that keeps Earth's atmosphere at a temperature that is comfortable for most living things. Over time, the amount of energy absorbed by the atmosphere and Earth's surface is in balance with the amount of energy radiated into space. In this way, Earth's average temperatures remain fairly constant. However, as you will learn later, emissions from human activities may be altering this process.

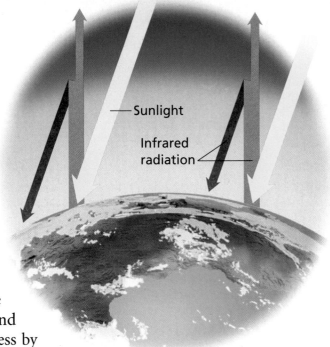

FIGURE 3
Greenhouse Effect
Sunlight travels through the atmosphere to Earth's surface. Earth's surface then gives off infrared radiation. Much of this energy is held by the atmosphere, warming it.

Sunlight

Infrared radiation

 **Reading Checkpoint** What is the greenhouse effect?

Section 1 Assessment

Target Reading Skill

Sequencing Refer to your flowchart about how the sun's energy reaches Earth's surface as you answer Question 2.

Reviewing Key Concepts

1. **a. Listing** List three forms of radiation from the sun.
   b. Comparing and Contrasting Which form of radiation from the sun has the longest wavelength? The shortest wavelength?
2. **a. Summarizing** What happens to most of the sunlight that reaches Earth?
   b. Interpreting Diagrams What percentage of incoming sunlight is reflected by clouds, dust, and gases in the atmosphere?
   c. Applying Concepts Why are sunsets red?

3. **a. Describing** What happens to the energy from the sun that is absorbed by Earth's surface?
   b. Predicting How might conditions on Earth be different without the greenhouse effect?

Lab zone At-Home Activity

Heating Your Home With an adult family member, explore the role radiation from the sun plays in heating your home. Does it make some rooms warmer in the morning? Are other rooms warmer in the afternoon? How does opening and closing curtains or blinds affect the temperature of a room? Explain your observations to your family.

Heating Earth's Surface

Problem

How do the heating and cooling rates of sand and water compare?

Skills Focus

developing hypotheses, graphing, drawing conclusions

Materials

- 2 thermometers or temperature probes
- 2 beakers, 400-mL
- sand, 300 mL
- water, 300 mL
- lamp with 150-W bulb
- metric ruler
- clock or stopwatch
- string
- graph paper
- ring stand and two ring clamps

Procedure

1. Which do you think will heat up faster—sand or water? Record your hypothesis. Then follow these steps to test your hypothesis.

2. Copy the data table into your notebook. Add enough rows to record data for 15 minutes.

3. Fill one beaker with 300 mL of dry sand.

4. Fill the second beaker with 300 mL of water at room temperature.

5. Arrange the beakers side by side beneath the ring stand.

6. Place one thermometer in each beaker. If you are using a temperature probe, see your teacher for instructions.

7. Suspend the thermometers from the ring stand with string. This will hold the thermometers in place so they do not fall.

8. Adjust the height of the clamp so that the bulb of each thermometer is covered by about 0.5 cm of sand or water in a beaker.

9. Position the lamp so that it is about 20 cm above the sand and water. There should be no more than 8 cm between the beakers. **CAUTION:** *Be careful not to splash water onto the hot light bulb.*

10. Record the temperature of the sand and water in your data table.

11. Turn on the lamp. Read the temperature of the sand and water every minute for 15 minutes. Record the temperatures in the *Temperature With Light On* column in the data table.

12. Which material do you think will cool off more quickly? Record your hypothesis. Again, give reasons why you think your hypothesis is correct.

13. Turn the light off. Read the temperature of the sand and water every minute for another 15 minutes. Record the temperatures in the *Temperature With Light Off* column (16–30 minutes).

Data Table					
Temperature With Light On (°C)			Temperature With Light Off (°C)		
Time (min)	Sand	Water	Time (min)	Sand	Water
Start			16		
1			17		
2			18		
3			19		
4			20		
5			21		

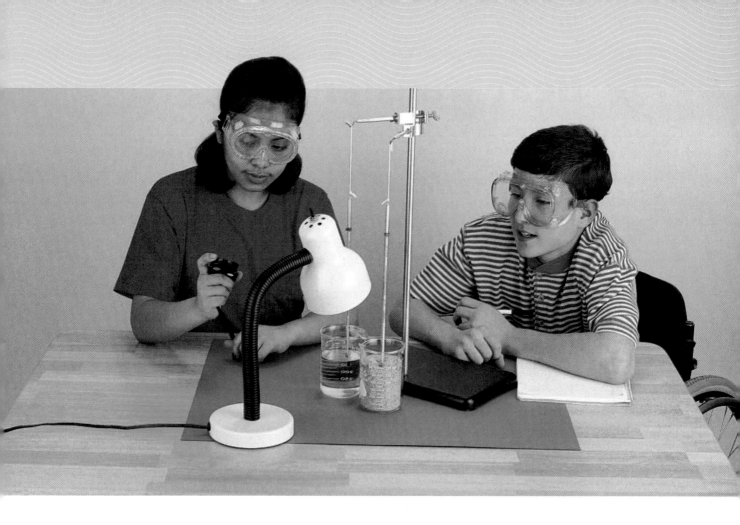

Analyze and Conclude

1. **Graphing** Draw two line graphs to show the data for the temperature change in sand and water over time. Label the horizontal axis from 0 to 30 minutes and the vertical axis in degrees Celsius. Draw both graphs on the same piece of graph paper. Use a dashed line to show the temperature change in water and a solid line to show the temperature change in sand.

2. **Calculating** Calculate the total change in temperature for each material.

3. **Interpreting Data** Based on your data, which material had the greater increase in temperature?

4. **Drawing Conclusions** What can you conclude about which material absorbed heat faster? How do your results compare with your hypothesis?

5. **Interpreting Data** Review your data again. In 15 minutes, which material cooled faster?

6. **Drawing Conclusions** How do these results compare to your second hypothesis?

7. **Developing Hypotheses** Based on your results, which do you think will heat up more quickly on a sunny day: the water in a lake or the sand surrounding it? After dark, which will cool off more quickly?

8. **Communicating** If your results did not support either of your hypotheses, why do you think the results differed from what you expected? Write a paragraph in which you discuss the results and how they compared to your hypotheses.

Design an Experiment

Do you think all solid materials heat up as fast as sand? For example, consider gravel, crushed stone, or different types of soil. Write a hypothesis about their heating rates as an "If … then…." statement. With the approval and supervision of your teacher, develop a procedure to test your hypothesis. Was your hypothesis correct?

Heat Transfer

Reading Preview

Key Concepts
- How is temperature measured?
- In what three ways is heat transferred?
- How is heat transferred in the troposphere?

Key Terms
- temperature
- thermal energy
- thermometer
- heat
- conduction
- convection
- convection currents

Target Reading Skill

Outlining As you read, make an outline about how heat is transferred. Use the red headings for the main topics and the blue headings for the subtopics.

Heat Transfer
I. Thermal energy and temperature
A. Measuring temperature
B.
II. How heat is transferred
A.

Discover **Activity**

What Happens When Air Is Heated?

1. Use heavy scissors to cut the flat part out of an aluminum pie plate. Use the tip of the scissors to poke a small hole in the middle of the flat part of the plate.
2. Cut the part into a spiral shape, as shown in the photo. Tie a 30-centimeter piece of thread to the middle of the spiral.
3. Hold the spiral over a source of heat, such as a candle, hot plate, or incandescent light bulb.

Think It Over
Inferring What happened to the spiral? Why do you think this happened?

You pour a cup of steaming tea from a teapot. Your teacup is warm to the touch. Somehow, heat was transferred from one object (the cup) to another (your hand) that it was touching. This is an example of conduction, one of three ways that heat can be transferred. As you'll learn in this section, heat transfer in the troposphere plays an important role in influencing Earth's weather.

It takes only a small amount of energy to heat up a cup of tea. ▶

FIGURE 4
Movement of Molecules The iced tea is cold, so its molecules move slowly. The herbal tea is hot, so its molecules move faster than the molecules in the iced tea.
Inferring *Which liquid has a higher temperature?*

Thermal Energy and Temperature

The tea in the cup and in the teapot are at the same temperature but have a different amount of total energy. To understand this, you need to know that all substances are made up of tiny particles that are constantly moving. The faster the particles are moving, the more energy they have. Figure 4 shows how the motion of the particles is related to the amount of energy they hold. **Temperature** is the *average* amount of energy of motion of each particle of a substance. That is, temperature is a measure of how hot or cold a substance is. In contrast, the *total* energy of motion in the particles of a substance is called **thermal energy.** The hot tea in the teapot has more thermal energy than the hot tea in the cup because it has more particles.

Measuring Temperature Temperature is one of the most important factors affecting the weather. **Air temperature is usually measured with a thermometer.** A **thermometer** is a thin glass tube with a bulb on one end that contains a liquid, usually mercury or colored alcohol.

Thermometers work because liquids expand when they are heated and contract when they are cooled. When the air temperature increases, the temperature of the liquid in the bulb also increases. This causes the liquid to expand and rise up the column.

Temperature Scales Temperature is measured in units called degrees. Two temperature scales are commonly used: the Celsius scale and the Fahrenheit scale. Scientists use the Celsius scale. On the Celsius scale, the freezing point of pure water is 0°C (read "zero degrees Celsius"). The boiling point of pure water at sea level is 100°C. Weather reports in the United States use the Fahrenheit scale. On the Fahrenheit scale, the freezing point of water is 32°F and the boiling point is 212°F.

Reading Checkpoint **Which temperature scale do scientists use?**

Converting Units

Temperatures in weather reports use the Fahrenheit scale, but scientists use the Celsius scale. Temperature readings can be converted from the Fahrenheit scale to the Celsius scale using the following equation:

$$°C = \frac{5}{9}(°F - 32)$$

If the temperature is 68°F, what is the temperature in degrees Celsius?

$$°C = \frac{5}{9}(68 - 32)$$

$$°C = 20°C$$

Practice Problem Use the equation to convert the following temperatures from Fahrenheit to Celsius: 35.0°F, 60.0°F, and 72.0°F.

Lab zone Try This Activity

Temperature and Height

How much difference is there between air temperatures near the ground and higher up? Give reasons for your prediction.

1. Take all of your measurements outside at a location that is sunny all day.

2. Early in the morning, measure the air temperature 1 cm and 1.25 m above the ground. Record the time and temperature for each height. Repeat your measurements late in the afternoon.

3. Repeat Step 2 for two more days.

4. Graph your data for each height with temperature on the vertical axis and time of day on the horizontal axis. Use the same graph paper and same scale for each graph. Label each graph.

Interpreting Data At which height did the temperature vary the most? How can you explain the difference?

How Heat Is Transferred

Heat is the transfer of thermal energy from a hotter object to a cooler one. **Heat is transferred in three ways: radiation, conduction, and convection.**

Radiation Have you ever felt the warmth of the sun's rays on your face? You were feeling energy coming directly from the sun as radiation. Recall that radiation is the direct transfer of energy by electromagnetic waves. Most of the heat you feel from the sun travels to you as infrared radiation. You cannot see infrared radiation, but you can feel it as heat.

Conduction Have you ever walked barefoot on hot sand? Your feet felt hot because heat moved directly from the sand into your feet. The direct transfer of heat from one substance to another substance that it is touching is called **conduction.** When a fast-moving sand molecule bumps into a slower-moving molecule, the faster molecule transfers some of its energy.

The closer together the atoms or molecules in a substance are, the more effectively they can conduct heat. Conduction works well in some solids, such as metals, but not as well in liquids and gases. Air and water do not conduct heat very well.

Convection In fluids (liquids and gases), particles can move easily from one place to another. As the particles move, their energy goes along with them. The transfer of heat by the movement of a fluid is called **convection.**

Heating the Troposphere Radiation, conduction, and convection work together to heat the troposphere. During the day, the sun's radiation heats Earth's surface. The land becomes warmer than the air. Air near Earth's surface is warmed by both radiation and conduction. However, heat is not easily transferred from one air particle to another by conduction. Only the first few meters of the troposphere are heated by conduction. Thus, the air close to the ground is usually warmer than the air a few meters up.

Within the troposphere, heat is transferred mostly by convection. When the air near the ground is heated, its particles move more rapidly. As a result, they bump into each other and move farther apart. The air becomes less dense. Cooler, denser air sinks toward the surface, forcing the warmer air to rise. The upward movement of warm air and the downward movement of cool air form **convection currents.** Convection currents move heat throughout the troposphere.

 **Reading Checkpoint** How is the air near Earth's surface heated?

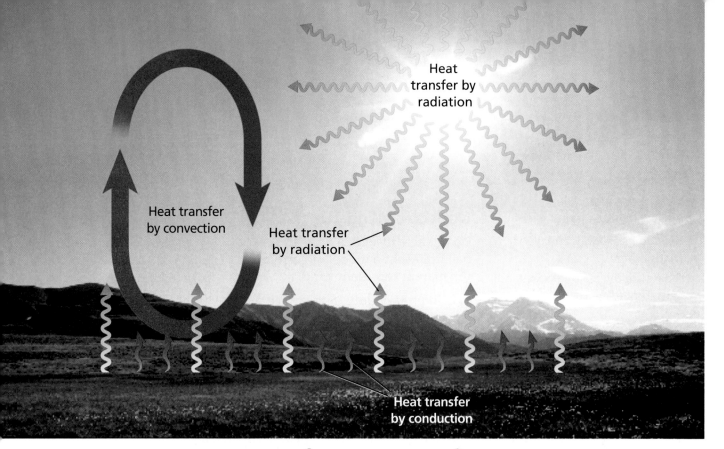

Heat transfer by radiation

Heat transfer by convection

Heat transfer by radiation

Heat transfer by conduction

Radiation

Conduction

Convection

FIGURE 5
Heat Transfer
All three types of heat transfer—radiation, conduction, and convection—help to warm the troposphere.

Section 2 Assessment

Target Reading Skill Outlining Use the information in your outline about heat transfer to help you answer the questions below.

Reviewing Key Concepts

1. **a. Defining** What is temperature?
   b. Identifying What instrument is used to measure air temperature?
   c. Comparing and Contrasting A pail of water is the same temperature as a lake. Compare the amount of thermal energy of the water in the lake and the water in the pail.
2. **a. Naming** Name three ways that heat can be transferred.
   b. Describing How do the three types of heat transfer work together to heat the troposphere?

   c. Identifying What is the major way that heat is transferred in the troposphere?
   d. Applying Concepts Explain how a hawk or eagle can sometimes soar upward without flapping its wings.

Math Practice

3. **Converting Units** Use the equation from the Math Skills Activity to convert the following temperatures from Fahrenheit to Celsius: 52°F, 86°F, 77°F, and 97°F.

Reading Preview

Key Concepts
- What causes winds?
- How do local winds and global winds differ?
- Where are the major global wind belts located?

Key Terms
- wind • anemometer
- wind-chill factor • local winds
- sea breeze • land breeze
- global winds • Coriolis effect
- latitude • jet stream

Target Reading Skill

Relating Cause and Effect As you read, identify how the unequal heating of the atmosphere causes the air to move. Write the information in a graphic organizer like the one below.

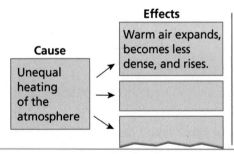

Cause

Unequal heating of the atmosphere

Effects

Warm air expands, becomes less dense, and rises.

Lab zone Discover **Activity**

Does the Wind Turn?

Do this activity with a partner. Let the ball represent a model of Earth and the marker represent wind.

1. Using heavy-duty tape, attach a pencil to a large smooth ball so that you can spin the ball from the top without touching it.
2. One partner should hold the pencil. Slowly turn the ball counterclockwise when seen from above.
3. While the ball is turning, the second partner should use a marker to try to draw a straight line from the "North Pole" to the "equator" of the ball. What shape does the line form?

Think It Over

Making Models If cold air were moving south from Canada into the continental United States, how would its movement be affected by Earth's rotation?

Have you ever flown a kite? Start by unwinding a few meters of string with the kite downwind from you. Have a friend hold the kite high overhead. Then, as your friend releases the kite, run directly into the wind. If you're lucky, the kite will start to rise. Once the kite is stable, you can unwind your string to let the wind lift the kite high into the sky. But what exactly is the wind that lifts the kite, and what causes it to blow?

A kite festival in Cape Town, South Africa ▶

What Is Wind?

Because air is a fluid, it can move easily from place to place. Differences in air pressure cause the air to move. A **wind** is the horizontal movement of air from an area of high pressure to an area of lower pressure. **Winds are caused by differences in air pressure.**

Most differences in air pressure are caused by the unequal heating of the atmosphere. Convection currents form when an area of Earth's surface is heated by the sun's rays. Air over the heated surface expands and becomes less dense. As the air becomes less dense, its air pressure decreases. If a nearby area is not heated as much, the air above the less-heated area will be cooler and denser. The cool, dense air with a higher pressure flows underneath the warm, less dense air. This forces the warm air to rise.

Measuring Wind Winds are described by their direction and speed. Wind direction is determined with a wind vane. The wind swings the wind vane so that one end points into the wind. The name of a wind tells you where the wind is coming from. For example, a south wind blows from the south toward the north. A north wind blows to the south.

Wind speed can be measured with an **anemometer** (an uh MAHM uh tur). An anemometer has three or four cups mounted at the ends of spokes that spin on an axle. The force of the wind against the cups turns the axle. A meter on the axle shows the wind speed.

Wind-Chill Factor On a warm day, a cool breeze can be refreshing. But during the winter, the same breeze can make you feel uncomfortably cold. The wind blowing over your skin removes body heat. The stronger the wind, the colder you feel. The increased cooling a wind can cause is called the **wind-chill factor.** Thus a weather report may say, "The temperature outside is 20 degrees Fahrenheit. But with a wind speed of 30 miles per hour, the wind-chill factor makes it feel like 1 degree above zero."

 **Reading Checkpoint** **Toward what direction does a west wind blow?**

Try This Activity

Build a Wind Vane

1. ✂ Use scissors to cut out a pointer and a slightly larger tail fin from construction paper.
2. Make a slit 1 cm deep in each end of a soda straw.
3. Slide the pointer and tail fin into place on the straw, securing them with small pieces of tape.

4. Hold the straw on your finger to find the point at which it balances.
5. Carefully push a pin through the balance point and into the eraser of a pencil. Make sure the wind vane can spin freely.

Observing How can you use your wind vane to tell the direction of the wind?

FIGURE 6
Wind Direction and Speed
The wind vane on the left points in the direction the wind is blowing from. The anemometer on the right measures wind speed. The cups catch the wind, turning faster when the wind blows faster.

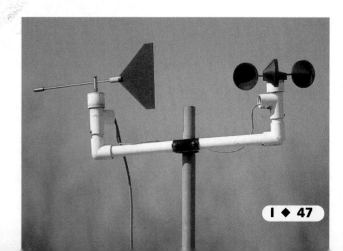

Local Winds

Have you ever noticed a breeze at the beach on a hot summer day? Even if there is no wind inland, there may be a cool breeze blowing in from the water. This breeze is an example of a local wind. **Local winds** are winds that blow over short distances. **Local winds are caused by the unequal heating of Earth's surface within a small area.** Local winds form only when large-scale winds are weak.

Sea Breeze Unequal heating often occurs along the shore of a large body of water. It takes more energy to warm up a body of water than it does to warm up an equal area of land. As the sun heats Earth's surface during the day, the land warms up faster than the water. As a result, the air over the land becomes warmer than the air over the water. The warm air expands and rises, creating a low-pressure area. Cool air blows inland from over the water and moves underneath the warm air, causing a sea breeze. A **sea breeze** or a lake breeze is a local wind that blows from an ocean or lake. Figure 7 shows a sea breeze.

Land Breeze At night, the process is reversed. Land cools more quickly than water, so the air over the land becomes cooler than the air over the water. As the warmer air over the water expands and rises, cooler air from the land moves beneath it. The flow of air from land to a body of water is called a **land breeze.**

FIGURE 7
Local Winds
During the day, cool air moves from the sea to the land, creating a sea breeze. At night, cooler air moves from the land to the sea.
Forming Operational Definitions *What type of breeze occurs at night?*

Global Winds

Global winds are winds that blow steadily from specific directions over long distances. **Like local winds, global winds are created by the unequal heating of Earth's surface. But unlike local winds, global winds occur over a large area.** Recall how the sun's radiation strikes Earth. In the middle of the day near the equator, the sun is almost directly overhead. The direct rays from the sun heat Earth's surface intensely. Near the poles, the sun's rays strike Earth's surface at a lower angle. The sun's energy is spread out over a larger area, so it heats the surface less. As a result, temperatures near the poles are much lower than they are near the equator.

Global Convection Currents How do global winds develop? Temperature differences between the equator and the poles produce giant convection currents in the atmosphere. Warm air rises at the equator, and cold air sinks at the poles. Therefore air pressure tends to be lower near the equator and greater near the poles. This difference in pressure causes winds at Earth's surface to blow from the poles toward the equator. Higher in the atmosphere, however, air flows away from the equator toward the poles. Those air movements produce global winds.

The Coriolis Effect If Earth did not rotate, global winds would blow in a straight line from the poles toward the equator. Because Earth is rotating, however, global winds do not follow a straight path. As the winds blow, Earth rotates from west to east underneath them, making it seem as if the winds have curved. The way Earth's rotation makes winds curve is called the **Coriolis effect** (kawr ee OH lis).

Because of the Coriolis effect, global winds in the Northern Hemisphere gradually turn toward the right. As Figure 9 shows, a wind blowing toward the south gradually turns toward the southwest. In the Southern Hemisphere, winds curve toward the left.

✓ **Reading Checkpoint** Which way do winds turn in the Southern Hemisphere?

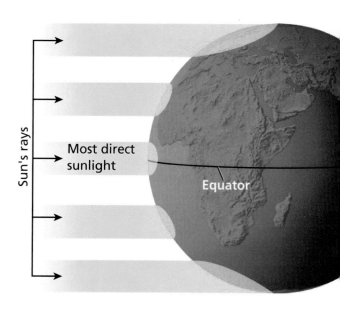

FIGURE 8
Angle of Sun's Rays
Near the equator, energy from the sun strikes Earth almost directly. Near the poles, the same amount of energy is spread out over a larger area.

Sun's rays

Most direct sunlight

Equator

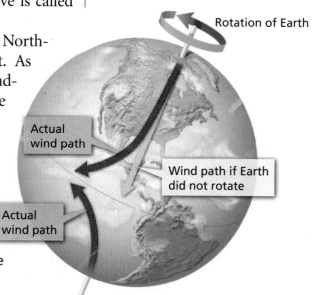

Rotation of Earth

Actual wind path

Wind path if Earth did not rotate

Actual wind path

FIGURE 9
Coriolis Effect
As Earth rotates, the Coriolis effect turns winds in the Northern Hemisphere toward the right.

FIGURE 10
Ocean Sailing
Sailing ships relied on global winds to speed their journeys to various ports around the world. *Applying Concepts How much effect do you think the prevailing winds have on shipping today?*

Global Wind Belts

The Coriolis effect and other factors combine to produce a pattern of calm areas and wind belts around Earth, as shown in Figure 11. The calm areas include the doldrums and the horse latitudes. **The major global wind belts are the trade winds, the polar easterlies, and the prevailing westerlies.**

Doldrums Near the equator, the sun heats the surface strongly. Warm air rises steadily, creating an area of low pressure. Cool air moves into the area, but is warmed rapidly and rises before it moves very far. There is very little horizontal motion, so the winds near the equator are very weak. Regions near the equator with little or no wind are called the doldrums.

Horse Latitudes Warm air that rises at the equator divides and flows both north and south. **Latitude** is distance from the equator, measured in degrees. At about 30° north and south latitudes, the air stops moving toward the poles and sinks. In each of these regions, another belt of calm air forms. Hundreds of years ago, sailors becalmed in these waters ran out of food and water for their horses and had to throw the horses overboard. Because of this, the latitudes 30° north and south of the equator came to be called the horse latitudes.

Trade Winds When the cold air over the horse latitudes sinks, it produces a region of high pressure. This high pressure causes surface winds to blow both toward the equator and away from it. The winds that blow toward the equator are turned west by the Coriolis effect. As a result, winds in the Northern Hemisphere between 30° north latitude and the equator generally blow from the northeast. In the Southern Hemisphere between 30° south latitude and the equator, the winds blow from the southeast. For hundreds of years, sailors relied on these winds to move ships carrying valuable cargoes from Europe to the West Indies and South America. As a result, these steady easterly winds are called the trade winds.

Prevailing Westerlies In the mid-latitudes, between 30° and 60° north and south, winds that blow toward the poles are turned toward the east by the Coriolis effect. Because they blow from the west to the east, they are called prevailing westerlies. The prevailing westerlies blow generally from the southwest in north latitudes and from the northwest in south latitudes. The prevailing westerlies play an important part in the weather of the United States.

FIGURE 11
Global Winds

A series of wind belts circles Earth. Between the wind belts are calm areas where air is rising or falling. **Interpreting Diagrams** *Which global wind belt would a sailor choose to sail from eastern Canada to Europe?*

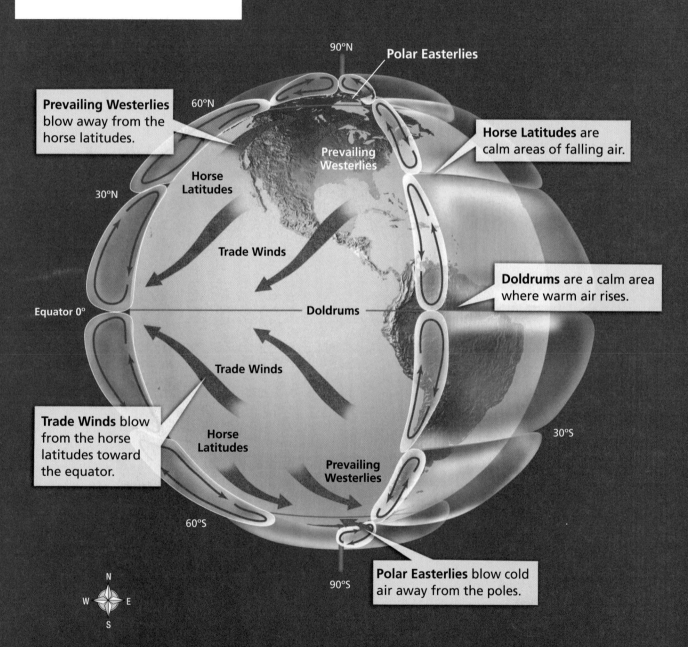

90°N — **Polar Easterlies**

Prevailing Westerlies blow away from the horse latitudes.

60°N

Horse Latitudes are calm areas of falling air.

Prevailing Westerlies

Horse Latitudes

30°N

Trade Winds

Doldrums are a calm area where warm air rises.

Equator 0° — Doldrums

Trade Winds

Trade Winds blow from the horse latitudes toward the equator.

Horse Latitudes

30°S

Prevailing Westerlies

60°S

Polar Easterlies blow cold air away from the poles.

90°S

N
W · E
S

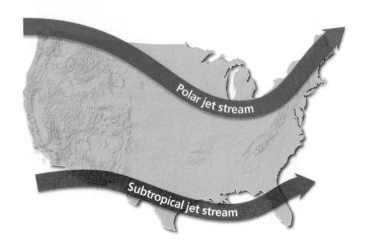

FIGURE 12
Jet Streams
The jet streams are high-speed bands of winds occurring at the top of the troposphere. By traveling east in a jet stream, pilots can save time and fuel.

Polar Easterlies Cold air near the poles sinks and flows back toward lower latitudes. The Coriolis effect shifts these polar winds to the west, producing the polar easterlies. The polar easterlies meet the prevailing westerlies at about 60° north and 60° south latitudes, along a region called the polar front. The mixing of warm and cold air along the polar front has a major effect on weather in the United States.

Jet Streams About 10 kilometers above Earth's surface are bands of high-speed winds called **jet streams.** These winds are hundreds of kilometers wide but only a few kilometers deep. Jet streams generally blow from west to east at speeds of 200 to 400 kilometers per hour, as shown in Figure 12. As jet streams travel around Earth, they wander north and south along a wavy path.

 **Reading Checkpoint** **What are the jet streams?**

Section 3 Assessment

Target Reading Skill

Relating Cause and Effect Refer to your graphic organizer about the effects of unequal heating to help you answer Question 1 below.

Reviewing Key Concepts

1. a. Defining What is wind?
  b. Relating Cause and Effect How is wind related to air temperature and air pressure?
  c. Applying Concepts It's fairly warm but windy outside. Use the concept of wind-chill factor to explain why it may be a good idea to wear a jacket.
2. a. Defining What are local winds?
  b. Summarizing What causes local winds?
  c. Comparing and Contrasting Compare the conditions that cause a sea breeze with those that cause a land breeze.

3. a. Identifying Name the three major global wind belts.
  b. Describing Briefly describe the three major global wind belts and where they are located.
  c. Interpreting Diagrams Use Figure 9 and Figure 11 to describe how the Coriolis effect influences the direction of the trade winds in the Northern Hemisphere. Does it have the same effect in the Southern Hemisphere? Explain.

Writing in Science

Explanation Imagine that you are a hot-air balloonist. You want to fly your balloon across the continental United States. To achieve the fastest time, would it make more sense to fly east-to-west or west-to-east? Explain how the prevailing winds influenced your decision.

Measuring the Wind

Problem

Can you design and build an anemometer to measure the wind?

Design Skills

evaluating the design, redesigning

Materials

- pen • round toothpick • masking tape
- 2 wooden coffee stirrers • meter stick
- corrugated cardboard sheet, 15 cm × 20 cm
- wind vane

Procedure ✂

1. Begin by making a simple anemometer that uses wooden coffee stirrers to indicate wind speed. On a piece of cardboard, draw a curved scale like the one shown in the diagram. Mark it in equal intervals from 0 to 10.

2. Carefully use the pen to make a small hole where the toothpick will go. Insert the toothpick through the hole.

3. Tape the wooden coffee stirrers to the toothpick as shown in the diagram, one on each side of the cardboard.

4. Copy the data table into your notebook.

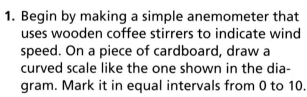

Data Table		
Location	Wind Direction	Wind Speed

5. Take your anemometer outside the school. Stand about 2–3 m away from the building and away from any corners or large plants.

6. Use the wind vane to find out what direction the wind is coming from. Hold your anemometer so that the card is straight, vertical, and parallel to the wind direction.

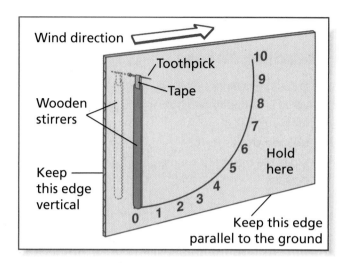

7. Observe the wooden stirrer on your anemometer for one minute. Record the highest wind speed that occurs during that time.

8. Repeat your measurements on all the other sides of the building. Record your data.

Analyze and Conclude

1. **Interpreting Data** Was the wind stronger on one side of the school than on the other sides? Explain your observations.

2. **Applying Concepts** Based on your data, which side of the building provides the best location for a door?

3. **Evaluating the Design** Do you think your anemometer accurately measured all of the winds you encountered? How could you improve its accuracy?

4. **Redesigning** What was the hardest part of using your anemometer? How could you change your design to make it more useful at very low or at very high wind speeds? Explain.

5. **Working With Design Constraints** How did having to use the materials provided by your teacher affect your anemometer? How would your design have changed if you could have used any materials you wanted to?

Communicate

Write a brochure describing the benefits of your anemometer. Make sure your brochure explains how the anemometer works and its potential uses.

4 Water in the Atmosphere

Reading Focus

Key Concepts
- What is humidity and how is it measured?
- How do clouds form?
- What are the three main types of clouds?

Key Terms
- water cycle • evaporation
- humidity • relative humidity
- psychrometer • condensation
- dew point • cirrus
- cumulus • stratus

Target Reading Skill

Asking Questions Before you read, preview the red headings. In a graphic organizer like the one below, ask *what* or *how* questions for each heading. As you read, write answers to your questions.

The Water Cycle

Question	Answer
How does the water cycle work?	During the water cycle . . .

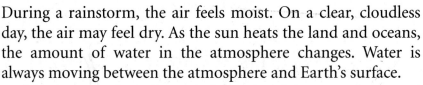

Lab zone Discover **Activity**

How Does Fog Form?

1. Fill a narrow-necked plastic bottle with hot tap water. Pour out most of the water, leaving about 3 cm at the bottom. **CAUTION:** *Avoid spilling hot water. Do not use water that is so hot that you cannot safely hold the bottle.*

2. Place an ice cube on the mouth of the bottle. What happens?

3. Repeat Steps 1 and 2 using cold water instead of hot water. What happens?

Think It Over
Developing Hypotheses How can you explain your observations? Why is there a difference between what happens with the hot water and what happens with the cold water?

During a rainstorm, the air feels moist. On a clear, cloudless day, the air may feel dry. As the sun heats the land and oceans, the amount of water in the atmosphere changes. Water is always moving between the atmosphere and Earth's surface.

The movement of water between the atmosphere and Earth's surface is called the **water cycle.** As you can see in Figure 13, water vapor enters the air by evaporation from the oceans and other bodies of water. **Evaporation** is the process by which water molecules in liquid water escape into the air as water vapor. Water vapor is also added to the air by living things. Water enters the roots of plants, rises to the leaves, and is released as water vapor.

As part of the water cycle, some of the water vapor in the atmosphere condenses to form clouds. Rain and snow fall from the clouds toward the surface. The water then runs off the surface or moves through the ground, back into the lakes, streams, and eventually the oceans.

Humidity

How is the quantity of water vapor in the atmosphere measured? **Humidity** is a measure of the amount of water vapor in the air. Air's ability to hold water vapor depends on its temperature. Warm air can hold more water vapor than cool air.

Relative Humidity Weather reports usually refer to the water vapor in the air as relative humidity. **Relative humidity** is the percentage of water vapor that is actually in the air compared to the maximum amount of water vapor the air can hold at a particular temperature. For example, at 10°C, 1 cubic meter of air can hold at most 8 grams of water vapor. If there actually were 8 grams of water vapor in the air, then the relative humidity of the air would be 100 percent. Air with a relative humidity of 100 percent is said to be saturated. If the air had 4 grams of water vapor, the relative humidity would be half, or 50 percent.

FIGURE 13

Water Cycle

In the water cycle, water moves from oceans, lakes, rivers, and plants into the atmosphere and then falls back to Earth.

Go **O**nline
active art

For: Water Cycle activity
Visit: PHSchool.com
Web Code: cfp-4024

Condensation

Precipitation

Evaporation from plants

Evaporation from oceans, lakes, and streams

Surface runoff

FIGURE 14
Sling Psychrometer
A sling psychrometer is used to measure relative humidity.

Measuring Relative Humidity Relative humidity can be measured with an instrument called a psychrometer. A **psychrometer** (sy KRAHM uh tur) has two thermometers, a wet-bulb thermometer and a dry-bulb thermometer, as shown in Figure 14. The bulb of the wet-bulb thermometer has a cloth covering that is moistened with water. When the psychrometer is "slung," or spun by its handle, air blows over both thermometers. Because the wet-bulb thermometer is cooled by evaporation, its reading drops below that of the dry-bulb thermometer.

If the relative humidity is high, the water on the wet bulb evaporates slowly, and the wet-bulb temperature does not change much. If the relative humidity is low, the water on the wet bulb evaporates rapidly, and the wet-bulb temperature drops. The relative humidity can be found by comparing the temperatures of the wet-bulb and dry-bulb thermometers.

 Reading Checkpoint **What instrument measures relative humidity?**

Math Analyzing Data

Determining Relative Humidity

Relative humidity is affected by temperature. Use the data table to answer the questions below. First, find the dry-bulb temperature in the left column of the table. Then find the difference between the wet- and dry-bulb temperatures across the top of the table. The number in the table where these two readings intersect indicates the relative humidity in percent.

Relative Humidity					
Dry-Bulb Reading (°C)	Difference Between Wet- and Dry-Bulb Readings (°C)				
	1	2	3	4	5
10	88	76	65	54	43
12	88	78	67	57	48
14	89	79	69	60	50
16	90	80	71	62	54
18	91	81	72	64	56
20	91	82	74	66	58
22	92	83	75	68	60

1. **Interpreting Data** At noon, the readings on a sling psychrometer are 18°C for the dry-bulb thermometer and 14°C for the wet-bulb thermometer. What is the relative humidity?

2. **Interpreting Data** At 5 P.M., the psychrometer is used again. The reading on the dry-bulb thermometer is 12°C, and the reading on the wet-bulb thermometer is 11°C. Determine the new relative humidity.

3. **Interpreting Data** How did the temperature change between noon and 5 P.M.?

4. **Interpreting Data** How did relative humidity change during the course of the day?

5. **Drawing Conclusions** How was the relative humidity affected by air temperature? Explain your answer.

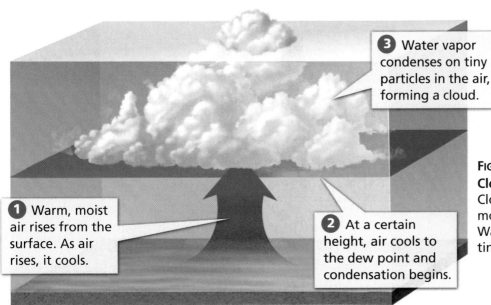

3 Water vapor condenses on tiny particles in the air, forming a cloud.

1 Warm, moist air rises from the surface. As air rises, it cools.

2 At a certain height, air cools to the dew point and condensation begins.

FIGURE 15
Cloud Formation
Clouds form when warm, moist air rises and cools. Water vapor condenses onto tiny particles in the air.

How Clouds Form

When you look at a cloud, you are seeing millions of tiny water droplets or ice crystals. **Clouds form when water vapor in the air condenses to form liquid water or ice crystals.** Molecules of water vapor in the air become liquid water in the process of **condensation.** How does water in the atmosphere condense? Two conditions are required for condensation: cooling of the air and the presence of particles in the air.

The Role of Cooling As you have learned, cold air holds less water vapor than warm air. As air cools, the amount of water vapor it can hold decreases. The water vapor condenses into tiny droplets of water or ice crystals.

The temperature at which condensation begins is called the **dew point.** If the dew point is above freezing, the water vapor forms water droplets. If the dew point is below freezing, the water vapor may change directly into ice crystals.

The Role of Particles But something else besides a change in temperature is needed for cloud formation. For water vapor to condense, tiny particles must be present so the water has a surface on which to condense. In cloud formation, most of these particles are salt crystals, dust from soil, and smoke. Water vapor also condenses onto solid surfaces, such as blades of grass or window panes. Liquid water that condenses from the air onto a cooler surface is called dew. Ice that has been deposited on a surface that is below freezing is called frost.

 **Reading Checkpoint** What two factors are required for condensation to occur?

FIGURE 16
Condensation
Water vapor condensed on this insect to form dew. **Predicting** *What would happen if the surface were below freezing?*

Cirrus clouds

Cumulus clouds

Stratus clouds

Types of Clouds

Clouds come in many different shapes, as shown in Figure 17. **Scientists classify clouds into three main types based on their shape: cirrus, cumulus, and stratus. Clouds are further classified by their altitude.** Each type of cloud is associated with a different type of weather.

Cirrus Clouds Wispy, feathery clouds are known as **cirrus** (SEER us) clouds. *Cirrus* comes from a word meaning a curl of hair. Cirrus clouds form only at high levels, above about 6 kilometers, where temperatures are very low. As a result, cirrus clouds are made of ice crystals.

Cirrus clouds that have feathery "hooked" ends are sometimes called mare's tails. Cirrocumulus clouds, which look like rows of cotton balls, often indicate that a storm is on its way. The rows of cirrocumulus clouds look like the scales of a fish. For this reason, the term "mackerel sky" is used to describe a sky full of cirrocumulus clouds.

Cumulus Clouds Clouds that look like fluffy, rounded piles of cotton are called **cumulus** (KYOO myuh lus) clouds. The word *cumulus* means "heap" or "mass" in Latin. Cumulus clouds form less than 2 kilometers above the ground, but they may grow in size and height until they extend upward as much as 18 kilometers. Cumulus clouds that are not very tall usually indicate fair weather. These clouds, which are common on sunny days, are called "fair weather cumulus." Towering clouds with flat tops, called cumulonimbus clouds, often produce thunderstorms. The suffix *-nimbus* means "rain."

Stratus Clouds Clouds that form in flat layers are called **stratus** (STRAT us) clouds. Recall that *strato* means "spread out." Stratus clouds usually cover all or most of the sky and are a uniform dull, gray color. As stratus clouds thicken, they may produce drizzle, rain, or snow. They are then called nimbostratus clouds.

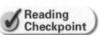 **Reading Checkpoint** What are stratus clouds?

FIGURE 17

Clouds

The three main types of clouds are cirrus, cumulus, and stratus. A cloud's name contains clues about its height and structure. **Interpreting Diagrams** *What type of cloud is found at the highest altitudes?*

(km)
13
12
11
10
9
8
7
6
5
4
3
2
1

Cirrus

Cirrocumulus

Altocumulus

Cumulonimbus

Altostratus

Cumulus

Nimbostratus

Stratus

Fog

FIGURE 18
Fog Around the Golden Gate Bridge
The cold ocean water of San Francisco Bay is often covered by fog in the early morning.
Predicting *What will happen as the sun rises and warms the air?*

Altocumulus and Altostratus Part of a cloud's name may be based on its height. The names of clouds that form between 2 and 6 kilometers above Earth's surface have the prefix *alto-*, which means "high." The two main types of these clouds are altocumulus and altostratus. These are "middle-level" clouds that are higher than regular cumulus and stratus clouds, but lower than cirrus and other "high" clouds.

Fog Clouds that form at or near the ground are called fog. Fog often forms when the ground cools at night after a warm, humid day. The ground cools the air just above the ground to the air's dew point. The next day the heat of the morning sun "burns" the fog off as its water droplets evaporate. Fog is more common in areas near bodies of water or low-lying marshy areas. In mountainous areas, fog can form as warm, moist air moves up the mountain slopes and cools.

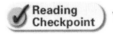 **Reading Checkpoint** **What is fog?**

Section 4 Assessment

Target Reading Skill

Asking Questions Use the answers to the questions you wrote about the headings to help answer the questions below.

Reviewing Key Concepts

1. **a. Reviewing** What is humidity?
   b. Comparing and Contrasting How are humidity and relative humidity different?
   c. Calculating Suppose a sample of air can at most hold 10 grams of water vapor. If the sample actually has 2 grams of water vapor, what is its relative humidity?

2. **a. Identifying** What process is involved in cloud formation?
   b. Summarizing What two conditions are needed for clouds to form?
   c. Inferring When are clouds formed by ice crystals instead of drops of liquid water?

3. **a. Listing** What are the three main types of clouds?

   b. Describing Briefly describe each of the three main types of clouds.
   c. Classifying Classify each of the following cloud types as low-level, medium-level, or high-level: altocumulus, altostratus, cirrostratus, cirrus, cumulus, fog, nimbostratus, and stratus.

Lab zone **At-Home Activity**

Water in the Air Fill a large glass half full with cold water. Show your family members what happens as you add ice cubes to the water. Explain to your family that the water that appears on the outside of the glass comes from water vapor in the atmosphere. Also explain why the water on the outside of the glass only appears after you add ice to the water in the glass.

Precipitation

Reading Focus

Key Concepts

- What are the common types of precipitation?
- How is precipitation measured?

Key Terms

- precipitation
- drought
- cloud seeding
- rain gauge

⟳ Target Reading Skill

Using Prior Knowledge Before you read, write what you know about precipitation in a graphic organizer like the one below. As you read, write what you learn.

What You Know
1. Precipitation can be rain or snow.
2.

What You Learned
1.
2.

Lab zone — Discover **Activity**

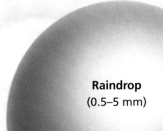

How Can You Make Hail?

1. Put on your goggles.
2. Put 15 g of salt into a beaker. Add 50 mL of water. Stir the solution until most of the salt is dissolved.
3. Put 15 mL of cold water in a clean test tube.
4. Place the test tube in the beaker.
5. Fill the beaker almost to the top with crushed ice. Stir the ice mixture every minute for six minutes.
6. Remove the test tube from the beaker and drop an ice chip into the test tube. What happens?

Think It Over

Inferring Based on your observation, what conditions are necessary for hail to form?

In Arica, Chile, the average rainfall is less than 1 millimeter per year. But in Hawaii, the average rainfall on Mount Waialeale is about 12 meters per year. As you can see, rainfall varies greatly around the world.

Water evaporates from every water surface on Earth and from living things. This water eventually returns to the surface as precipitation. **Precipitation** (pree sip uh TAY shun) is any form of water that falls from clouds and reaches Earth's surface.

Not all clouds produce precipitation. For precipitation to occur, cloud droplets or ice crystals must grow heavy enough to fall through the air. One way that cloud droplets grow is by colliding and combining with other droplets. As the droplets grow larger, they move faster and collect more small droplets. Finally, the droplets become heavy enough to fall out of the cloud as raindrops.

Typical Droplet Size
(Diameter)

Cloud droplet
(0.02 mm)

Mist droplet
(0.005–0.05 mm)

Drizzle droplet
(0.05–0.5 mm)

Raindrop
(0.5–5 mm)

FIGURE 19
Water Droplets
Droplets come in many sizes. Believe it or not, a raindrop has about one million times as much water in it as a cloud droplet.

Go Online
SCi LINKS NSTA

For: Links on precipitation
Visit: www.SciLinks.org
Web Code: scn-0925

Types of Precipitation

In warm parts of the world, precipitation is almost always in the form of rain. In colder regions, precipitation may fall as snow or ice. **Common types of precipitation include rain, sleet, freezing rain, snow, and hail.**

Rain The most common kind of precipitation is rain. Drops of water are called rain if they are at least 0.5 millimeter in diameter. Precipitation made up of smaller drops of water is called drizzle. Precipitation of even smaller drops is called mist. Drizzle and mist usually fall from stratus clouds.

Sleet Sometimes raindrops fall through a layer of air that is below 0°C, the freezing point of water. As they fall, the raindrops freeze into solid particles of ice. Ice particles smaller than 5 millimeters in diameter are called sleet.

Freezing Rain Sometimes raindrops falling through cold air near the ground do not freeze in the air. Instead, they freeze when they touch a cold surface. This kind of precipitation is called freezing rain. In an ice storm, a smooth, thick layer of ice builds up on every surface. The weight of the ice may break tree branches and cause them to fall onto power lines, causing power failures. Freezing rain and sleet can make sidewalks and roads slippery and dangerous.

 Reading Checkpoint   **What is sleet?**

FIGURE 20
Rain and Freezing Rain
Rain is the most common form of precipitation. Freezing rain coats objects with a layer of ice.
Relating Cause and Effect *What conditions are necessary for freezing rain to occur?*

Snow Often water vapor in a cloud is converted directly into ice crystals called snowflakes. Snowflakes have an endless number of different shapes and patterns, all with six sides or branches. Snowflakes often join together into larger clumps of snow in which the six-sided crystals are hard to see.

FIGURE 21
Snowflake
Snowflakes are tiny ice crystals. They all have six sides or branches.

Hail Round pellets of ice larger than 5 millimeters in diameter are called hailstones. Hail forms only inside cumulonimbus clouds during thunderstorms. A hailstone starts as an ice pellet inside a cold region of a cloud. Strong updrafts carry the hailstone up through the cold region many times. Each time the hailstone goes through the cold region, a new layer of ice forms around it. Eventually the hailstone becomes heavy enough to fall to the ground. If you cut a hailstone in half, you often see shells of ice, like the layers of an onion, as shown in Figure 22. Because hailstones can grow quite large before finally falling to the ground, hail can cause tremendous damage to crops, buildings, and vehicles.

FIGURE 22
How Hail Forms
Hailstones start as small pellets of ice in cumulonimbus clouds. They grow larger as they are repeatedly tossed up and down, until they become so heavy that they fall to the ground.

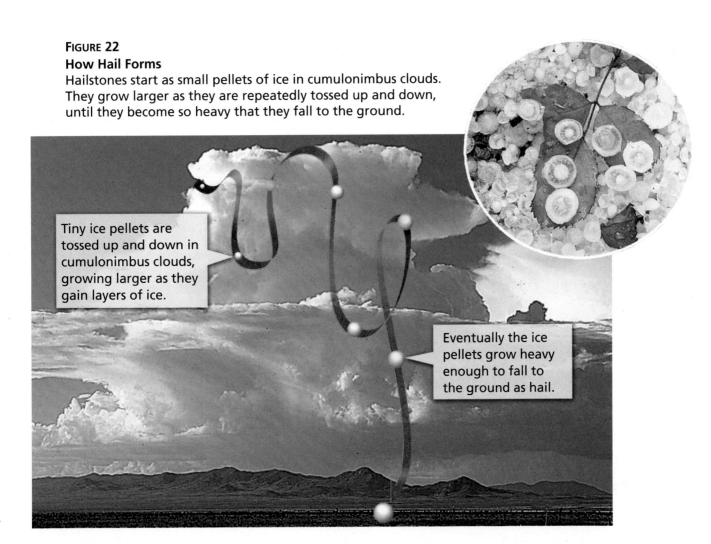

Tiny ice pellets are tossed up and down in cumulonimbus clouds, growing larger as they gain layers of ice.

Eventually the ice pellets grow heavy enough to fall to the ground as hail.

FIGURE 23
Cloud Seeding
Small planes are used to sprinkle chemicals into clouds to try to produce rain.

Modifying Precipitation Sometimes a region goes through a period of weather that is much drier than usual. Long periods of unusually low precipitation are called **droughts.** Droughts can cause great hardship.

Since the 1940s, scientists have been trying to produce rain during droughts. One method used to modify precipitation is called **cloud seeding.** In cloud seeding, tiny crystals of silver iodide and dry ice (solid carbon dioxide) are sprinkled into clouds from airplanes. Many clouds contain droplets of water which are supercooled below 0°C. The droplets don't freeze because there aren't enough solid particles around which ice crystals can form. Water vapor can condense on the particles of silver iodide, forming rain or snow. Dry ice cools the droplets even further, so that they will freeze without particles being present. However, to date cloud seeding has not been very effective in producing precipitation.

 **Reading Checkpoint** What is a drought?

Measuring Precipitation

There are various ways to measure the amount of rain or snow. **Scientists measure precipitation with various instruments, including rain gauges and measuring sticks.**

Snowfall Measurement Snowfall is usually measured in two ways; using a simple measuring stick or by melting collected snow and measuring the depth of water it produces. On average, 10 centimeters of snow contains about the same amount of water as 1 centimeter of rain. However, light, fluffy snow contains far less water than heavy, wet snow.

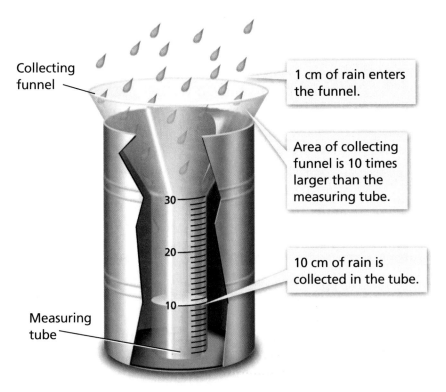

Collecting funnel

1 cm of rain enters the funnel.

Area of collecting funnel is 10 times larger than the measuring tube.

10 cm of rain is collected in the tube.

Measuring tube

30
20
10

FIGURE 24
Rain Gauge
A rain gauge measures the depth of rain that falls.
Observing *How much rain was collected in the measuring tube of this rain gauge?*

Rain Measurements An open-ended can or tube that collects rainfall is called a **rain gauge.** The amount of rainfall is measured by dipping a ruler into the water or by reading a marked scale. To increase the accuracy of the measurement, the top of a rain gauge may have a funnel that collects ten times as much rain as the tube alone, as shown in Figure 24. The funnel collects a greater depth of water that is easier to measure. To get the actual depth of rain, it is necessary to divide by ten. The narrow opening of the tube helps to minimize evaporation.

Section 5 Assessment

Target Reading Skill Using Prior Knowledge
Review your graphic organizer about precipitation and revise it based on what you have learned.

Reviewing Key Concepts

1. a. **Listing** Name the five common types of precipitation.
   b. **Comparing and Contrasting** Compare and contrast freezing rain and sleet.
   c. **Classifying** A thunderstorm produces precipitation in the form of ice particles that are about 6 millimeters in diameter. What type of precipitation would this be?
   d. **Relating Cause and Effect** How do hailstones become so large in cumulonimbus clouds?

2. a. **Identifying** How can a rain gauge be used to measure precipitation?
   b. **Explaining** How does the funnel in a rain gauge increase the accuracy of the measurement?

Writing in Science

Firsthand Account Think about the most exciting experience you have had with precipitation. Write a paragraph about that event. Make sure you describe the precipitation itself as well as the effect it had on you.

The BIG Idea **Transfer of Energy** Energy transfers resulting from differences in air pressure, air temperature, winds, and humidity produce changes in weather.

1 Energy in Earth's Atmosphere

Key Concepts

- Most energy from the sun travels to Earth in the form of visible light and infrared radiation. A small amount arrives as ultraviolet radiation.
- Some sunlight is absorbed or reflected by the atmosphere before it can reach the surface. The rest passes through to the surface.
- When the surface is heated, it radiates energy back into the atmosphere as infrared radiation.

Key Terms

electromagnetic waves   ultraviolet radiation
radiation   scattering
infrared radiation   greenhouse effect

2 Heat Transfer

Key Concepts

- Air temperature is usually measured with a thermometer.
- Heat is transferred in three ways: radiation, conduction, and convection.
- Radiation, conduction, and convection work together to heat the troposphere.

Key Terms

temperature   conduction
thermal energy   convection
thermometer   convection currents
heat

3 Winds

Key Concepts

- Winds are caused by differences in air pressure.
- Local winds are caused by the unequal heating of Earth's surface within a small area.
- Like local winds, global winds are created by the unequal heating of Earth's surface. But unlike local winds, global winds occur over a large area.
- The major global wind belts are the trade winds, the polar easterlies, and the prevailing westerlies.

Key Terms

wind   land breeze
anemometer   global winds
wind-chill factor   Coriolis effect
local winds   latitude
sea breeze   jet stream

4 Water in the Atmosphere

Key Concepts

- Relative humidity can be measured with an instrument called a psychrometer.
- Clouds form when water vapor in the air condenses to form liquid water or ice crystals.
- Scientists classify clouds into three main types based on their shape: cirrus, cumulus, and stratus. Clouds are also classified by altitude.

Key Terms

water cycle   condensation
evaporation   dew point
humidity   cirrus
relative humidity   cumulus
psychrometer   stratus

5 Precipitation

Key Concepts

- Common types of precipitation include rain, sleet, freezing rain, snow, and hail.
- Scientists measure precipitation with various instruments, including rain gauges and measuring sticks.

Key Terms

precipitation   cloud seeding
drought   rain gauge

Review and Assessment

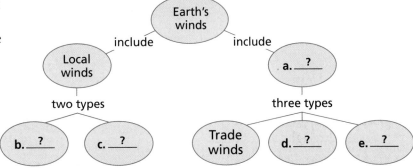
Organizing Information

Concept Mapping Copy the concept map about Earth's winds onto a separate sheet of paper. Then complete it and add a title. (For more on Concept Mapping, see the Skills Handbook).

Earth's winds
include → Local winds
include → a. ___?___

Local winds → two types → b. ___?___   c. ___?___

a. ___?___ → three types → Trade winds   d. ___?___   e. ___?___

Reviewing Key Terms

Choose the letter of the best answer.

1. Energy from the sun travels to Earth's surface by
   a. radiation.
   b. convection.
   c. evaporation.
   d. conduction.

2. Rising warm air transports thermal energy by
   a. conduction.
   b. convection.
   c. radiation.
   d. condensation.

3. Bands of high-altitude, high-speed winds are called
   a. jet streams.
   b. sea breezes.
   c. land breezes.
   d. local winds.

4. A type of cloud that forms in flat layers and often covers much of the sky is
   a. cirrus.
   b. cumulus.
   c. fog.
   d. stratus.

5. Rain, sleet, and hail are all forms of
   a. evaporation.
   b. condensation.
   c. precipitation.
   d. convection.

If the statement is true, write *true*. If it is false, change the underlined word or words to make the statement true.

6. Infrared radiation and <u>ultraviolet radiation</u> make up most of the energy Earth receives from the sun.

7. The transfer of heat by the movement of a fluid is called <u>conduction.</u>

8. Winds that blow steadily from specific directions for long distances are called <u>sea breezes.</u>

9. <u>Cirrus</u> clouds are made mostly of ice crystals.

10. Rainfall is measured by a(n) <u>anemometer.</u>

Writing in Science

Descriptive Paragraph Suppose you are preparing for an around-the-world sailing trip. Select a route. Then write a description of the types of winds you would expect to find along different parts of your route.

Discovery CHANNEL SCHOOL

Weather Factors
Video Preview
Video Field Trip
▶ Video Assessment

Review and Assessment

Checking Concepts

11. What causes the greenhouse effect? How does it affect Earth's atmosphere?

12. Describe examples of radiation, conduction, and convection from your daily life.

13. Describe how the movements of hot air at the equator and cold air at the poles produce global wind patterns.

14. Why are solid particles required for cloud formation?

15. Why do clouds usually form high in the air instead of near Earth's surface?

16. Describe sleet, hail, and snow in terms of how each one forms.

Math Practice

17. Converting Units Suppose the outside temperature is 60°F. What is the temperature in degrees Celsius?

18. Converting Units What is 30°C in degrees Fahrenheit?

Thinking Critically

19. Inferring Venus has an atmosphere that is mostly carbon dioxide. How do you think the greenhouse effect has altered Venus?

20. Interpreting Diagrams Describe the journey of a small particle of water through the water cycle, using the terms in the diagram below.

21. Applying Concepts What type of heat transfer is responsible for making you feel cold when you are swimming in a pool that is cold throughout?

22. Relating Cause and Effect What circumstances could cause a nighttime land breeze in a city near the ocean?

23. Problem Solving A psychrometer gives the same reading on both thermometers. What is the relative humidity?

Applying Skills

Use the table to answer questions 24–26.

Average Monthly Rainfall

Month	Rainfall	Month	Rainfall
January	1 cm	July	49 cm
February	1 cm	August	57 cm
March	1 cm	September	40 cm
April	2 cm	October	20 cm
May	25 cm	November	4 cm
June	52 cm	December	1 cm

24. Graphing Use the information in the table to draw a bar graph that shows the rainfall for each month at this location.

25. Calculating What is the total amount of rainfall each year at this location?

26. Classifying Which months of the year would you classify as "dry"? Which months would you classify as "wet"?

Lab zone Chapter **Project**

Performance Assessment Decide how to present the findings from your weather station to the class. For example, you could put your graphs and predictions on a poster or use a computer to make a slide show. Make sure your graphs are neatly drawn and easy to understand.

Standardized Test Prep

Choose the letter of the best answer.

1. When the temperature equals the dew point, the relative humidity is

  A zero.

  B about 10 percent.

  C about 50 percent.

  D 100 percent.

2. What equipment would you need to design an experiment to determine the relative humidity of the air?

  F a rain gauge and a thermometer

  G an anemometer or a thermometer

  H a psychrometer or two thermometers

  J an anemometer and a rain gauge

3. What is the temperature in degrees Celsius when a room thermometer reads 77°F?

  A 25°C   **B** 32°C

  C 45°C   **D** 77°C

The table below shows the actual air temperature when the wind speed is zero. Use the table and your knowledge of science to answer Questions 4 and 5.

Wind-Chill Temperature Index

Wind Speed	Equivalent Air Temperature (°C)			
0 km/h	5°	0°	–5°	–10°
10 km/h	2.7°	–3.3°	–9.3°	–15.3°
15 km/h	1.7°	–4.4°	–10.6°	–16.7°
20 km/h	1.1°	–5.2°	–11.6°	–17.9°

4. On a windy winter's day, the actual air temperature is −5°C and the wind speed is 15 kilometers per hour. What would the wind-chill factor make the temperature feel like to a person outdoors?

  F 1.7°C   **G** −5°C

  H −10.6°C   **J** −16.7°C

5. Use trends shown in the data table to predict how cold the air temperature would feel if the actual temperature was 0°C, and the wind speed was 25 km/h.

  A about 0°C   **B** about −6°C

  C about −15°C   **D** about 25°C

Constructed Response

6. Describe the process by which a cloud forms. What two conditions are necessary for this process to occur? How does this process compare to the process by which dew or frost is formed?

The **BIG Idea**
Weather Systems

 How do air masses produce changes in weather?

Chapter Preview

❶ **Air Masses and Fronts**
Discover How Do Fluids of Different Densities Behave?
Skills Activity Calculating
Skills Activity Classifying
Active Art Weather Fronts

❷ **Storms**
Discover Can You Make a Tornado?
Try This Lightning Distances
Science and History Weather That Changed History
At-Home Activity Storm Eyewitness
Skills Lab Tracking a Hurricane

❸ **Predicting the Weather**
Discover What's the Weather?
Analyzing Data Computer Weather Forecasting
Skills Activity Interpreting Data
Skills Lab Reading a Weather Map
Technology and Society Doppler Radar

Hurricane Hugo approaches ▶ the Florida coast.

◢Lab zone™ Chapter **Project**

The Weather Tomorrow

When the sky turns dark and threatening, it's not hard to predict the weather. A storm is likely on its way. But wouldn't you rather know about an approaching storm before it arrives? In this project you will get a chance to make your own weather forecasts and compare them to the forecasts of professionals. Good luck!

Your Goal To predict the weather for your own community and two other locations in the United States

To complete the project you must

- compare weather maps for several days at a time
- look for patterns in the weather
- draw maps to show your weather predictions

Plan It! Begin by previewing the chapter to learn about weather maps and symbols. Start a project folder to store daily national weather maps and a description of the symbols used on the maps. Choose two locations that are at least 1,000 kilometers away from your town and from each other. As you collect weather maps, look for patterns in day-to-day weather changes. Then predict the next day's weather and compare your predictions to professional forecasts and to the actual weather.

Air Masses and Fronts

Reading Preview

Key Concepts
- What are the major types of air masses in North America, and how do they move?
- What are the main types of fronts?
- What type of weather is associated with cyclones and anticyclones?

Key Terms
- air mass • tropical • polar
- maritime • continental
- front • occluded • cyclone
- anticyclone

Target Reading Skill

Comparing and Contrasting As you read, compare and contrast the four types of fronts by completing a table like the one below.

Types of Fronts

Front	How Forms	Type of Weather
Cold front	A cold air mass overtakes a warm air mass.	
Warm front		
Occluded front		

How Do Fluids of Different Densities Behave?

1. Put on your apron. Place a cardboard divider across the middle of a plastic shoe box.
2. Add a few drops of red food coloring to a liter of warm water. Pour the red liquid, which represents low-density warm air, into the shoe box on one side of the divider.

3. Add about 100 mL of table salt and a few drops of blue food coloring to a liter of cold water. Pour the blue liquid, which represents high-density cold air, into the shoe box on the other side of the divider.
4. What do you think will happen if you remove the divider?
5. Now quickly remove the divider. Watch carefully from the side. What happens?

Think It Over

Developing Hypotheses Based on this activity, write a hypothesis stating what would happen if a mass of cold air ran into a mass of warm air.

Listen to the evening news in the winter and you may hear a weather forecast like this: "A huge mass of Arctic air is moving our way, bringing freezing temperatures." Today's weather can be influenced by air from thousands of kilometers away—perhaps from Canada or the Pacific Ocean. A huge body of air that has similar temperature, humidity, and air pressure at any given height is called an **air mass.** A single air mass may spread over millions of square kilometers and be up to 10 kilometers deep.

FIGURE 1
Major Snowstorm
In winter, humid air masses bring heavy snowstorms to areas like New York City.

Types of Air Masses

Scientists classify air masses according to two characteristics: temperature and humidity. **Four major types of air masses influence the weather in North America: maritime tropical, continental tropical, maritime polar, and continental polar.**

The characteristics of an air mass depend on the temperatures and moisture content of the region over which the air mass forms. Remember that temperature affects air pressure. Cold, dense air has a higher pressure, while warm, less dense air has a lower pressure. **Tropical,** or warm, air masses form in the tropics and have low air pressure. **Polar,** or cold, air masses form north of 50° north latitude and south of 50° south latitude. Polar air masses have high air pressure.

Whether an air mass is humid or dry depends on whether it forms over water or land. **Maritime** air masses form over oceans. Water evaporates from the oceans, so the air can become very humid. **Continental** air masses form over land. Continental air masses have less exposure to large amounts of moisture from bodies of water. Therefore, continental air masses are drier than maritime air masses.

Maritime Tropical Warm, humid air masses form over tropical oceans. Maritime tropical air masses that form over the Gulf of Mexico and the Atlantic Ocean move first into the southeastern United States. These air masses then move north and northeast, where they influence weather in the central and eastern United States. In the west, maritime tropical air masses form over the Pacific Ocean. They mainly affect the weather on the West Coast. As they cross the coastal mountain ranges, the Pacific air masses lose moisture.

In summer, maritime tropical air masses usually bring hot, humid weather. Many summer showers and thunderstorms in the eastern United States develop in air masses that have formed over the Gulf of Mexico. In winter, a humid air mass can bring heavy rain or snow.

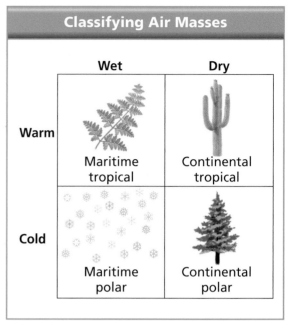

Classifying Air Masses

	Wet	Dry
Warm	Maritime tropical	Continental tropical
Cold	Maritime polar	Continental polar

Figure 2
Air masses can be classified according to their temperature and humidity. **Identifying** *What type of air mass consists of warm, moist air?*

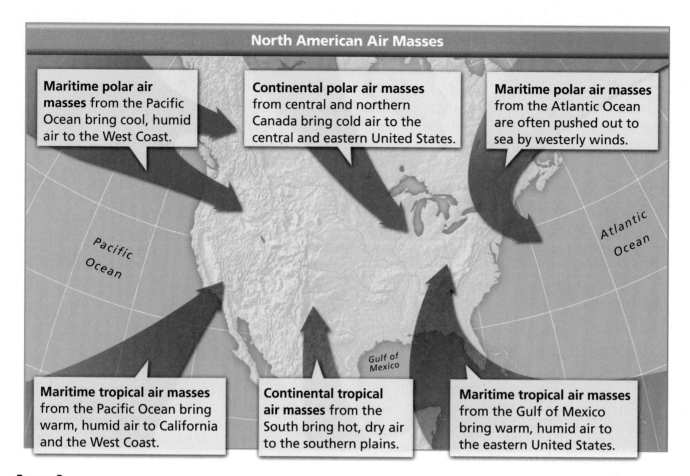

North American Air Masses

Maritime polar air masses from the Pacific Ocean bring cool, humid air to the West Coast.

Continental polar air masses from central and northern Canada bring cold air to the central and eastern United States.

Maritime polar air masses from the Atlantic Ocean are often pushed out to sea by westerly winds.

Pacific Ocean

Atlantic Ocean

Gulf of Mexico

Maritime tropical air masses from the Pacific Ocean bring warm, humid air to California and the West Coast.

Continental tropical air masses from the South bring hot, dry air to the southern plains.

Maritime tropical air masses from the Gulf of Mexico bring warm, humid air to the eastern United States.

FIGURE 3
Air masses can be warm or cold, and humid or dry. As an air mass moves into an area, the weather changes.

Maritime Polar Cool, humid air masses form over the icy cold North Pacific and North Atlantic oceans. Maritime polar air masses affect the West Coast more than the East Coast. Even in summer, these masses of cool, humid air often bring fog, rain, and cool temperatures to the West Coast.

Continental Tropical Hot, dry air masses form mostly in summer over dry areas of the Southwest and northern Mexico. Continental tropical air masses cover a smaller area than other air masses. They occasionally move northeast, bringing hot, dry weather to the southern Great Plains.

Continental Polar Large continental polar air masses form over central and northern Canada and Alaska, as shown in Figure 3. Air masses that form near the Arctic Circle can bring bitterly cold weather with very low humidity. In winter, continental polar air masses bring clear, cold, dry air to much of North America. In summer, the air mass is milder. Storms may occur when continental polar air masses move south and collide with maritime tropical air masses moving north.

 **Reading Checkpoint** Where do continental polar air masses come from?

How Air Masses Move

When an air mass moves into an area and interacts with other air masses, it causes the weather to change. **In the continental United States, air masses are commonly moved by the prevailing westerlies and jet streams.**

Prevailing Westerlies The prevailing westerlies, the major wind belts over the continental United States, generally push air masses from west to east. For example, maritime polar air masses from the Pacific Ocean are blown onto the West Coast, bringing low clouds and showers.

Jet Streams Embedded within the prevailing westerlies are jet streams. Recall that jet streams are bands of high-speed winds about 10 kilometers above Earth's surface. As jet streams blow from west to east, air masses are carried along their tracks.

Fronts As huge masses of air move across the land and the oceans, they collide with each other. But the air masses do not easily mix. Think about a bottle of oil and water. The less dense oil floats on top of the denser water. Something similar happens when two air masses with a different temperature and humidity collide. The air masses do not easily mix. The boundary where the air masses meet becomes a **front.** Storms and changeable weather often develop along fronts, as shown in Figure 4.

Lab zone Skills **Activity**

Calculating

When planes fly from west to east, they fly with the jet stream, and therefore can fly faster. When traveling from east to west, planes fly against the jet stream, and travel slower. To calculate the rate at which the planes fly, divide the distance traveled by the time it takes.

$$\text{Rate} = \frac{\text{Distance}}{\text{Time}}$$

If a plane flies from Denver, Colorado, to New York City, a distance of about 2,618 kilometers, it takes about 3 hours and 30 minutes. The return flight takes about 4 hours. Calculate the rates of air travel, in km/h, in each direction. How much extra speed does the jet stream add to the west-to-east flight?

Reading Checkpoint In what direction does the jet stream move storms?

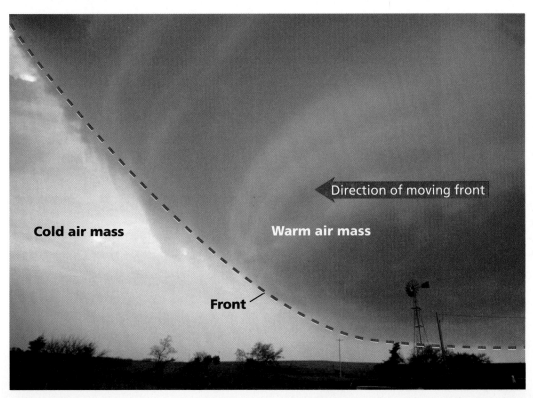

Cold air mass

Warm air mass

Direction of moving front

Front

FIGURE 4
How a Front Forms
The boundary where unlike air masses meet is called a front. A front may be 15 to 600 kilometers wide and extend high into the troposphere.

FIGURE 5
Types of Fronts

There are four types of fronts: cold fronts, warm fronts, stationery fronts, and occluded fronts. **Interpreting Diagrams** *What kind of weather occurs at a warm front?*

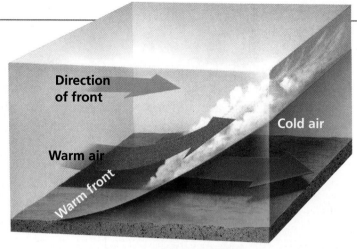

▲ **Warm Front**
A warm air mass overtakes a slow-moving cold air mass.

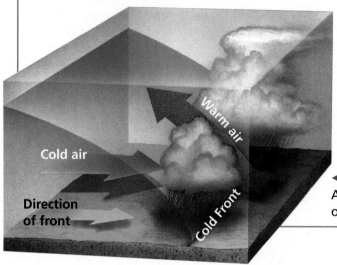

◄ **Cold Front**
A fast-moving cold air mass overtakes a warm air mass.

Types of Fronts

Colliding air masses can form four types of fronts: cold fronts, warm fronts, stationary fronts, and occluded fronts. The kind of front that develops depends on the characteristics of the air masses and how they are moving.

Cold Fronts As you have learned, cold air is dense and tends to sink. Warm air is less dense and tends to rise. When a rapidly moving cold air mass runs into a slowly moving warm air mass, the denser cold air slides under the lighter warm air. The warm air is pushed upward along the leading edge of the colder air, as shown in Figure 5. A cold front forms.

As the warm air rises, it expands and cools. Remember that warm air can hold more water vapor than cool air. The rising air soon reaches the dew point, the temperature at which the water vapor in the air condenses into droplets of liquid water or forms tiny ice crystals. Clouds form. If there is a lot of water vapor in the warm air, heavy rain or snow may fall. If the warm air mass contains only a little water vapor, then the cold front may be accompanied by only cloudy skies.

Since cold fronts tend to move quickly, they can cause abrupt weather changes, including thunderstorms. After a cold front passes through an area, colder, drier air moves in, often bringing clear skies, a shift in wind, and lower temperatures.

 **Reading Checkpoint** What type of weather do cold fronts bring?

Classifying

At home, watch the weather forecast on television. Make a note of each time the weather reporter mentions a front. Classify the fronts mentioned or shown as cold, warm, stationary, or occluded. What type of weather is predicted to occur when the front arrives? Note the specific weather conditions, such as temperature and air pressure, associated with the front. Is each type of front always associated with the same type of weather?

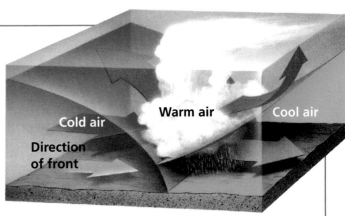

▲ Occluded Front
A warm air mass is caught
between two cooler air masses.

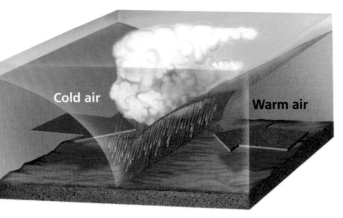

▼ Stationary Front
Cold and warm air masses meet,
but neither can move the other.

Go Online
active art

For: Weather Fronts activity
Visit: PHSchool.com
Web Code: cfp-4031

Warm Fronts Clouds and precipitation also accompany warm fronts. At a warm front, a fast-moving warm air mass overtakes a slowly moving cold air mass. Because cold air is denser than warm air, the warm air moves over the cold air. If the warm air is humid, light rain or snow falls along the front. If the warm air is dry, scattered clouds form. Because warm fronts move slowly, the weather may be rainy or cloudy for several days. After a warm front passes through an area, the weather is likely to be warm and humid.

Stationary Fronts Sometimes cold and warm air masses meet, but neither one can move the other. The two air masses face each other in a "standoff." In this case, the front is called a stationary front. Where the warm and cool air meet, water vapor in the warm air condenses into rain, snow, fog, or clouds. If a stationary front remains stalled over an area, it may bring many days of clouds and precipitation.

Occluded Fronts The most complex weather situation occurs at an occluded front, where a warm air mass is caught between two cooler air masses. The denser cool air masses move underneath the less dense warm air mass and push the warm air upward. The two cooler air masses meet in the middle and may mix. The temperature near the ground becomes cooler. The warm air mass is cut off, or **occluded,** from the ground. As the warm air cools and its water vapor condenses, the weather may turn cloudy and rain or snow may fall.

FIGURE 6
Structure of Cyclones and Anticyclones
Winds spiral inward towards the low-pressure center of a cyclone. Winds spiral outward from the high-pressure center of an anticyclone.
Interpreting Diagrams *Do cyclone winds spin clockwise or counter-clockwise in the Northern Hemisphere?*

Cyclone (Low)

Anticyclone (High)

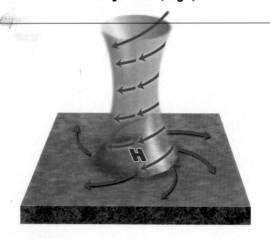

Cyclones and Anticyclones

As air masses collide to form fronts, the boundary between the fronts sometimes becomes distorted. This distortion can be caused by surface features, such as mountains, or strong winds, such as the jet stream. When this happens, bends can develop along the front. The air begins to swirl. The swirling air can cause a low-pressure center to form.

Cyclones If you look at a weather map, you will see areas marked with an *L*. The L stands for "low," and indicates an area of relatively low air pressure. A swirling center of low air pressure is called a **cyclone,** from a Greek word meaning "wheel."

As warm air at the center of a cyclone rises, the air pressure decreases. Cooler air blows toward this low-pressure area from nearby areas where the air pressure is higher. As shown in Figure 6, winds spiral inward toward the center of the system. Recall that, in the Northern Hemisphere, the Coriolis effect deflects winds to the right. Because of this deflection, winds in a cyclone spin counterclockwise in the Northern Hemisphere when viewed from above.

Cyclones play a large part in the weather of the United States. As air rises in a cyclone, the air cools, forming clouds and precipitation. **Cyclones and decreasing air pressure are associated with clouds, wind, and precipitation.**

Anticyclones As its name suggests, an anticyclone is the opposite of a cyclone. **Anticyclones** are high-pressure centers of dry air. Anticyclones are usually called "highs"—*H* on a weather map. Winds spiral outward from the center of an anticyclone, moving toward areas of lower pressure. Because of the Coriolis effect, winds in an anticyclone spin clockwise in the Northern Hemisphere. Because air moves out from the center of the anticyclone, cool air moves downward from higher in the troposphere. As the cool air falls, it warms up, so its relative humidity drops. **The descending air in an anticyclone generally causes dry, clear weather.**

 **Reading Checkpoint** What is an anticyclone?

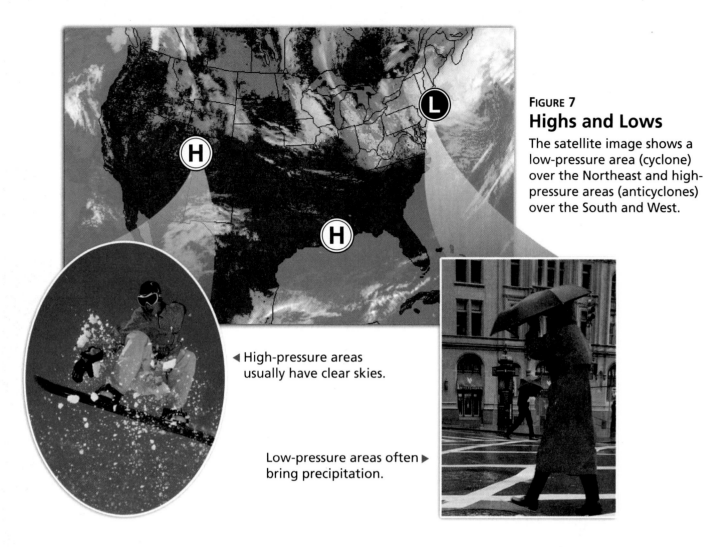

FIGURE 7
Highs and Lows
The satellite image shows a low-pressure area (cyclone) over the Northeast and high-pressure areas (anticyclones) over the South and West.

◄ High-pressure areas usually have clear skies.

Low-pressure areas often ► bring precipitation.

Section 1 Assessment

Target Reading Skill Comparing and Contrasting Use the information in your table about fronts to help you answer Question 2 below.

Reviewing Key Concepts

1. a. **Reviewing** What two characteristics are used to classify air masses?
   b. **Classifying** Classify the four major types of air masses according to whether they are dry or humid.
   c. **Applying Concepts** What type of air mass would form over the northern Atlantic Ocean?
2. a. **Defining** What is a front?
   b. **Describing** Name the four types of fronts and describe the type of weather each brings.
   c. **Classifying** What type of front would most likely be responsible for several days of rain and clouds?

3. a. **Identifying** What is a cyclone?
   b. **Relating Cause and Effect** How does air move in an anticyclone? How does this movement affect the weather?
   c. **Comparing and Contrasting** Compare cyclones and anticyclones. What type of weather is associated with each?

Writing in Science

News Report Suppose you are a television weather reporter covering a severe thunderstorm. Write a brief report to explain to viewers the conditions that caused the thunderstorm.

2 Storms

Reading Preview

Key Concepts
- What are the main kinds of storms, and how do they form?
- What measures can you take to ensure safety in a storm?

Key Terms
- storm • thunderstorm
- lightning • tornado
- hurricane • storm surge
- evacuate

Target Reading Skill
Sequencing As you read, make a flowchart like the one below that shows how a hurricane forms. Write each step of the process in the flowchart in a separate box in the order in which it occurs.

Hurricane Formation

Begins as a low-pressure area over warm water, or a tropical disturbance.

↓

Warm, humid air rises and begins to spiral.

↓

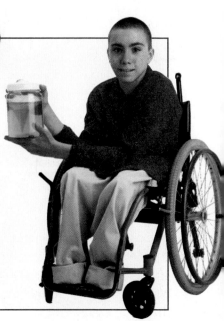

Lab zone | Discover **Activity**

Can You Make a Tornado?
1. Fill a large jar three-quarters full with water. Add a drop of liquid dish detergent and a penny or a marble.
2. Put the lid on the jar tightly. Now move the jar in a circle until the water inside begins to spin.

Think It Over
Observing What happens to the water in the jar? Describe the pattern that forms. How is it like a tornado? Unlike a tornado?

As a storm rages, lightning flashes and thunder rumbles. After the sky clears, dripping trees and numerous puddles are the only evidence of the passing storm. Right? Not always. Scientists search for other evidence—"fossil lightning"! When lightning strikes sand or sandy soil, the sand grains are fused together to form a fulgurite. The shape of the fulgurite reflects the path of the lightning bolt that formed it, as shown in Figure 8. These structures clearly show the tremendous power of storms.

A **storm** is a violent disturbance in the atmosphere. Storms involve sudden changes in air pressure, which in turn cause rapid air movements. Conditions that bring one kind of storm often cause other kinds of storms in the same area. For example, the conditions that cause thunderstorms can also cause tornadoes. There are several types of severe storms.

FIGURE 8
Fulgurites
A fulgurite forms when lightning strikes sand or sandy soil. The temperature of the lightning is so high that it melts the sand and forms a tube.

Storm movement

Cold air moves downward.

Warm, humid air rises.

Heavy rain

FIGURE 9
Thunderstorm Formation
A thunderstorm forms when warm, humid air rises rapidly within a cumulonimbus cloud. **Applying Concepts** *Why do cumulonimbus clouds often form along cold fronts?*

Thunderstorms

Do you find thunderstorms frightening? Exciting? As you watch the brilliant flashes of lightning and listen to long rolls of thunder, you may wonder what caused them.

How Thunderstorms Form A **thunderstorm** is a small storm often accompanied by heavy precipitation and frequent thunder and lightning. **Thunderstorms form in large cumulonimbus clouds, also known as thunderheads.** Most cumulonimbus clouds form on hot, humid afternoons. They also form when warm air is forced upward along a cold front. In both cases, the warm, humid air rises rapidly. The air cools, forming dense thunderheads. Heavy rain falls, sometimes along with hail. Within the thunderhead are strong upward and downward winds—updrafts and downdrafts—as shown in Figure 9. Many thunderstorms form in the spring and summer in southern states or on the Western Plains.

Lightning and Thunder During a thunderstorm, areas of positive and negative electrical charges build up in the storm clouds. **Lightning** is a sudden spark, or electrical discharge, as these charges jump between parts of a cloud, between nearby clouds, or between a cloud and the ground. Lightning is similar to the shocks you sometimes feel when you touch a metal object on a very dry day, but on a much larger scale.

What causes thunder? A lightning bolt can heat the air near it to as much as 30,000°C, much hotter than the sun's surface. The rapidly heated air expands suddenly and explosively. Thunder is the sound of the explosion. Because light travels much faster than sound, you see lightning before you hear thunder.

Lab zone Try This Activity

Lightning Distances
Because light travels faster than sound, you see a lightning flash before you hear the clap of thunder. Here's how to calculate your distance from a thunderstorm. **CAUTION:** *Only do this activity inside a building.*

1. Count the number of seconds between the moment when you see the lightning and when you hear the thunder.

2. Divide the number of seconds you counted by three to get the approximate distance in kilometers. Example:

$$\frac{15 \text{ s}}{3 \text{ s/km}} = 5 \text{ km}$$

Calculating Wait for another lightning flash and calculate the distance again. How can you tell whether a thunderstorm is moving toward you or away from you?

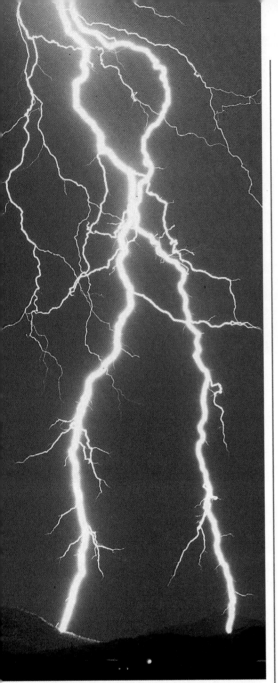

Thunderstorm Damage Thunderstorms can cause severe damage. The heavy rains associated with thunderstorms can flood low-lying areas. Lightning can also cause damage. When lightning strikes the ground, the hot, expanding air can shatter tree trunks or start forest fires. When lightning strikes people or animals, it acts like a powerful electric shock. Lightning can cause unconsciousness, serious burns, or even heart failure.

Floods A major danger during severe thunderstorms is flooding. Floods occur when so much water pours into a stream or river that its banks overflow, covering the surrounding land. In urban areas, floods can occur when the ground is already saturated by heavy rains. The water can't soak into the water-logged ground or the many areas covered with buildings, roads, and parking lots. A flash flood is a sudden, violent flood that occurs shortly after a storm.

Thunderstorm Safety The safest place to be during a thunderstorm is indoors. If you are inside a house, avoid touching telephones, electrical appliances, or plumbing fixtures, all of which can conduct electricity. It is usually safe to stay in a car with a hard top during a thunderstorm. The electricity will move along the metal skin of the car and jump to the ground. However, do not touch any metal inside the car. **During thunderstorms, avoid places where lightning may strike. Also avoid objects that can conduct electricity, such as metal objects and bodies of water.**

How can you remain safe if you are caught outside during a thunderstorm? It is dangerous to seek shelter under a tree, because lightning may strike the tree and you. Instead, find a low area away from trees, fences, and poles. Crouch with your head down. If you are swimming or in a boat, get to shore and find shelter away from the water.

FIGURE 10
Lightning Striking Earth
Lightning occurs when electricity jumps within clouds, between clouds, or between clouds and the ground. Lightning can cause fires or serious injuries.

Go Online
PLANET DIARY

For: More on thunder and lightning
Visit: PHSchool.com
Web Code: cfd-4032

 **Reading Checkpoint** How can lightning be dangerous?

Tornadoes

A tornado is one of the most frightening and destructive types of storms. A **tornado** is a rapidly whirling, funnel-shaped cloud that reaches down from a storm cloud to touch Earth's surface. If a tornado occurs over a lake or ocean, the storm is known as a waterspout. Tornadoes are usually brief, but can be deadly. They may touch the ground for 15 minutes or less and be only a few hundred meters across. But wind speeds in the most intense tornadoes may approach 500 kilometers per hour.

FIGURE 11

Tornado Formation

Tornadoes can form when warm, humid air rises rapidly in a cumulonimbus cloud. Varying winds at different heights can spin the rising air like a top.

2 The warm air begins to rotate as it meets winds blowing in different directions at different altitudes.

Cumulonimbus cloud

1 Warm, moist air flows in at the bottom of a cumulonimbus cloud and moves upward. A low pressure area forms inside the cloud.

3 A tornado forms as part of the cloud descends to earth in a funnel.

Rain

How Tornadoes Form Tornadoes can form in any situation that produces severe weather. **Tornadoes most commonly develop in thick cumulonimbus clouds—the same clouds that bring thunderstorms.** Tornadoes are most likely to occur when thunderstorms are likely—in spring and early summer, often late in the afternoon when the ground is warm. The Great Plains often have the kind of weather pattern that is likely to create tornadoes: A warm, humid air mass moves north from the Gulf of Mexico into the lower Great Plains. A cold, dry air mass moves south from Canada. When the air masses meet, the cold air moves under the warm air, forcing it to rise. A squall line of thunderstorms is likely to form, with storms traveling from southwest to northeast. A single squall line can produce ten or more tornadoes.

Tornado Alley Tornadoes occur more often in the United States than in any other country. About 800 tornadoes occur in the United States every year. Weather patterns on the Great Plains result in a "tornado alley," as shown in Figure 12. However, tornadoes can and do occur in nearly every part of the United States.

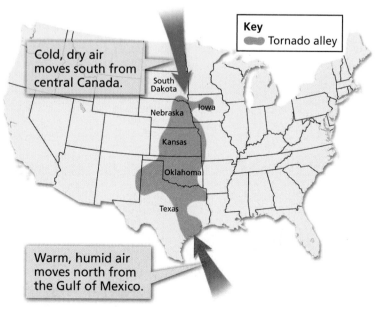

Key
Tornado alley

Cold, dry air moves south from central Canada.

South Dakota

Iowa

Nebraska

Kansas

Oklahoma

Texas

Warm, humid air moves north from the Gulf of Mexico.

FIGURE 12
Tornado Alley
Tornadoes in the U.S. are most likely to occur in a region known as Tornado Alley. **Interpreting Maps** *Name five states that Tornado Alley crosses.*

Tornado Damage Tornado damage comes from both strong winds and flying debris. The low pressure inside the tornado sucks dust and other objects into the funnel. Tornadoes can move large objects—sheds, trailers, cars—and scatter debris many miles away. One tornado tore off a motel sign in Broken Bow, Oklahoma, and dropped it 30 miles away in Arkansas! One of the reasons that tornadoes are so frightening is that they are unpredictable. A tornado can level houses on one street but leave neighboring houses standing.

Tornadoes are ranked on the Fujita scale by the amount of damage they cause. The Fujita scale was named for the scientist who devised it, Dr. T. Theodore Fujita. The scale goes from light damage (F0) to extreme damage (F5). Luckily, only about one percent of tornadoes are ranked as F4 or F5.

Science and History

Weather That Changed History

Unanticipated storms have caused incredible damage, killed large numbers of people, and even changed the course of history.

1588 England
King Philip II of Spain sent the Spanish Armada, a fleet of 130 ships, to invade England. Strong winds in the English Channel trapped the Armada near shore. Some Spanish ships escaped, but storms wrecked most of them.

1620 Massachusetts
English Pilgrims set sail for the Americas in the *Mayflower*. They had planned to land near the mouth of the Hudson River, but turned back north because of rough seas and storms. When the Pilgrims landed farther north, they decided to stay and so established Plymouth Colony.

1281 Japan
In an attempt to conquer Japan, Kublai Khan, the Mongol emperor of China, sent a fleet of ships carrying a huge army. A hurricane from the Pacific brought high winds and towering waves that sank the ships. The Japanese named the storm *kamikaze*, meaning "divine wind."

| 1200 | 1600 | 1700 |

Tornado Safety What should you do if a tornado is predicted in your area? A "tornado watch" is an announcement that tornadoes are possible in your area. Watch for approaching thunderstorms. A "tornado warning" is an announcement that a tornado has been seen in the sky or on weather radar. If you hear a tornado warning, move to a safe area as soon as you can. Do not wait until you actually see the tornado.

The safest place to be during a tornado is in a storm shelter or the basement of a well-built building. If the building you are in does not have a basement, move to the middle of the ground floor. Stay away from windows and doors to avoid flying debris. Lie on the floor under a sturdy piece of furniture, such as a large table. If you are outdoors, lie flat in a ditch.

 Reading Checkpoint What is a tornado warning?

Writing in Science

Research and Write
Many of these events happened before forecasters had the equipment to predict weather scientifically. Research one of the events in the timeline. Write a paragraph describing the event and how history might have been different if the people involved had had accurate weather predictions.

1837 North Carolina
The steamship *Home* sank during a hurricane off Ocracoke, North Carolina. In one of the worst storm-caused disasters at sea, 90 people died. In response, the U.S. Congress passed a law requiring sea-going ships to carry a life preserver for every passenger.

1870 Great Lakes
Learning that more than 1,900 boats had sunk in storms on the Great Lakes in 1869, Congress set up a national weather service, the Army Signal Corps. In 1891 the job of issuing weather warnings and forecasts went to a new agency, the U.S. Weather Bureau.

1900 and 1915 Texas
When a hurricane struck the port city of Galveston in 1900, it killed at least 8,000 people and destroyed much of the city. As a result, a seawall 5 meters high and 16 kilometers long was built. When another hurricane struck in 1915, the seawall greatly reduced the amount of damage.

1800   **1900**   **2000**

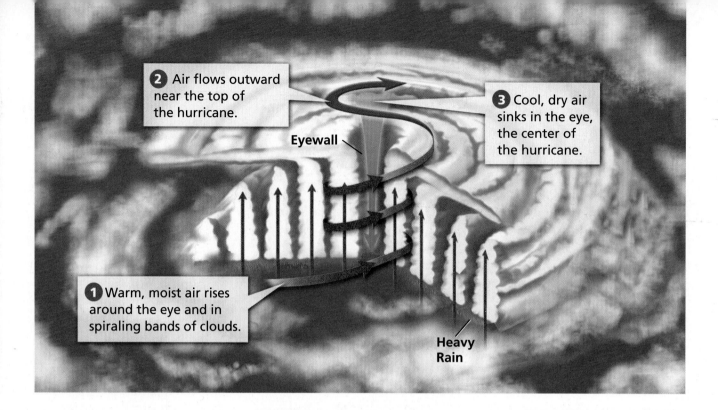

2 Air flows outward near the top of the hurricane.

3 Cool, dry air sinks in the eye, the center of the hurricane.

Eyewall

1 Warm, moist air rises around the eye and in spiraling bands of clouds.

Heavy Rain

FIGURE 13
Structure of a Hurricane
In a hurricane, air moves rapidly around a low-pressure area called the eye.

Hurricanes

A **hurricane** is a tropical cyclone that has winds of 119 kilometers per hour or higher. A typical hurricane is about 600 kilometers across. Hurricanes form in the Atlantic, Pacific, and Indian oceans. In the western Pacific Ocean, hurricanes are called typhoons.

How Hurricanes Form A typical hurricane that strikes the United States forms in the Atlantic Ocean north of the equator in August, September, or October. **A hurricane begins over warm ocean water as a low-pressure area, or tropical disturbance.** If the tropical disturbance grows in size and strength, it becomes a tropical storm, which may then become a hurricane.

A hurricane draws its energy from the warm, humid air at the ocean's surface. As this air rises and forms clouds, more air is drawn into the system. Inside the storm are bands of very high winds and heavy rains. Winds spiral inward toward the area of lowest pressure at the center. The lower the air pressure at the center of a storm, the faster the winds blow toward the center. Hurricane winds may be as strong as 320 kilometers per hour.

Look at Figure 13. Hurricane winds are strongest in a narrow band around the center of the storm. At the center is a ring of clouds, called the eyewall, that enclose a quiet "eye." The wind gets stronger as the eye approaches. When the eye arrives, the weather changes suddenly. The air grows calm and the sky may clear. After the eye passes, the storm resumes, but the wind blows from the opposite direction.

How Hurricanes Move Hurricanes last longer than other storms, usually a week or more. During that period, they can travel quite a distance. Hurricanes that form in the Atlantic Ocean are steered by easterly trade winds toward the Caribbean islands and the southeastern United States. After a hurricane passes over land, it no longer has warm, moist air to draw energy from. The hurricane gradually loses strength, although heavy rainfall may continue for several days.

August 25

August 24

August 23

Hurricane Damage When a hurricane comes ashore, it brings high waves and severe flooding as well as wind damage. The low pressure and high winds of the hurricane over the ocean raise the level of the water up to 6 meters above normal sea level. The result is a **storm surge,** a "dome" of water that sweeps across the coast where the hurricane lands. Storm surges can cause great damage, washing away beaches, destroying buildings along the coast, and eroding the coastlines.

Hurricane Safety Until the 1950s, a fast-moving hurricane could strike with little warning. People now receive information well in advance of an approaching hurricane.

A "hurricane watch" indicates that hurricane conditions are possible in an area within the next 36 hours. You should be prepared to **evacuate** (ee VAK yoo ayt), or move away temporarily. A "hurricane warning" means that hurricane conditions are expected within 24 hours. **If you hear a hurricane warning and are told to evacuate, leave the area immediately.**

FIGURE 14
Hurricane Andrew
The path of Hurricane Andrew over three consecutive days can be seen in this photo montage.

FIGURE 15
Hurricane Katrina
Hurricane Katrina caused tremendous damage to New Orleans and the Gulf Coast in 2005. Here, a rescue crew in Bay St. Louis, Mississippi, assists a family that was trapped atop their car by rising flood waters.

Reading Checkpoint What is a storm surge?

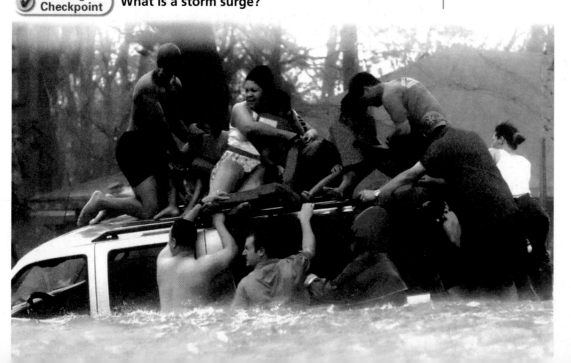

Winter Storms

In the winter in the northern United States, a large amount of precipitation falls as snow. **All year round, most precipitation begins in clouds as snow. If the air is colder than 0°C all the way to the ground, the precipitation falls as snow.** Heavy snowfalls can block roads, trapping people in their homes and making it hard for emergency vehicles to move. Extreme cold can damage crops and cause water pipes to freeze and burst.

Lake-Effect Snow Two of the snowiest cities in the United States are Buffalo and Rochester in upstate New York. On average, nearly three meters of snow falls on each of these cities every winter. Why do Buffalo and Rochester get so much snow?

Study Figure 16. Notice that Buffalo is located east of Lake Erie, and Rochester is located south of Lake Ontario. In the fall and winter, the land near these lakes cools much more rapidly than the water in the lakes. Although the water in these lakes is cold, it is still much warmer than the surrounding land and air.

When a cold, dry air mass from central Canada moves southeast across one of the Great Lakes, it picks up water vapor and heat from the lake. As soon as the air mass reaches the other side of the lake, the air rises and cools again. The water vapor condenses and falls as snow, usually within 40 kilometers of the lake.

FIGURE 16
Lake-Effect Snow
As cold dry air moves across the warmer water, it becomes more humid as water vapor evaporates from the lake surface. When the air reaches land and cools, lake-effect snow falls.
Interpreting Maps *Which two cities on the map receive large amounts of lake-effect snow?*

Great Lakes Snow Belts

Cold, dry air

Key
Snow Belt

Lake Superior
Lake Huron
Lake Michigan
Lake Ontario
Lake Erie
Rochester
Buffalo
Detroit
Chicago

N
W   E
S

0   100   200 mi
0   100   200 km

FIGURE 17
Winter Storm Damage
Major winter storms can cause a great deal of damage. Here, utility workers in Maine remove a pole snapped by a fierce winter storm.

Snowstorm Safety Imagine being caught in a snowstorm when the wind suddenly picks up. High winds can blow falling snow sideways or pick up snow from the ground and suspend it in the air. This situation can be extremely dangerous because the blowing snow limits your vision and makes it easy to get lost. Also, strong winds cool a person's body rapidly. **If you are caught in a snowstorm, try to find shelter from the wind.** Cover exposed parts of your body and try to stay dry. If you are in a car, the driver should keep the engine running only if the exhaust pipe is clear of snow.

 **Reading Checkpoint** How can snowstorms be dangerous?

Section 2 Assessment

Target Reading Skill Sequencing Refer to your flowchart about hurricane formation as you answer Question 3.

Reviewing Key Concepts

1. a. **Defining** What is a thunderstorm?
   b. **Listing** List two dangers associated with thunderstorms.
   c. **Describing** What safety precautions should you follow during a thunderstorm?
2. a. **Identifying** What weather conditions are most likely to produce tornadoes?
   b. **Developing Hypotheses** Why do tornadoes occur most often in the area known as "tornado alley"?
3. a. **Defining** What is a hurricane?
   b. **Relating Cause and Effect** How do hurricanes form?

4. a. **Explaining** What is lake-effect snow?
   b. **Inferring** Why doesn't lake-effect snow fall to the north or west of the Great Lakes?
   c. **Describing** What should you do if you are caught in a snowstorm?

Lab zone At-Home **Activity**

Storm Eyewitness Interview a family member or other adult about a dramatic storm that he or she has experienced. Before the interview, make a list of questions you would like to ask. For example, when and where did the storm occur? Write up your interview in a question-and-answer format, beginning with a short introduction.

Tracking a Hurricane

Problem

How can you predict when and where a hurricane will come ashore?

Skills Focus

interpreting data, predicting, drawing conclusions

Materials

- ruler   • red, blue, green, and brown pencils
- tracing paper

Procedure

1. Look at the plotted path of the hurricane on the map. Each dot represents the location of the eye of the hurricane at six-hour intervals. The last dot shows where the hurricane was located at noon on August 30.

2. Predict the path you think the hurricane will take. Place tracing paper over the map below. Using a red pencil, place an *X* on your tracing paper where you think the hurricane will first reach land. Next to your *X*, write the date and time you think the hurricane will come ashore.

3. Hurricane warnings are issued for an area that is likely to experience a hurricane within 24 hours. On your tracing paper, shade in red the area for which you would issue a hurricane warning.

4. Using the following data table, plot the next five positions for the storm using a blue pencil. Use your ruler to connect the dots to show the hurricane's path.

Data Table

Date and Time	Latitude	Longitude
August 30, 6:00 P.M.	28.3° N	86.8° W
August 31, midnight	28.4° N	86.0° W
August 31, 6:00 A.M.	28.6° N	85.3° W
August 31, noon	28.8° N	84.4° W
August 31, 6:00 P.M.	28.8° N	84.0° W

5. Based on the new data, decide if you need to change your prediction of where and when the hurricane will come ashore. Mark your new predictions in blue pencil on your tracing paper.

6. During September 1, you obtain four more positions. (Plot these points only after you have completed Step 5.) Based on these new data, use the green pencil to indicate when and where you now think the hurricane will come ashore.

Data Table

Date and Time	Latitude	Longitude
September 1, midnight	28.8° N	83.8° W
September 1, 6:00 A.M.	28.6° N	83.9° W
September 1, noon	28.6° N	84.2° W
September 1, 6:00 P.M.	28.9° N	84.8° W

7. The next day, September 2, you plot four more positions using a brown pencil. (Plot these points only after you have completed Step 6.)

Data Table

Date and Time	Latitude	Longitude
September 2, midnight	29.4° N	85.9° W
September 2, 6:00 A.M.	29.7° N	87.3° W
September 2, noon	30.2° N	88.8° W
September 2, 6:00 P.M.	31.0° N	90.4° W

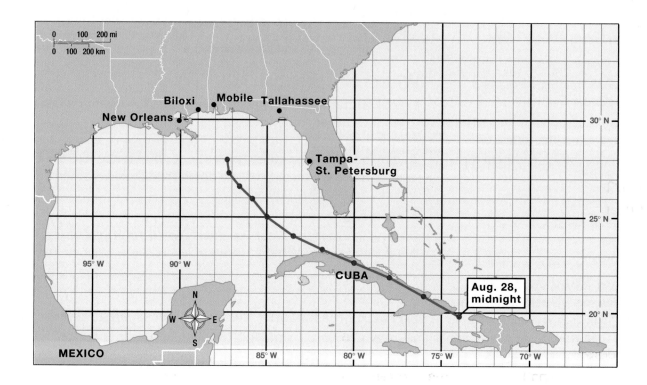

Analyze and Conclude

1. **Interpreting Data** Describe in detail the complete path of the hurricane you tracked. Include where it came ashore and identify any cities that were in the vicinity.

2. **Predicting** How did your predictions in Steps 2, 5, and 6 compare to what actually happened?

3. **Interpreting Data** What was unusual about your hurricane's path?

4. **Inferring** How do you think hurricanes with a path like this one affect the issuing of hurricane warnings?

5. **Drawing Conclusions** Why do you have to be so careful when issuing warnings? What problems might be caused if you issued an unnecessary hurricane warning? What might happen if a hurricane warning were issued too late?

6. **Communicating** In this activity you only had data for the hurricane's position. If you were tracking a hurricane and issuing warnings, what other types of information would help you make decisions about the hurricane's path? Write a paragraph describing the additional information you would need.

More to Explore

With your teacher's help, search the Internet for more hurricane tracking data. Map the data and try to predict where the hurricane will come ashore.

Predicting the Weather

Reading Preview

Key Concepts
- How do weather forecasters predict the weather?
- How has technology helped to improve weather forecasts?
- What can be learned from the information on weather maps?

Key Terms
- meteorologist
- isobar
- isotherm

Target Reading Skill
Previewing Visuals Before you read, look at Figure 21, a weather map. Then write three questions about the map in a graphic organizer like the one below. As you read, answer your questions.

Weather Map

Q. What type of front is located west of Oklahoma City?
A.
Q.

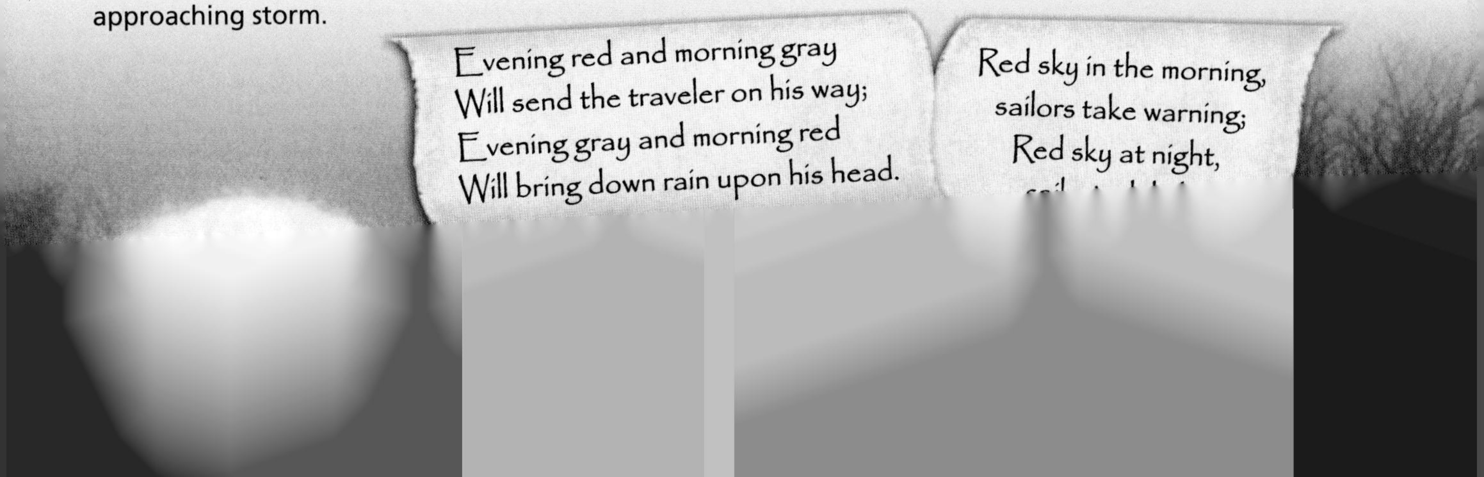

FIGURE 18
Red Sky
The red sky shown in this sunrise may indicate an approaching storm.

Discover Activity

Lab zone

What's the Weather?

1. Look at the weather report in your local newspaper. Note what weather conditions are predicted for your area today, including temperature, precipitation, and wind speed.
2. Look out the window or think about what it was like the last time you were outside. Write down the actual weather conditions where you are.

Think It Over
Observing Does the weather report match what you observe? What is the same? What is different?

Every culture's folklore includes weather sayings. Many of these sayings are based on long-term observations. Sailors, pilots, farmers, and others who work outdoors are usually careful observers of clouds, winds, and other signs of changes in the weather. Two examples are shown below.

Why do these two weather sayings agree that a red morning sky means bad weather? Recall that in the United States storms usually move from west to east. Clouds in the west may indicate an advancing low-pressure area, bringing stormy weather. If there are high clouds in the west in the morning, the rising sun in the east turns these clouds red. The reverse is true at sunset. As the sun sets in the west, it turns clouds in the east red. Clouds in the east may indicate that a storm is moving away to the east. A red sky is one kind of observation that helps people to predict the weather.

Evening red and morning gray
Will send the traveler on his way;
Evening gray and morning red
Will bring down rain upon his head.

Red sky in the morning,
sailors take warning;
Red sky at night,

FIGURE 19
Meteorologist at Work
Professional meteorologists use computers to help track and forecast the weather. *Inferring Why might a meteorologist need to refer to more than one computer screen?*

Weather Forecasting

The first step in forecasting is to collect data, either from simple, direct observations or through the use of instruments. For example, if a barometer shows that the air pressure is falling, you can expect a change in the weather. Falling air pressure usually indicates an approaching low-pressure area, possibly bringing rain or snow.

Making Simple Observations You can read weather signs in the clouds, too. Cumulus clouds often form on warm afternoons when warm air rises. If you see these clouds growing larger and taller, you can expect them to become cumulonimbus clouds, which may produce a thunderstorm. If you can see thin cirrus clouds high in the sky, a warm front may be approaching.

Even careful weather observers often turn to professional meteorologists for weather information. **Meteorologists** (mee tee uh RAHL uh jists) are scientists who study the causes of weather and try to predict it.

Interpreting Complex Data Meteorologists are able to interpret information from a variety of sources, including local weather observers, instruments carried by balloons, satellites, and weather stations around the world. **Meteorologists use maps, charts, and computers to analyze weather data and to prepare weather forecasts.** They often use radar to track areas of rain or snow and to locate severe storms such as tornadoes. Forecasters can also follow the path of a storm system.

Where do weather reporters get their information? Most weather information comes from the National Weather Service. The National Weather Service uses balloons, satellites, radar, and surface instruments to gather weather data.

 **Reading Checkpoint** What is a meteorologist?

Weather Technology

Techniques for predicting weather have changed dramatically in recent years. Short-range forecasts—forecasts for up to five days—are now fairly reliable. Meteorologists can also make somewhat accurate long-range predictions. **Technological improvements in gathering weather data and using computers have improved the accuracy of weather forecasts.**

Weather Balloons Weather balloons carry instruments high into the troposphere and lower stratosphere. Remember that these are the two lowest layers of the atmosphere. The instruments measure temperature, air pressure, and humidity.

Weather Satellites The first weather satellite, *TIROS-1*, was launched in 1960. Satellites orbit Earth in the exosphere, the uppermost layer of the atmosphere. Cameras on weather satellites in the exosphere can make images of Earth's surface, clouds, storms, and snow cover. These images are then transmitted to meteorologists on Earth, who interpret the information. New technologies, such as NASA's *Terra* satellite, shown in Figure 20, provide large amounts of data to meteorologists. Modern satellites collect data on temperature, humidity, solar radiation, wind speed and wind direction, and provide images of clouds and storm systems.

FIGURE 20
Satellite Technology
The large satellite image shows an intense cyclone over Ireland and Great Britain. The *Terra* satellite (right) collects data on weather and environmental conditions.

Automated Weather Stations Data are also gathered from surface locations for temperature, air pressure, relative humidity, rainfall, and wind speed and direction. The National Weather Service has established a network of over 1,700 surface weather observation sites.

Computer Forecasts Computers are widely used to help forecast weather. Instruments can now gather large amounts of data, including temperature, humidity, air pressure, wind speed and direction, and other factors. Computers process such information quickly to help forecasters make predictions. To make a forecast, the computer starts with weather conditions reported from various weather stations over a large area. The computer then works through thousands of calculations using equations from weather models. These data are used to make forecasts for 12 hours, 24 hours, 36 hours, and so on. Each forecast builds on the previous forecast. When new weather data come in, the computer forecasts are revised.

Go Online
PLANET DIARY

For: More on weather maps
Visit: PHSchool.com
Web Code: cfd-4033

✓ **Reading Checkpoint** How are computers used to produce weather forecasts?

Math ➤ Analyzing Data

Computer Weather Forecasting

Scientists use computers to develop different models of how a front may move. These predictions are then used to make weather forecasts. As more data become available, some models are found to be incorrect, while others are found to closely fit the predicted conditions. The upper graph shows predicted air pressure from two models. The lower graph shows actual data for air pressure.

1. **Reading Graphs** What two variables are being graphed?

2. **Interpreting Data** How is air pressure predicted to change according to each model in the top graph?

3. **Inferring** Which computer model most closely matches the actual air pressure data?

4. **Predicting** What weather would you forecast for Monday and Tuesday? Explain. (*Hint:* Remember that falling air pressure usually means an approaching low-pressure area and possible precipitation.)

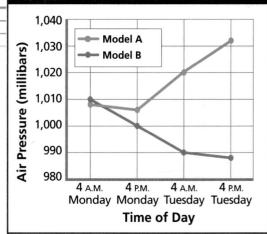

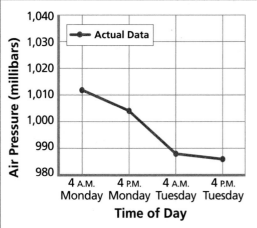

FIGURE 21
Reading Weather Map Symbols

The figure below shows what various weather symbols mean. At right, the weather map shows data collected from many weather stations.

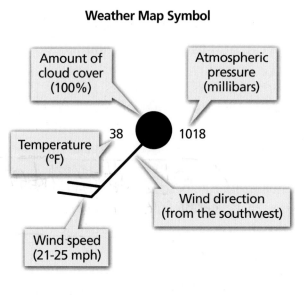

Wind Speed (mph)	Symbol
1 – 2	
3 – 8	
9 – 14	
15 – 20	
21 – 25	
26 – 31	
32 – 37	
38 – 43	
44 – 49	
50 – 54	
55 – 60	
61 – 66	
67 – 71	
72 – 77	

Weather Map Symbol

Amount of cloud cover (100%)

Atmospheric pressure (millibars)

Temperature (°F)

38 1018

Wind direction (from the southwest)

Wind speed (21-25 mph)

Cloud Cover (%)	Symbol
0	
10	
20–30	
40	
50	
60	
70–80	
90	
100	

Reading Weather Maps

A weather map is a "snapshot" of conditions at a particular time over a large area. There are many types of weather maps. Weather forecasters often present maps generated by computers from surface data, radar, or satellite information.

Weather Service Maps Data from many local weather stations all over the country are assembled into weather maps at the National Weather Service. The data collected by a typical station is summarized in Figure 21 above. The simplified weather map on the next page includes most of the weather station data shown in the key.

On some weather maps, you see curved lines. These lines connect places where certain conditions—temperature or air pressure—are the same. **Isobars** are lines joining places on the map that have the same air pressure. (*Iso* means "equal" and *bar* means "pressure.") The numbers on the isobars are the pressure readings. Air pressure readings may be given in inches of mercury or in millibars or both. The isobars in Figure 21 are shown in both millbars and inches of mercury.

Isotherms are lines joining places that have the same temperature. The isotherm may be labeled with the temperature in degrees Fahrenheit, degrees Celsius, or both.

Interpreting Data

Use Figure 21 to help you answer questions about this weather station data.

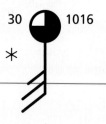

30 1016

1. What is the temperature at this station?
2. What is the wind speed?
3. Which way is the wind blowing?
4. What is the air pressure?
5. What percent of the sky is covered by clouds?
6. What type of precipitation, if any, is falling?

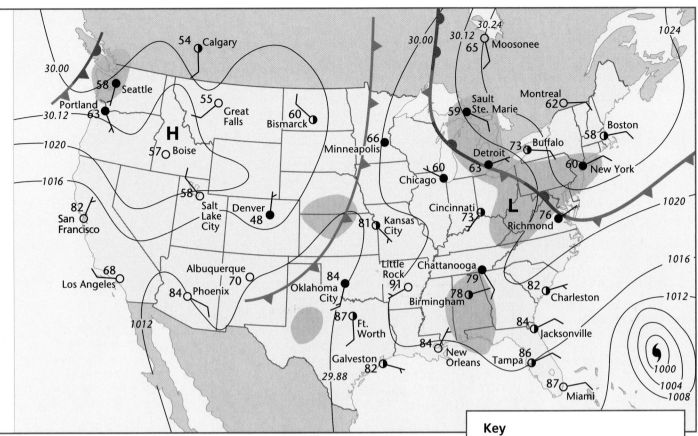

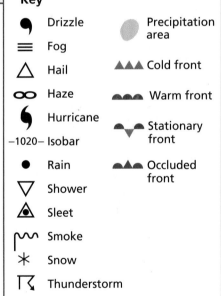

Key

🌢	Drizzle	Precipitation area	
≡	Fog		
△	Hail	▲▲▲ Cold front	
∞	Haze	●●● Warm front	
🌢	Hurricane		
–1020–	Isobar	⌣⌣ Stationary front	
●	Rain		
▽	Shower	▲●▲ Occluded front	
⊿	Sleet		
⌇⌇	Smoke		
＊	Snow		
⌐	Thunderstorm		

Newspaper Weather Maps Maps in newspapers are simplified versions of maps produced by the National Weather Service. Figure 22 on the next page shows a typical newspaper weather map. From what you have learned in this chapter, you can probably interpret most of the symbols on this map. **Standard symbols on weather maps show fronts, areas of high and low pressure, types of precipitation, and temperatures.** Note that the high and low temperatures are given in degrees Fahrenheit instead of Celsius.

Limits of Weather Forecasts As computers have grown more powerful, and new satellites and radar technologies have been developed, scientists have been able to make better forecasts. But even with extremely fast computers, it is unlikely that forecasters will ever be able to predict the weather a month in advance with great accuracy. This has to do with the so-called "butterfly effect." The atmosphere works in such a way that a small change in the weather today can mean a larger change in the weather a week later! The name refers to a scientist's suggestion that even the flapping of a butterfly's wings causes a tiny disturbance in the atmosphere. This tiny event might cause a larger disturbance that could—eventually—grow into a large storm.

 **Reading Checkpoint** What is the "butterfly effect"?

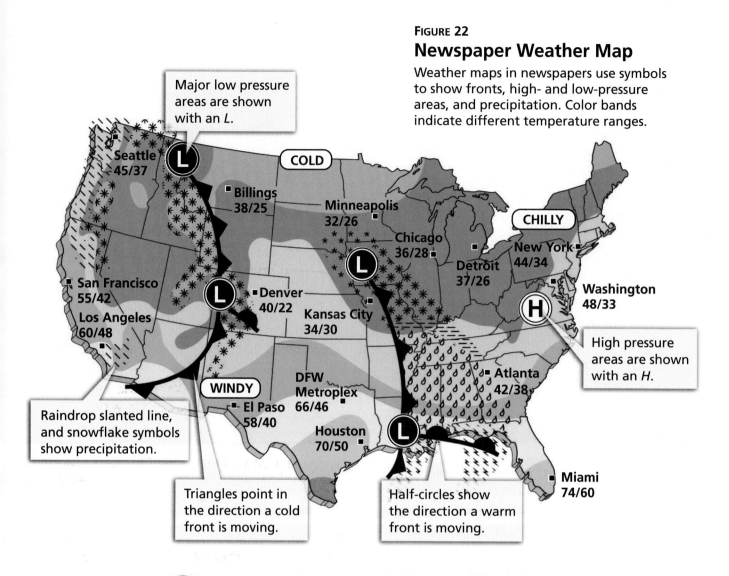

FIGURE 22
Newspaper Weather Map
Weather maps in newspapers use symbols to show fronts, high- and low-pressure areas, and precipitation. Color bands indicate different temperature ranges.

Major low pressure areas are shown with an *L*.

COLD

Seattle
45/37

Billings
38/25

Minneapolis
32/26

CHILLY

Chicago
36/28

Detroit
37/26

New York
44/34

San Francisco
55/42

Denver
40/22

Kansas City
34/30

Washington
48/33

Los Angeles
60/48

High pressure areas are shown with an *H*.

Raindrop slanted line, and snowflake symbols show precipitation.

WINDY

DFW
Metroplex 66/46

El Paso
58/40

Atlanta
42/38

Houston
70/50

Miami
74/60

Triangles point in the direction a cold front is moving.

Half-circles show the direction a warm front is moving.

Section 3 Assessment

Target Reading Skill Previewing Visuals Refer to your questions and answers about weather maps to help you answer Question 3 below.

Reviewing Key Concepts

1. a. Describing What is a meteorologist?
   b. Explaining What tools do meteorologists rely on to forecast the weather?
2. a. Listing List three technologies used to gather weather data.
   b. Summarizing Describe the types of weather data gathered by satellites.
   c. Drawing Conclusions How does the large amount of weather data gathered by various modern technologies affect the accuracy of weather forecasts?

3. a. Identifying What is the symbol for a cold front on a weather map?
   b. Explaining How is wind direction indicated on a weather map?
   c. Interpreting Diagrams According to Figure 22, what is the weather like in Chicago? How might this change in a few hours?

Writing in Science

Weather Report Find a current weather map from a newspaper. Use the map to write a brief weather report for your region. Include a description of the various weather symbols used on the map.

Reading a Weather Map

Problem

How does a weather map communicate data?

Skills Focus

interpreting maps, observing, drawing conclusions

Procedure

1. Examine the symbols on the weather map below. For more information about the symbols used on the map, refer to Figure 21 and Figure 22 earlier in this section.

2. Observe the different colors on the weather map below.

3. Find the symbols for snow and rain.

4. Locate the warm fronts and cold fronts.

5. Locate the symbols for high and low pressure.

Analyze and Conclude

1. **Interpreting Maps** What color represents the highest temperatures? What color represents the lowest temperatures?

2. **Interpreting Maps** Which city has the highest temperature? Which city has the lowest temperature?

3. **Interpreting Maps** Where on the map is it raining? Where on the map is it snowing?

4. **Interpreting Maps** How many different kinds of fronts are shown on the map?

5. **Observing** How many areas of low pressure are shown on the map? How many areas of high pressure are shown on the map?

6. **Drawing Conclusions** What season does this map represent? How do you know?

7. **Communicating** The triangles and semicircles on the front lines show which way the front is moving. What type of front is moving toward Minneapolis? What kind of weather do you think it will bring?

More to Explore

Compare this weather map to one shown on a television news report. Which symbols on these maps are similar? Which symbols are different?

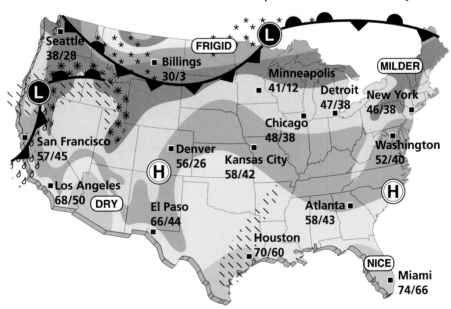

Doppler Radar

"Let's look at our Doppler radar screen," says a TV meteorologist pointing to a weather map with moving color blotches. The colors represent different locations and intensities of precipitation. "The purple area here shows a severe storm moving rapidly into our area." Doppler radar helps meteorologists make more accurate weather forecasts by tracking the speed and direction of precipitation.

What Is Doppler Radar?

Doppler radar gets its name from the "Doppler effect," which describes the changes that occur in radio waves as they bounce off a moving object. Nearly 150 Doppler radar stations throughout the United States continuously send out radio waves. These waves bounce off particles in the air, such as raindrops, snowflakes, hail, and even dust. Some of these radio waves are reflected back to the Doppler radar station where computers process the data.

Transmitter sends out radio waves that bounce off particles, such as raindrops, in the air. Some waves are reflected back to the station.

Antenna picks up the returning radio waves. Data from incoming waves are sent to a computer.

Computer is used to process data and generate a Doppler radar image for meteorologists.

Doppler Radar Station
Rotating continuously inside the protective housing, the station is supported by a tower that may be as tall as 30 meters.

How Effective Is Doppler Radar?

Before Doppler radar, it was hard to track fast-moving storms such as tornadoes. Tornado warnings were issued an average of just five minutes in advance. Today, Doppler radar can give people several extra minutes to prepare. People also use Doppler images to make decisions about everyday activities.

But the technology does have limitations. Doppler radar doesn't "see" everything. Sometimes mountains or buildings block the radio waves. In addition, Doppler radar doesn't always pick up light precipitation such as drizzle. Meteorologists must review the completeness of the data and decide how it might affect the forecast.

Tornado
Doppler radar can detect the air movements in thunderstorms that may lead to tornadoes. A tornado is a rapidly spinning, funnel-shaped cloud formed of condensed water particles.

Weigh the Impact

1. Identify the Need
How is Doppler radar an important technology in weather forecasting?

2. Research
Using the Internet, research Doppler radar reports for your city. Examine a Doppler image and explain each element on the map, including the different colors and the direction of motion.

3. Write
As a TV meteorologist, write the script for a local weather forecast. Describe areas with precipitation, the amount of precipitation, and the direction of weather systems. Use your research and notes.

Go Online
PHSchool.com

For: More on Doppler radar
Visit: PHSchool.com
Web Code: cfh-4030

Doppler Radar Screens

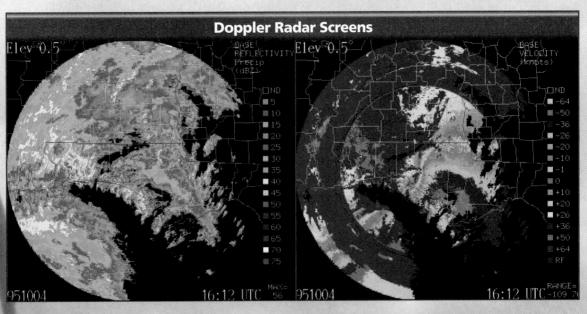

The amount of precipitation is shown above by using different colors.

The different colors above show the speed and direction of precipitation.

The BIG Idea **Weather Systems** When air masses collide, they form fronts. Storms and rapid changes in weather often develop along fronts.

1 Air Masses and Fronts

Key Concepts

- Four major types of air masses influence the weather in North America: maritime tropical, continental tropical, maritime polar, and continental polar.

- In the continental United States, air masses are commonly moved by the prevailing westerlies and jet streams.

- Colliding air masses can form four types of fronts: cold fronts, warm fronts, stationary fronts, and occluded fronts.

- Cyclones and decreasing air pressure are associated with clouds, wind, and precipitation.

- The descending air in an anticyclone generally causes dry, clear weather.

Key Terms

air mass	front
tropical	occluded
polar	cyclone
maritime	anticyclone
continental	

2 Storms

Key Concepts

- Thunderstorms form in large cumulonimbus clouds, also known as thunderheads.

- During thunderstorms, avoid places where lightning may strike. Also avoid objects that can conduct electricity, such as metal objects and bodies of water.

- Tornadoes most commonly develop in thick cumulonimbus clouds—the same clouds that bring thunderstorms.

- The safest place to be during a tornado is in a storm shelter or the basement of a well-built building.

- A hurricane begins over warm ocean water as a low-pressure area, or tropical disturbance.

- If you hear a hurricane warning and are told to evacuate, leave the area immediately.

- All year round, most precipitation begins in clouds as snow.

- If you are caught in a snowstorm, try to find shelter from the wind.

Key Terms

- storm • thunderstorm • lightning
- tornado • hurricane • storm surge
- evacuate

3 Predicting the Weather

Key Concepts

- Meteorologists use maps, charts, and computers to analyze weather data and to prepare weather forecasts.

- Technological improvements in gathering weather data and using computers have improved the accuracy of weather forecasts.

- Standard symbols on weather maps show fronts, areas of high and low pressure, types of precipitation, and temperatures.

Key Terms

meteorologist
isobar
isotherm

Review and Assessment

Go Online
PHSchool.com
For: Self-Assessment
Visit: PHSchool.com
Web Code: cfa-4030

Organizing Information

Comparing and Contrasting Copy the table, which compares and contrasts thunderstorms, tornadoes, and hurricanes, onto a separate sheet of paper. Then complete it and add a title. (For more on Comparing and Contrasting, see the Skills Handbook.)

Type of Storm	Where Forms	Typical Time of Year	Safety Rules
Thunderstorm	Within large cumulonimbus clouds	a. _____?_____	b. _____?_____
Tornado	c. _____?_____	Spring, early summer	d. _____?_____
Hurricane	e. _____?_____	f. _____?_____	Evacuate or move inside a well-built building

Reviewing Key Terms

Choose the letter of the best answer.

1. An air mass that forms over an ocean is called
   a. tropical.
   b. continental.
   c. maritime.
   d. polar.

2. Cool, clear weather usually follows a
   a. warm front.
   b. cold front.
   c. stationary front.
   d. occluded front.

3. A rotating funnel-shaped cloud with high winds that extends from a storm cloud to Earth's surface is a
   a. storm surge.
   b. thunderstorm.
   c. hurricane.
   d. tornado.

4. Very large tropical cyclones with high winds are called
   a. hurricanes.
   b. tornadoes.
   c. air masses.
   d. anticyclones.

5. Lines joining places that have the same temperature are
   a. isobars.
   b. isotherms.
   c. fronts.
   d. occluded.

If the statement is true, write *true*. If it is false, change the underlined word or words to make the statement true.

6. Summers in the Southwest are hot and dry because of <u>maritime tropical</u> air masses.

7. A <u>cyclone</u> is a high-pressure center of dry air.

8. Cumulonimbus clouds may produce both thunderstorms and <u>hurricanes.</u>

9. <u>Lightning</u> is a sudden spark or electrical discharge, as electrical charges jump between parts of a cloud, between nearby clouds, or between a cloud and the ground.

10. On a weather map, <u>isotherms</u> join places on the map with the same air pressure.

Writing in Science

Descriptive Paragraph Imagine that you are a hurricane hunter—a scientist who flies into a hurricane to collect data. Describe what it would feel like as you flew through the hurricane's eyewall into its eye.

Discovery CHANNEL SCHOOL™

Weather Patterns

Video Preview
Video Field Trip
▶ Video Assessment

Review

Checking Concepts

11. Describe how wind patterns affect the movement of air masses in North America.

12. How does a cold front form?

13. What safety precautions should you take if a tornado is predicted in your area? If a hurricane is predicted?

14. What happens to a hurricane when it moves onto land? Why?

15. Explain how lake-effect snow forms.

16. What are some of the sources of information that meteorologists use to predict the weather?

Thinking Critically

17. **Relating Cause and Effect** How do differences in air density influence the movement of air along cold and warm fronts?

18. **Making Generalizations** What type of weather is most likely to form at the front shown below?

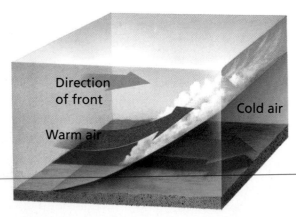

Direction of front

Cold air

Warm air

19. **Comparing and Contrasting** Compare thunderstorms and tornadoes. How are they similar? How are they different?

20. **Predicting** If you observe that air pressure is decreasing, what kind of weather do you think is coming?

21. **Applying Concepts** Would you expect hurricanes to form over the oceans off the northeast or northwest coasts of the United States? Explain.

22. **Making Judgments** What do you think is the most important thing people should do to reduce the dangers of storms?

23. **Applying Concepts** Why can't meteorologists accurately forecast the weather a month in advance?

Applying Skills

Use the map to answer Questions 24–27.

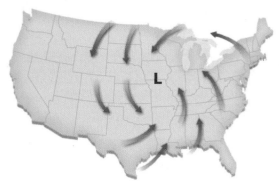

L

24. **Interpreting Maps** Does the map show a cyclone or an anticyclone? How can you tell?

25. **Interpreting Data** What do the arrows show about the movement of the winds in this pressure center? What else indicates wind direction?

26. **Making Models** Using this diagram as an example, draw a similar diagram to illustrate a high-pressure area. Remember to indicate wind direction in your diagram.

27. **Posing Questions** If you saw a pressure center like the one shown above on a weather map, what could you predict about the weather? What questions would you need to ask in order to make a better prediction?

Lab zone Chapter **Project**

Performance Assessment Present your weather maps and weather forecasts to the class. Discuss how accurate your weather predictions were. Explain why inaccuracies may have occurred in your forecasts.

Standardized Test Prep

Choose the letter of the best answer.

1. How are air masses classified?
  A by temperature and pressure
  B by pressure and humidity
  C by temperature and density
  D by temperature and humidity

2. A rapidly moving cold air mass meets a slowly moving warm air mass and forms a front. What will most likely occur at this front?
  F The two air masses will mix together.
  G The warm air will slide under the cold air. The cold air will rise and get warmer.
  H Cold air will slide under the warm air. Warm air will rise and cool. Clouds will form.
  J The less dense warm air will sink and cool. Clouds will form.

Use the graph below and your knowledge of science to answer Questions 3–4.

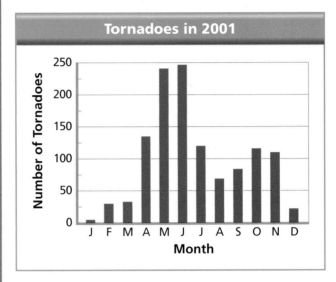

3. According to the graph, which two months in 2001 had the most tornadoes?
  A April and May
  B May and July
  C May and June
  D June and July

4. Which statement best summarizes the trend shown in the graph?
  F Tornadoes always occur most frequently in May and June.
  G Tornadoes occur when the weather is warmest.
  H In 2001, tornadoes were most frequent in April, May, and June.
  J Tornadoes are generally most frequent in the winter.

Constructed Response

5. Sound travels at a speed of about 330 m/s. How could you use this information to determine how far away lightning bolts are from you during a thunderstorm? Use an example to show how you would calculate the distance.

Chapter

4

Climate and Climate Change

The BIG Idea
Earth's Many Climates

Q **What are the major factors that influence a region's climate?**

Chapter Preview

❶ **What Causes Climate?**
Discover How Does Latitude Affect Climate?
Skills Activity Inferring
Math Skills Percentage
Active Art The Seasons
Skills Lab Sunny Rays and Angles

❷ **Climate Regions**
Discover How Do Climates Differ?
Try This Modeling a Climate
Skills Activity Classifying
At-Home Activity What's Your Climate?
Consumer Lab Cool Climate Graphs

❸ **Long-Term Changes in Climate**
Discover What Story Can Tree Rings Tell?
Analyzing Data Ice Ages and Temperature
Active Art Continental Drift

❹ **Global Changes in the Atmosphere**
Discover What Is the Greenhouse Effect?
Try This Activity It's Your Skin!
At-Home Activity Sun Protection

These emperor penguins thrive ▶
in Antarctica's polar climate.

Lab zone™ Chapter **Project**

Investigating Microclimates

A microclimate is a small area with its own climate. As you work through this chapter, you will investigate microclimates in your community.

Your Goal To compare weather conditions from at least three microclimates

To complete your project, you must

- hypothesize how the microclimates in three areas differ from each other
- collect data from your locations at the same time each day
- relate each microclimate to the plants and animals found there

Plan It! Begin by brainstorming a list of nearby places that may have different microclimates. How are the places different? Keep in mind weather factors such as temperature, precipitation, humidity, wind direction, and wind speed. Consider areas that are grassy, sandy, sunny, or shaded. You will need to measure daily weather conditions and record them in a logbook. Collect the instruments you need before you begin your investigation. Once you have collected all the data, construct your graphs and look for patterns. Then plan your presentation.

What Causes Climate?

Reading Preview

Key Concepts
- What factors influence temperature?
- What factors influence precipitation?
- What causes the seasons?

Key Terms
- climate • microclimate
- tropical zone • polar zone
- temperate zone
- marine climate
- continental climate
- windward • leeward
- monsoon

Target Reading Skill

Building Vocabulary After you read the section, reread the paragraphs that contain definitions of Key Terms. Use all the information you have learned to write a meaningful sentence using each Key Term.

An oasis in the Mojave Desert ▼

Lab zone Discover **Activity**

How Does Latitude Affect Climate?

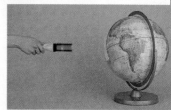

1. On a globe, tape a strip of paper from the equator to the North Pole. Divide the tape into three equal parts. Label the top section *poles,* the bottom section *equator,* and the middle section *mid-latitudes.*

2. Tape the end of an empty toilet paper roll to the end of a flashlight. Hold the flashlight about 30 cm from the equator. Turn on the flashlight to represent the sun. On the paper strip, have a partner draw the area the light shines on.

3. Move the flashlight up slightly to aim at the "mid-latitudes." Keep the flashlight horizontal and at the same distance from the globe. Again, draw the lighted area.

4. Repeat Step 3, but this time aim the light at the "poles."

Think It Over

Observing How does the size of the illuminated area change? Do you think the sun's rays heat Earth's surface evenly?

The weather in an area changes every day. At a given location, the weather may be cloudy and rainy one day and clear and sunny the next. **Climate,** on the other hand, refers to the average, year-after-year conditions of temperature, precipitation, winds, and clouds in an area. For example, California's Mojave Desert, shown below, has a hot, dry climate.

Scientists use two main factors—precipitation and temperature—to describe the climate of a region. A climate region is a large area that has similar climate conditions throughout. For example, the climate in the southwestern United States is dry, with hot summers.

The factors that affect large climate regions also affect smaller areas. Have you ever noticed that it is cooler and more humid in a grove of trees than in an open field? A small area with climate conditions that differ from those around it may have its own **microclimate.**

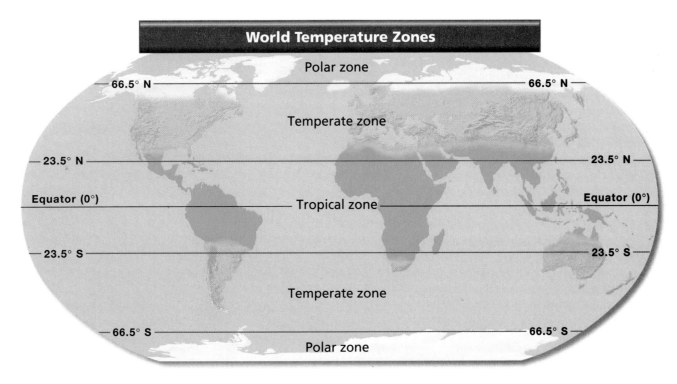

World Temperature Zones

Polar zone

66.5° N — 66.5° N

Temperate zone

23.5° N — 23.5° N

Equator (0°) — Tropical zone — Equator (0°)

23.5° S — 23.5° S

Temperate zone

66.5° S — 66.5° S

Polar zone

Factors Affecting Temperature

Why are some places warm and others cold? **The main factors that influence temperature are latitude, altitude, distance from large bodies of water, and ocean currents.**

Latitude In general, climates of locations near the equator are warmer than climates of areas far from the equator. The reason is that the sun's rays hit Earth's surface most directly at the equator. At the poles, the same amount of solar radiation is spread over a larger area, and therefore brings less warmth.

Recall that latitude is the distance from the equator, measured in degrees. Based on latitude, Earth's surface can be divided into the three temperature zones shown in Figure 1. The **tropical zone** is the area near the equator, between about 23.5° north latitude and 23.5° south latitude. The tropical zone receives direct or nearly direct sunlight all year round, making climates there warm.

In contrast, the sun's rays always strike at a lower angle near the North and South poles. As a result, the areas near both poles have cold climates. These **polar zones** extend from about 66.5° to 90° north and 66.5° to 90° south latitudes.

Between the tropical zones and the polar zones are the **temperate zones**. In summer, the sun's rays strike the temperate zones more directly. In winter, the sun's rays strike at a lower angle. As a result, the weather in the temperate zones ranges from warm or hot in summer to cool or cold in winter.

FIGURE 1
The tropical zone has the warmest climates. Cold climates occur in the polar zone. In between lies the temperate zone, where climates vary from warm to cool.
Interpreting Maps *In which temperature zone is most of the United States located?*

FIGURE 2
Effect of Altitude
Mount Kilimanjaro, in Tanzania, is near the equator.
Relating Cause and Effect *What factor is responsible for the difference between the climate at the mountaintop and the climate at the base?*

Altitude The peak of Mount Kilimanjaro towers high above the plains of East Africa. Kilimanjaro is covered in snow all year round, as shown in Figure 2. Yet it is located near the equator, at 3° south latitude. Why is Mount Kilimanjaro so cold?

In the case of high mountains, altitude is a more important climate factor than latitude. In the troposphere, temperature decreases about 6.5 Celsius degrees for every 1-kilometer increase in altitude. As a result, highland areas everywhere have cool climates, no matter what their latitude. At nearly 6 kilometers, the air at the top of Kilimanjaro is about 39 Celsius degrees colder than the air at sea level at the same latitude.

Distance From Large Bodies of Water Oceans or large lakes can also affect temperatures. Oceans greatly moderate, or make less extreme, the temperatures of nearby land. Water heats up more slowly than land. It also cools down more slowly. Therefore, winds off the ocean often prevent extremes of hot and cold in coastal regions. Much of the west coasts of North America, South America, and Europe have mild **marine climates,** with relatively mild winters and cool summers.

The centers of North America and Asia are too far inland to be warmed or cooled by the ocean. Most of Canada and of Russia, as well as the central United States, have continental climates. **Continental climates** have more extreme temperatures than marine climates. Winters are cold, while summers are warm or hot.

Ocean Currents Marine climates are influenced by ocean currents, streams of water within the oceans that move in regular patterns. Some warm ocean currents move from the tropics towards the poles. This affects climate as the warm ocean water warms the air above it. The warmed air then moves over nearby land. In the same way, cold currents bring cold water from the polar zones toward the equator. A cold current brings cool air.

As you read about the following currents, trace their paths on the map in Figure 3. The best-known warm-water current is the Gulf Stream. The Gulf Stream begins in the Gulf of Mexico, then flows north along the east coast of the United States. When it crosses the North Atlantic, it becomes the North Atlantic Drift. This warm current brings mild, humid air to Ireland and southern England. As a result, these areas have a mild, wet climate despite their relatively high latitude.

In contrast, the cool California Current flows southward down the West Coast of the United States. The California Current makes climates along the West Coast cooler than you would expect at those latitudes.

Reading Checkpoint What effect do oceans have on the temperatures of nearby land areas?

Lab zone Skills **Activity**

Inferring
Look at the currents in the South Pacific, South Atlantic, and Indian oceans. What pattern can you observe? Now compare currents in the South Atlantic to those in the North Atlantic. What might be responsible for differences in the current patterns?

FIGURE 3
On this map, warm currents are shown in red and cold currents in blue. Interpreting Maps *What type of current occurs around Antarctica?*

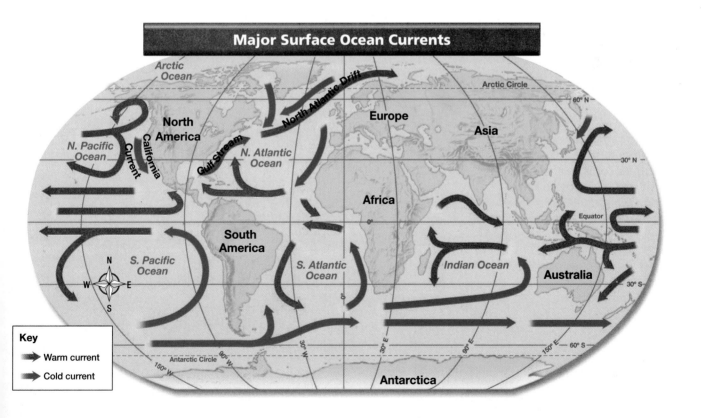

Major Surface Ocean Currents

Key
→ Warm current
→ Cold current

Factors Affecting Precipitation

The air masses that pass over an area may bring rain or snow. The amount of precipitation varies from year to year. But over time, total precipitation tends toward a yearly average. What determines the amount of precipitation an area receives? **The main factors that affect precipitation are prevailing winds, the presence of mountains, and seasonal winds.**

Prevailing Winds As you know, weather patterns depend on the movement of huge air masses. Air masses are moved from place to place by prevailing winds, the directional winds that usually blow in a region. Air masses can be warm or cool, dry or humid. The amount of water vapor in the air mass influences how much rain or snow will fall.

The amount of water vapor in prevailing winds also depends on where the winds come from. Winds that blow inland from oceans or large lakes carry more water vapor than winds that blow from over land. For example, winter winds generally blow from west to east across the Great Lakes. The winds pick up moisture that evaporates from the lakes. As a result, areas that are downwind can receive large amounts of snow.

Mountain Ranges A mountain range in the path of prevailing winds can also influence where precipitation falls. When humid winds blow from the ocean toward coastal mountains, they are forced to rise, as shown in Figure 4. The rising air cools and its water vapor condenses, forming clouds. Rain or snow falls on the **windward** side of the mountains, the side the wind hits.

By the time the air has moved over the mountains, it has lost much of its water vapor, so it is cool and dry. The land on the **leeward** side of the mountains—downwind—is in a rain shadow. Little precipitation falls there.

FIGURE 4
Rain Shadow
A mountain range can form a barrier to the movement of humid air. Humid air cools as it is blown up the side of a mountain range.
Applying Concepts *Where does the heaviest rainfall occur?*

Warm, moist air blows in from the ocean and is pushed up by the mountains.

Warm, moist air

As the air rises, it cools and water vapor condenses. Moisture in the air is released as precipitation.

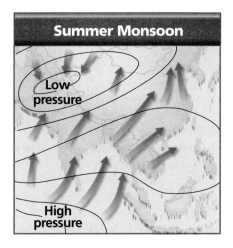

Summer Monsoon

Low pressure

High pressure

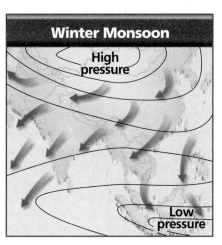

Winter Monsoon

High pressure

Low pressure

FIGURE 5
Monsoons
In a summer monsoon, wind blows from the ocean to the land. In the winter, the monsoon reverses and blows from the land to the ocean. Summer monsoons in Nepal cause heavy rain (above).

Seasonal Winds A seasonal change in wind patterns can affect precipitation. These seasonal winds are similar to land and sea breezes, but occur over a wider area. Sea and land breezes over a large region that change direction with the seasons are called **monsoons.** What produces a monsoon? In the summer in South and Southeast Asia, the land gradually gets warmer than the ocean. A "sea breeze" blows steadily inland from the ocean all summer, even at night. The air blowing from the ocean during this season is very warm and humid. As the humid air rises over the land, the air cools. This causes water vapor to condense into clouds, producing heavy rains.

Thailand and parts of India receive much of their rain from the summer monsoons. These rains supply the water needed by rice and other crops. Monsoon winds also bring rain to coastal areas in West Africa and northeastern South America.

Regions affected by monsoon winds receive very little rain in winter. In the winter, the land cools and becomes colder than the ocean. A "land breeze" blows steadily from the land to the ocean. These winds carry little moisture.

Reading Checkpoint Why does precipitation fall mainly on the windward sides of mountains?

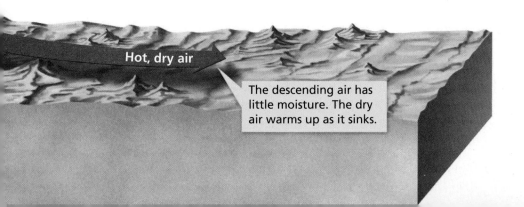

Hot, dry air

The descending air has little moisture. The dry air warms up as it sinks.

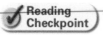
Percentage

Light from the sun strikes Earth's surface at different angles. An angle is made up of two lines that meet at a point. Angles are measured in degrees. A full circle has 360 degrees.

When the sun is directly overhead near the equator, it is at an angle of 90° to Earth's surface. A 90° angle is called a right angle. What percentage of a circle is it?

$$\frac{90 \text{ degrees}}{360 \text{ degrees}} = \frac{d\%}{100\%}$$

$$90 \times 100 = 360 \times d$$

$$\frac{90 \times 100}{360} = d = 25$$

A 90° angle is 25 percent of a full circle.

Practice Problem Earth's axis is tilted at an angle of 23.5°. About what percentage of a right angle is this?

The Seasons

Although you can describe the average weather conditions of a climate region, these conditions are not constant all year long. Instead, most places outside the tropics have four seasons: winter, spring, summer, and autumn. When it is summer in the Northern Hemisphere it is winter in the Southern Hemisphere. So the seasons are not a result of changes in the distance between Earth and the sun. In fact, Earth is farthest from the sun during the summer in the Northern Hemisphere.

Tilted Axis **The seasons are caused by the tilt of Earth's axis as Earth travels around the sun.** The axis is an imaginary line through Earth's center that passes through both poles. Earth rotates, or turns, around this axis once each day. Earth's axis is not straight up and down, but is tilted at an angle of 23.5°. As Earth travels around the sun, its axis always points in the same direction. So the north end of the axis is pointed away from the sun for one part of the year and toward the sun for another part of the year.

Effect of the Tilted Axis Look at Figure 7. Which way is the north end of Earth's axis tilted in June? Notice that the Northern Hemisphere receives more direct rays from the sun. Also, in June the days in the Northern Hemisphere are longer than the nights. The combination of more direct rays and longer days makes Earth's surface warmer in the Northern Hemisphere than at any other time of the year. It is summer in the Northern Hemisphere. At the same time, the Southern Hemisphere is experiencing winter.

In December, on the other hand, the north end of Earth's axis is tilted away from the sun. It is winter in the Northern Hemisphere and summer in the Southern Hemisphere.

Reading Checkpoint In June, what season is it in the Southern Hemisphere?

FIGURE 6
Summer and Winter
There can be a striking difference between summer and winter in the same location. **Inferring** *During which season does the area shown receive more solar energy?*

FIGURE 7
The Seasons

The seasons are a result of Earth's tilted axis. The seasons change as the amount of energy each hemisphere receives from the sun changes.

March

Go Online
active art

For: The Seasons activity
Visit: PHSchool.com
Web Code: cfp-5012

23.5°

June

December

September

June
The north end of Earth's axis is tilted toward the sun. It is summer in the Northern Hemisphere and winter in the Southern Hemisphere.

March and September
Neither end of Earth's axis is tilted toward the sun. Both hemispheres receive the same amount of energy.

December
The south end of Earth's axis is tilted toward the sun. It is summer in the Southern Hemisphere and winter in the Northern Hemisphere.

Section 1 Assessment

Target Reading Skill Building Vocabulary
Use your sentences to help answer the questions.

Reviewing Key Concepts

1. a. Identifying Name four factors that affect temperature.
   b. Describing How does temperature vary in Earth's temperature zones?
   c. Comparing and Contrasting Two locations are at the same latitude in the temperate zone. One is in the middle of a continent. The other is on a coast affected by a warm ocean current. How will their climates differ?

2. a. Listing List three factors that affect precipitation.
   b. Summarizing How do prevailing winds affect the amount of precipitation an area receives?

   c. Relating Cause and Effect How does a mountain range in the path of prevailing winds affect precipitation on either side of the mountains?

3. a. Reviewing What causes the seasons?
   b. Describing Describe how the seasons are related to Earth's orbit around the sun.
   c. Developing Hypotheses How might Earth's climates be different if Earth were not tilted on its axis?

Math Practice

4. Percentage At noon at a particular location, the sun makes an angle of 66.5° with Earth's surface. What percentage of a full circle is this?

Sunny Rays and Angles

Problem

How does the angle of a light source affect the rate at which the temperature of a surface changes?

Skills Focus

controlling variables, graphing, interpreting data, making models

Materials

- books • graph paper • pencil
- watch or clock • ruler • clear tape
- 3 thermometers or temperature probes
- protractor • 100-W incandescent lamp
- scissors • black construction paper

Procedure

1. Cut a strip of black construction paper 5 cm by 10 cm. Fold the paper in half and tape two sides to form a pocket.

2. Repeat Step 1 to make two more pockets.

Data Table			
Time (min.)	Temperature (°C)		
	0° Angle	45° Angle	90° Angle
Start			
1			
2			
3			
4			
5			

3. Place the bulb of a thermometer inside each pocket. If you're using a temperature probe, see your teacher for instructions.

4. Place the pockets with thermometers close together, as shown in the photo. Place one thermometer in a vertical position (90° angle), one at a 45° angle, and the third one in a horizontal position (0° angle). Use a protractor to measure the angles. Support the thermometers with books.

5. Position the lamp so that it is 30 cm from each of the thermometer bulbs. Make sure the lamp will not move during the activity.

6. Copy a data table like the one above into your notebook.

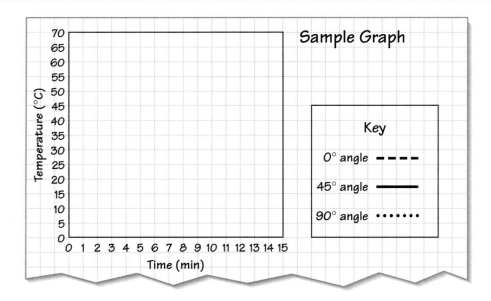

Sample Graph

Key

0° angle ----

45° angle ———

90° angle ·······

7. In your data table, record the temperature on all three thermometers. (All three temperatures should be the same.)

8. Switch on the lamp. In your data table, record the temperature on each thermometer every minute for 15 minutes. **CAUTION:** *Be careful not to touch the hot lampshade.*

9. After 15 minutes, switch off the lamp.

Analyze and Conclude

1. **Controlling Variables** In this experiment, what was the manipulated variable? What was the responding variable?

2. **Graphing** Graph your data. Label the horizontal axis and vertical axis of your graph as shown on the sample graph. Use solid, dashed, and dotted lines to show the results from each thermometer, as shown in the key.

3. **Interpreting Data** Based on your data, at which angle did the temperature increase the most?

4. **Interpreting Data** At which angle did the temperature increase the least?

5. **Making Models** What part of Earth's surface does each thermometer represent?

6. **Drawing Conclusions** Why is air at the North Pole still very cold in the summer even though the Northern Hemisphere is tilted toward the sun?

7. **Communicating** Write a paragraph explaining what variables were held constant in this experiment.

Design an Experiment

Design an experiment to find out how the results of the investigation would change if the lamp were placed farther from the thermometers. Then, design another experiment to find out what happened if the lamp were placed closer to the thermometers.

2 Climate Regions

Reading Preview

Key Concepts
- What factors are used to classify climates?
- What are the six main climate regions?

Key Terms
- rain forest • savanna
- desert • steppe
- humid subtropical • subarctic
- tundra • permafrost

Target Reading Skill
Comparing and Contrasting
As you read, compare and contrast the six main climate regions by completing a table like the one below.

Climate Regions

Climate Region	Precipitation	Temperature
Tropical Rainy	Heavy precipitation	
Dry		
Temperate Marine		

Lab zone Discover **Activity**

How Do Climates Differ?

1. Collect pictures from magazines and newspapers of a variety of land areas around the world.
2. Sort the pictures into categories according to common weather characteristics.

Think It Over
Forming Operational Definitions Choose several words that describe the typical weather for each category. What words would you use to describe the typical weather where you live?

Suppose you lived for an entire year near the equator. It would be very different from where you live now. The daily weather, the amount of sunlight, and the pattern of seasons would all be new to you. You would be in another climate region.

Scientists classify climates according to two major factors: temperature and precipitation. They use a system developed around 1900 by Wladimir Köppen (KEP un). Besides temperature and precipitation, Köppen also looked at the distinct vegetation in different areas. This system identifies broad climate regions, each of which has smaller subdivisions.

There are six main climate regions: tropical rainy, dry, temperate marine, temperate continental, polar, and highlands. These climate regions are shown in Figure 10.

Maps can show boundaries between the climate regions. In the real world, of course, no clear boundaries mark where one climate region ends and another begins. Each region blends gradually into the next.

Tropical Rainy Climates

The tropics have two types of rainy climates: tropical wet and tropical wet-and-dry. Tropical wet climates are found in low-lying lands near the equator.

Tropical Wet In areas that have a tropical wet climate, many days are rainy, often with afternoon thunderstorms. These thunderstorms are triggered by midday heating. Another source of precipitation is prevailing winds. In many areas with a tropical wet climate, the trade winds bring moisture from the oceans. With year-round heat and heavy rainfall, vegetation grows lush and green. Dense rain forests grow in these rainy tropical climates. **Rain forests** are forests in which large amounts of rain fall year-round. Tropical rain forests are important because it is thought that at least half of the world's species of land plants and animals are found there.

In the United States, only the windward sides of the Hawaiian islands have a tropical wet climate. Rainfall is very heavy—over 10 meters per year on the windward side of the Hawaiian island of Kauai. The rain forests of Hawaii have a large variety of plants, including ferns, orchids, and many types of vines and trees.

Tropical Wet-and-Dry Areas that have tropical wet-and-dry climates receive slightly less rain than tropical climates and have distinct dry and rainy seasons. Instead of rain forests, there are tropical grasslands called **savannas.** Scattered clumps of trees that can survive the dry season dot the coarse grasses. Only a small part of the United States—the southern tip of Florida—has a tropical wet-and-dry climate. The graphs in Figure 9 show how temperature and precipitation vary in Makindu, Kenya, in East Africa.

Reading Checkpoint What parts of the United States have tropical rainy climates?

FIGURE 8
Tropical Rain Forests
Lush tropical rain forests grow in the tropical wet climate.

FIGURE 9
Climate Graphs
A graph of average temperature (left) can be combined with a graph of average precipitation (middle) to form a climate graph. These graphs show data for a tropical wet-and-dry region.

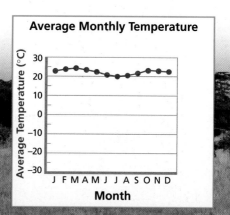

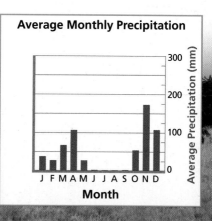

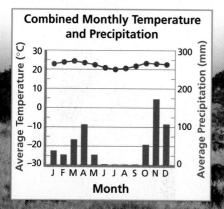

FIGURE 10

Climate Regions

Climate regions are classified according to a combination of temperature and precipitation. Climates in highland regions change rapidly as altitude changes.

Key

Tropical Rainy
- Tropical wet
- Tropical wet-and-dry

Dry
- Semiarid
- Arid

Temperate Marine
- Mediterranean
- Humid subtropical
- Marine west coast

Temperate Continental
- Humid continental
- Subarctic

Polar
- Tundra
- Ice cap

Highlands

Tropical Rainy
Temperature always 18°C or above

Tropical wet Always hot and humid, with heavy rainfall (at least 6 centimeters per month) all year round

Tropical wet-and-dry Always hot; alternating wet and dry seasons; heavy rainfall in the wet season

Dry
Occurs wherever potential evaporation is greater than precipitation; may be hot or cold

Semiarid Dry but receives about 25 to 50 centimeters of precipitation per year

Arid Desert, with little precipitation, usually less than 25 centimeters per year

Temperate Marine
Averages 10°C or above in warmest month, between –3°C and 18°C in the coldest month

Mediterranean Warm, dry summers and rainy winters

Humid subtropical Hot summers and cool winters

Marine west coast Mild winters and cool summers, with moderate precipitation all year

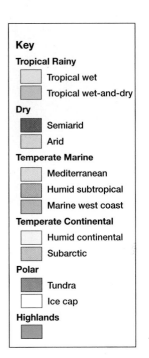

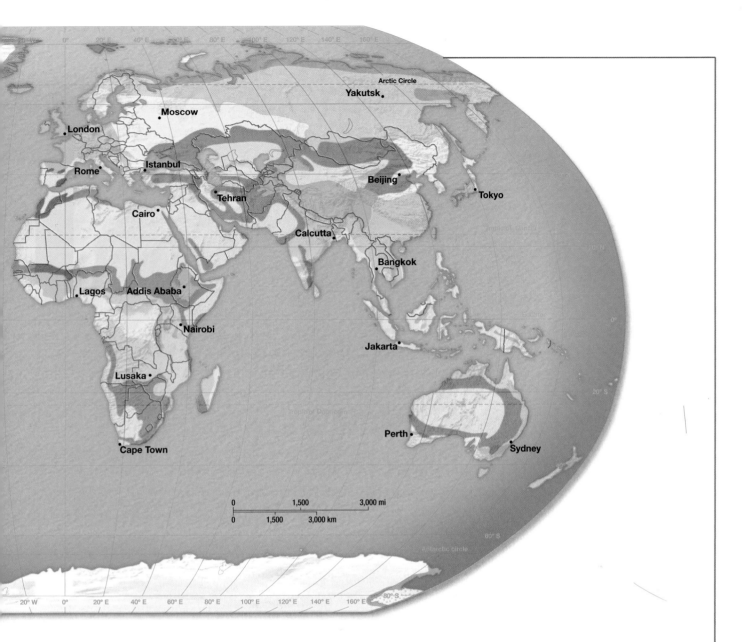

Arctic Circle

Yakutsk

Moscow

London

Istanbul

Rome

Tehran

Beijing

Tokyo

Cairo

Calcutta

Bangkok

Lagos

Addis Ababa

Nairobi

Jakarta

Lusaka

Cape Town

Perth

Sydney

Antarctic circle

| 0 | | 1,500 | | 3,000 mi |
| 0 | 1,500 | | 3,000 km | |

Temperate Continental

Average temperature 10°C or above in the warmest month, –3°C or below in the coldest month

Humid continental Hot, humid summers and cold winters, with moderate precipitation year round

Subarctic Short, cool summers and long, cold winters; light precipitation, mainly in summer

Polar

Average temperature below 10°C in the warmest month

Tundra Always cold with a short, cool summer—warmest temperature about 10°C

Ice cap Always cold, average temperature at or below 0°C

Highlands

Generally cooler and wetter than nearby lowlands; temperature decreasing with altitude

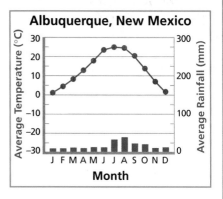

FIGURE 11
Arid Climate
Deserts of the southwestern United States are home to the western patchnose snake.
Interpreting Graphs Which month has the highest average temperature?

Albuquerque, New Mexico

Average Temperature (°C) / *Average Rainfall (mm)*

Month: J F M A M J J A S O N D

Dry Climates

A climate is "dry" if the amount of precipitation that falls is less than the amount of water that could potentially evaporate. Because water evaporates more slowly in cool weather, a cool place with low rainfall may not be as dry as a warmer place that receives the same amount of rain. **Dry climates include arid and semiarid climates.**

Look at the map of world climate regions in Figure 10. What part of the United States is dry? Why is precipitation in this region so low? As you can see, dry regions often lie inland, far from oceans that are the source of humid air masses. In addition, much of the region lies in the rain shadow east of the Sierra Nevada and Rocky Mountains. Humid air masses from the Pacific Ocean lose much of their water as they cross the mountains. Little rain or snow is carried to dry regions.

Arid When you think about **deserts,** or arid regions, you may picture blazing heat and drifting sand dunes. Some deserts are hot and sandy, but others are cold or rocky. On average, arid regions, or deserts, get less than 25 centimeters of rain a year. Some years may bring no rain at all. Only specialized plants such as cactus and yucca can survive the desert's dryness and extremes of hot and cold. In the United States there are arid climates in portions of California, the Great Basin, and the Southwest.

Semiarid Locate the semiarid regions in Figure 10. As you can see, large semiarid areas are usually located on the edges of deserts. These semiarid areas are called steppes. A **steppe** is dry but gets enough rainfall for short grasses and low bushes to grow. For this reason, a steppe may also be called a prairie or grassland. The Great Plains are the steppe region of the United States.

 **Reading Checkpoint** What is a desert?

Temperate Marine Climates

Look once again at Figure 10. Along the coasts of continents in the temperate zones, you will find the third main climate region, temperate marine. **There are three kinds of temperate marine climates: marine west coast, humid subtropical, and Mediterranean.** Because of the moderating influence of oceans, all three are humid and have mild winters.

Marine West Coast The coolest temperate marine climates are found on the west coasts of continents north of 40° north latitude and south of 40° south latitude. Humid ocean air brings mild, rainy winters. Summer precipitation can vary considerably.

In North America, the marine west coast climate extends from northern California to southern Alaska. In the northwestern United States, humid air from the Pacific Ocean hits the western slopes of the Coastal Ranges. The air rises up the slopes of the mountains, and it cools. As the air cools, large amounts of rain or snow fall on the western slopes. The eastern slopes lie in the rain shadow of the mountains and receive little precipitation.

Because of the heavy precipitation, thick forests of tall trees grow in this region, including coniferous, or cone-bearing, trees such as Sitka spruce, Douglas fir, redwoods, and Western red cedar, as shown in Figure 12. One of the main industries of this region is harvesting and processing wood for lumber, paper, and furniture.

Eugene, Oregon

FIGURE 12
Marine West Coast Climate
Redwoods, Douglas firs, and Sitka spruce dominate the lush forests found in marine west coast climates.

Santa Barbara, California

FIGURE 13

Mediterranean Climate
Santa Barbara, on the coast of southern California, has a Mediterranean climate. Mild temperatures throughout the year make the area ideal for growing olives and citrus fruits.
Interpreting Graphs *How much precipitation does Santa Barbara receive in July? In January?*

Classifying

The table shows some climate data for three cities.

	City A	City B	City C
Average Jan. Temp. (°C)	12.8	18.9	−5.6
Average July Temp. (°C)	21.1	27.2	20
Annual Precipitation (cm)	33	152	109

Describe the climate you would expect each city to have. Identify the cities of Miami, Florida; Los Angeles, California; and Portland, Maine. Use Figure 10 to help identify each city's climate.

Mediterranean A coastal climate that is drier and warmer than west coast marine is known as Mediterranean. Most areas with this climate are found around the Mediterranean Sea. In the United States, the southern coast of California has a Mediterranean climate. This climate is mild, with two seasons. In winter, marine air masses bring cool, rainy weather. Summers are somewhat warmer, with little rain.

Mediterranean climates have two main vegetation types. One is made up of dense shrubs and small trees, called chaparral (chap uh RAL). The other vegetation type includes grasses with a few large trees.

Agriculture is important to the economy of California's Mediterranean climate region. Using irrigation, farmers grow many different crops, including rice, many vegetables, fruits, and nuts.

Humid Subtropical The warmest temperate marine climates are along the edges of the tropics. **Humid subtropical** climates are wet and warm, but not as constantly hot as the tropics. Locate the humid subtropical climates in Figure 10.

The southeastern United States has a humid subtropical climate. Summers are hot, with much more rainfall than in winter. Maritime tropical air masses move inland, bringing tropical weather conditions, including thunderstorms and occasional hurricanes, to southern cities such as Houston, New Orleans, and Atlanta. Winters are cool to mild, with more rain than snow. However, polar air masses moving in from the north can bring freezing temperatures and frosts.

Mixed forests of oak, ash, hickory, and pines grow in the humid subtropical region of the United States. Important crops in this region include oranges, peaches, peanuts, sugar cane, and rice.

 **Reading Checkpoint** **What region of the United States has a humid subtropical climate?**

Temperate Continental Climates

Temperate continental climates are not influenced very much by oceans, so they commonly have extremes of temperature. **Temperate continental climates are only found on continents in the Northern Hemisphere, and include humid continental and subarctic.** The parts of continents in the Southern Hemisphere south of 40° south latitude are not far enough from oceans for dry continental air masses to form.

Humid Continental Shifting tropical and polar air masses bring constantly changing weather to humid continental climates. In winter, continental polar air masses move south, bringing bitterly cold weather. In summer, tropical air masses move north, bringing heat and high humidity. Humid continental climates receive moderate amounts of rain in the summer. Smaller amounts of rain or snow fall in winter.

What parts of the United States have a humid continental climate? The eastern part of the region—the Northeast—has a range of forest types, from mixed forests in the south to coniferous forests in the north. Much of the western part of this region—the Midwest—was once tall grasslands, but is now farmland.

Subarctic The **subarctic** climates lie north of the humid continental climates. Summers in the subarctic are short and cool. Winters are long and bitterly cold.

In North America, coniferous trees such as spruce and fir make up a huge northern forest that stretches from Alaska to eastern Canada. Wood products from this forest are an important part of the economy. Many large mammals, including bears and moose, live in the forest. Birds of many species breed in the subarctic.

 **Reading Checkpoint** Which area of the United States has a subarctic climate?

FIGURE 14
Subarctic Climate
Subarctic climates have cool summers and cold winters. The world's largest subarctic regions are in Russia, Canada, and Alaska. This emperor goose is breeding in the subarctic climate region in Alaska.

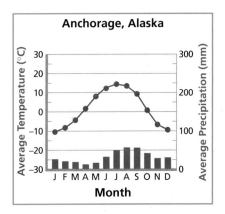

Polar Climates

The polar climate is the coldest climate region, and includes the ice cap and tundra climates. Ice cap and tundra climates are found only in the far north and south, near the North and South poles. Most polar climates are relatively dry, because the cold air holds little moisture.

Ice Cap As Figure 10 shows, ice cap climates are found mainly on Greenland and in Antarctica. With average temperatures always at or below freezing, the land in ice cap climate regions is covered with ice and snow. Intense cold makes the air dry. Lichens and a few low plants may grow on the rocks.

Tundra The **tundra** climate region stretches across northern Alaska, Canada, and Russia. Short, cool summers follow bitterly cold winters. Because of the cold, some layers of the tundra soil are always frozen. This permanently frozen tundra soil is called **permafrost.** Because of the permafrost, water cannot drain away, so the soil is wet and boggy in summer.

It is too cold on the tundra for trees to grow. Despite the harsh climate, during the short summers the tundra is filled with life. Mosquitoes and other insects hatch in the ponds and marshes above the frozen permafrost. Mosses, grasses, lichens, wildflowers, and shrubs grow quickly during the short summers. In North America, herds of caribou eat the vegetation and are in turn preyed upon by wolves. Some birds, such as the white-tailed ptarmigan, live on the tundra year-round. Others, such as the arctic tern and many waterfowl, spend only their summer breeding seasons there.

 **Reading Checkpoint** **What type of vegetation is found on the tundra?**

FIGURE 15
Tundra Climate
The Nenet people are reindeer herders on the tundra of northern Russia. These reindeer are grazing on some short shrubs typical of tundra plants.

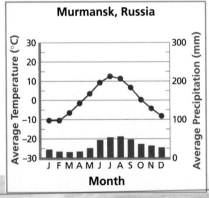

Murmansk, Russia

Average Temperature (°C) / Average Precipitation (mm)

Month J F M A M J J A S O N D

Highlands

Why are highlands a distinct climate region? **Temperature falls as altitude increases, so highland regions are colder than the regions that surround them.** Increasing altitude produces climate changes similar to the climate changes you would expect with increasing latitude. Precipitation also increases as air masses carrying moisture pass over highland areas.

The climate on the lower slopes of a mountain range is like that of the surrounding countryside. The Rocky Mountain foothills, for instance, share the semiarid climate of the Great Plains. But as you go higher up into the mountains, temperatures become lower and precipitation increases. Climbing 1,000 meters up in elevation is like traveling 1,200 kilometers toward the poles. The climate higher in the mountains is like that of the subarctic: cool with coniferous trees.

Above a certain elevation—the tree line—temperatures are too low for trees to grow. The climate above the tree line is like that of the tundra. Only low plants, mosses, and lichens can grow there.

FIGURE 16
Highland Climate
Highland climates are generally cooler than surrounding regions. The Mount Rainier area in Washington State has short summers and long, severe winters.
Classifying *What climate zone does the mountaintop resemble?*

Section 2 Assessment

Target Reading Skill Comparing and Contrasting Use the information in your table about climate regions to help you answer Question 1.

Reviewing Key Concepts

1. a. **Listing** What two major factors are used to classify climates?
   b. **Reviewing** What other factor did Köppen use in classifying climates?
2. a. **Identifying** What are the six main climate regions?
   b. **Comparing and Contrasting** How is a tropical wet climate similar to a tropical wet-and-dry climate? How are they different?
   c. **Inferring** In what climate region would you find plains covered with short grasses and small bushes? Explain.
   d. **Relating Cause and Effect** Why do marine west coast climates have abundant precipitation?

   e. **Predicting** Which place would have more severe winters—central Russia or the west coast of France? Why?
   f. **Sequencing** Place the following climates in order from coldest to warmest: tundra, subarctic, humid continental, ice cap.
   g. **Relating Cause and Effect** How could a forest grow on a mountain that is surrounded by a desert?

Lab zone At-Home Activity

What's Your Climate? Describe to your family the characteristics of the climate region in which you live. What plants and animals live in your climate region? What characteristics do these plants and animals have that make them well-adapted to the region?

Cool Climate Graphs

Problem

Based on climate data, what is the best time of year to visit various cities to enjoy particular recreational activities?

Skills Focus

graphing, interpreting data

Materials

- calculator • ruler • 3 pieces of graph paper
- black, blue, red, and green pencils
- climate map on pages 120–121
- U.S. map with city names and latitude lines

Procedure

1. Work in groups of three. Each person should graph the data for a different city, A, B, or C.

2. On graph paper, use a black pencil to label the axes as on the climate graph below. Title your climate graph City A, City B, or City C.

3. Use your green pencil to make a bar graph of the monthly average amount of precipitation. Place a star below the name of each month that has more than a trace of snow.

4. Use a red pencil to plot the average monthly maximum temperature. Make a dot for the temperature in the middle of each space for the month. When you have plotted data for all 12 months, connect the points into a smooth curved line.

5. Use a blue pencil to plot the average monthly minimum temperature for your city. Use the same procedure as in Step 4.

6. Calculate the total average annual precipitation for this city and include it in your observations. Do this by adding the average precipitation for each month.

Analyze and Conclude

Use all three climate graphs, plus the graph for Washington, D.C., to answer these questions.

1. **Interpreting Data** Which of the four cities has the least change in average temperatures during the year?

2. **Interpreting Maps** Use the map on pages 120–121 to help find the climate region in which each city is located.

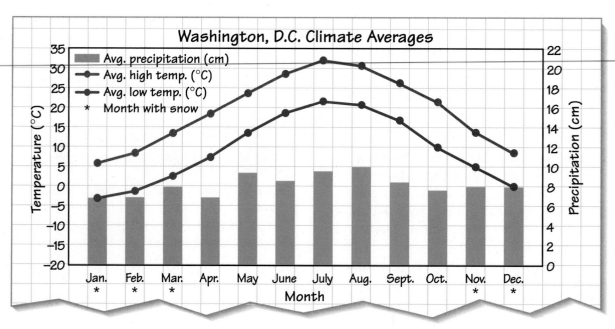

Climate Data

Washington, D.C.	Jan.	Feb.	Mar.	April	May	June	July	Aug.	Sept.	Oct.	Nov.	Dec.
Average High Temp. (°C)	6	8	14	19	24	29	32	31	27	21	14	8
Average Low Temp. (°C)	−3	−2	3	8	14	19	22	21	17	10	5	0
Average Precipitation (cm)	6.9	6.9	8.1	6.9	9.4	8.6	9.7	9.9	8.4	7.6	7.9	7.9
Months With Snow	*	*	*	trace	—	—	—	—	—	trace	*	*
City A	Jan.	Feb.	Mar.	April	May	June	July	Aug.	Sept.	Oct.	Nov.	Dec.
Average High Temp. (°C)	13	16	16	17	17	18	18	19	21	21	17	13
Average Low Temp. (°C)	8	9	9	10	11	12	12	13	13	13	11	8
Average Precipitation (cm)	10.4	7.6	7.9	3.3	0.8	0.5	0.3	0.3	0.8	3.3	8.1	7.9
Months With Snow	trace	trace	trace	—	—	—	—	—	—	—	—	trace
City B	Jan.	Feb.	Mar.	April	May	June	July	Aug.	Sept.	Oct.	Nov.	Dec.
Average High Temp. (°C)	5	7	10	16	21	26	29	27	23	18	11	6
Average Low Temp. (°C)	−9	−7	−4	1	6	11	14	13	8	2	−4	−8
Average Precipitation (cm)	0.8	1.0	2.3	3.0	5.6	5.8	7.4	7.6	3.3	2.0	1.3	1.3
Months With Snow	*	*	*	*	*	—	—	—	trace	*	*	*
City C	Jan.	Feb.	Mar.	April	May	June	July	Aug.	Sept.	Oct.	Nov.	Dec.
Average High Temp. (°C)	7	11	13	18	23	28	33	32	27	21	12	8
Average Low Temp. (°C)	−6	−4	−2	1	4	8	11	10	5	1	−3	−7
Average Precipitation (cm)	2.5	2.3	1.8	1.3	1.8	1	0.8	0.5	0.8	1	2	2.5
Months With Snow	*	*	*	*	*	trace	—	—	trace	trace	*	*

3. **Applying Concepts** Which of the cities below matches each climate graph?
   Colorado Springs, Colorado; latitude 39° N
   San Francisco, California; latitude 38° N
   Reno, Nevada; latitude 40° N

4. **Inferring** The four cities are at approximately the same latitude. Why are their climate graphs so different?

5. **Graphing** What factors do you need to consider when setting up and numbering the left and right *y*-axes of a climate graph so that your data will fit on the graph?

6. **Communicating** Imagine that you are writing a travel brochure for one of the four cities. Write a description of the climate of the city and discuss the best time to visit to do a selected outdoor activity.

More to Explore

What type of climate does the area where you live have? Find out what outdoor recreational opportunities your community has. How is each activity particularly suited to the climate of your area?

Long-Term Changes in Climate

Reading Preview

Key Concepts
- What principle do scientists follow in studying ancient climates?
- What changes occur on Earth's surface during an ice age?
- What factors can cause climate change?

Key Terms
- ice age
- sunspot

Target Reading Skill

Identifying Supporting Evidence As you read, identify the evidence that is used to show that climates change. Write the evidence in a graphic organizer like the one below.

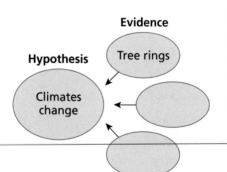

Evidence

Hypothesis

Tree rings

Climates change

Lab zone Discover **Activity**

What Story Can Tree Rings Tell?

1. Look at the photo of tree rings in Figure 18. Tree rings are the layers of new wood that form each year as a tree grows.
2. Look closely at the tree rings. Note whether they are all the same thickness.
3. What weather conditions might cause a tree to form thicker or thinner tree rings?

Think It Over

Inferring How could you use tree rings to tell you about weather in the past?

One of the greatest Native American cultures in the American Southwest was the Ancestral Pueblos. These farming people built great pueblos, or "apartment houses," of stone and sun-baked clay, with hundreds of rooms, as shown in Figure 17. By about the year 1000, the Ancestral Pueblos were flourishing. Evidence from tree rings indicates that several periods of intense drought then occurred. These droughts may have contributed to a breakdown in their society. By the late 1200s, they had abandoned the pueblos and moved to other areas.

Although weather varies from day to day, climates usually change more slowly. But climates do change, both in small areas and throughout the world. Although climate change is usually slow, its consequences are great.

FIGURE 17
Ancient Pueblo Dwellings
The Ancestral Pueblos lived in these buildings, now in Mesa Verde National Park in southwestern Colorado, about 1,000 years ago.

Studying Climate Change

Climate changes have affected many regions in addition to the Southwest. For example, Greenland today is mostly covered by an ice cap. But 80 million years ago, Greenland had a warm, moist climate. Fossils of magnolias and palm trees found in Greenland provide evidence for this climate change. Today magnolia and palm trees grow only in warm, moist climates. Scientists assume that the ancestors of these trees required similar conditions. **In studying ancient climates, scientists follow an important principle: If plants or animals today need certain conditions to live, then similar plants and animals in the past also required those conditions.**

Pollen One source of information about ancient climates is pollen records. Each type of plant has a particular type of pollen. The bottoms of some lakes are covered with thick layers of mud and plant material, including pollen that fell to the bottom of the lake over thousands of years. Scientists can drill down into these layers and bring up cores to examine. By looking at the pollen present in each layer, scientists can tell what types of plants lived in the area. From pollen data, scientists can infer that an ancient climate was similar to the climate where the same plants grow today.

Tree Rings Tree rings can also be used to learn about ancient climates. Every summer, a tree grows a new layer of wood just under its bark. These layers form rings, as shown in Figure 18. In cool climates, the amount the tree grows—the thickness of a ring—depends on the length of the warm growing season. In dry climates, the thickness of each ring depends on the amount of rainfall. Scientists study the pattern of thick or thin tree rings. From these data they can see whether previous years were warm or cool, wet or dry.

 **Reading Checkpoint** What are two ways scientists study ancient climates?

FIGURE 18
Evidence of Climate Change
The width of tree rings provides information on temperature and rainfall. A thin ring indicates that the year was cool or dry. A thick ring indicates that the year was warm or wet. *Inferring Which tree rings would provide information about climate close to the time that the tree was cut down?*

Glaciers in North America

Key
☐ Area covered by glaciers
▨ Mammoth steppe

FIGURE 19
The Last Ice Age
The map shows the parts of North America that were covered by glaciers 18,000 years ago. On the steppe near the glaciers lived many mammals that are now extinct, including woolly mammoths.

Climate and Climate Change

Video Preview
▶ Video Field Trip
Video Assessment

Ice Ages

Throughout Earth's history, climates have gradually changed. Over millions of years, warm periods have alternated with cold periods known as **ice ages,** or glacial episodes. **During each ice age, huge sheets of ice called glaciers covered large parts of Earth's surface.**

Glaciers transform the landscape by carving giant grooves in solid rock, depositing enormous piles of sediment, and moving huge boulders hundreds of kilometers. From this evidence and from fossils, scientists have concluded that in the past two million years there have been many major ice ages. Each one lasted 100,000 years or longer. Long, warmer periods occurred between the ice ages. Some scientists think that we are now in a warm period between ice ages.

The last ice age ended only about 10,500 years ago. Ice sheets covered much of northern Europe and North America, reaching as far south as present-day Iowa and Nebraska, as shown in Figure 19. In some places, the ice was more than 3 kilometers thick. So much water was frozen in the ice sheets that the average sea level was much lower than it is today. When the ice sheets melted, the rising oceans flooded coastal areas. Inland, the Great Lakes formed.

 **Reading Checkpoint** Why were the oceans lower during the ice ages than they are now?

Causes of Climate Change

Why do climates change? **Possible explanations for major climate changes include variations in the position of Earth relative to the sun, changes in the sun's energy output, major volcanic eruptions, and the movement of the continents.**

Earth's Position As Earth revolves around the sun, the time of year when Earth is closest to the sun shifts from January to July and back again over a period of about 23,000 years. The angle at which Earth's axis tilts and the shape of Earth's orbit around the sun also change slightly over long periods of time. The combined effects of these changes may be the main cause of ice ages.

Solar Energy Short-term changes in climate have been linked to changes in the number of **sunspots**—dark, cooler regions on the surface of the sun. Sunspots increase and decrease in fairly regular 11-year cycles. Satellite measurements have shown that the amount of energy the sun produces increases slightly when there are more sunspots. This may cause Earth's temperature to warm.

Volcanic Activity Major volcanic eruptions release huge quantities of gases and ash into the atmosphere. These materials can stay in the upper atmosphere for months or years. Scientists think that the gases and ash filter out some of the incoming solar radiation, and may lower temperatures.

Math Analyzing Data

Ice Ages and Temperature

The graph shows the estimated average worldwide temperature over the last 350,000 years. During this time, cold glacial periods (blue) alternated with warmer interglacial periods (pink).

1. **Reading Graphs** What does the x-axis of the graph represent? What does the y-axis represent?

2. **Interpreting Data** What pattern do you see in these data? How would you explain this pattern?

3. **Predicting** Based on the pattern over the last 350,000 years, predict how global temperature will change in the future.

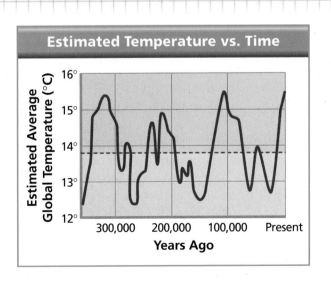

Estimated Temperature vs. Time

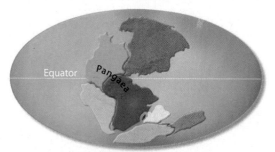

225 Million Years Ago

180–200 Million Years Ago

FIGURE 20
Moving Continents
The continents have moved over millions of years.
Interpreting Maps *Which present-day continents broke away from Gondwanaland? Which broke away from Laurasia?*

Go Online
active art

For: Continental Drift activity
Visit: PHSchool.com
Web Code: cfp-1015

Movement of Continents The continents have not always been located where they are now. About 225 million years ago, most of the land on Earth was part of a single continent called Pangaea (pan JEE uh), as Figure 20 shows. At that time, most continents were far from their present positions. Continents that are now in the polar zones were once near the equator. This movement explains how tropical plants such as magnolias and palm trees could once have grown in Greenland.

The movements of continents over time changed the locations of land and sea. These changes affected the global patterns of winds and ocean currents, which in turn slowly changed climates. And as the continents continue to move, climates will continue to change.

 **Reading Checkpoint** What was Pangaea?

Section 3 Assessment

Target Reading Skill

Identifying Supporting Evidence Refer to your graphic organizer about the hypothesis that climate changes as you answer Question 1 below.

Reviewing Key Concepts

1. **a. Reviewing** What principle do scientists follow in studying ancient climates?
   b. Describing What types of evidence do scientists gather to study changes in climate?
   c. Inferring Suppose that you are a scientist studying tree rings in a cross-section of an ancient tree. What could several narrow tree rings in a row tell you about the climate when those rings were formed?

2. **a. Defining** What is a glacier?
   b. Explaining What occurs during an ice age?
   c. Comparing and Contrasting Compare the climate today with it during an ice age.

3. **a. Listing** What are four factors that could be responsible for changing Earth's climate?
   b. Summarizing Select one of the four factors that could cause climate change and summarize how it may cause the climate to change.

Writing in Science

Procedure for Data Collection Suppose that you are a scientist who wants to use pollen data from a lake bed to learn about ancient climates. Write the steps for the procedure that you would follow to collect and analyze your data.

Global Changes in the Atmosphere

Reading Preview

Key Concepts
- What events can cause short-term climate changes?
- How might human activities be affecting the temperature of Earth's atmosphere?
- How have human activities affected the ozone layer?

Key Terms
- El Niño • La Niña
- global warming
- greenhouse gas
- chlorofluorocarbon

Target Reading Skill
Asking Questions Before you read, preview the red headings. Ask a *what* or *how* question for each heading, for example, "How does short-term climate change occur?" As you read, write the answers to your questions.

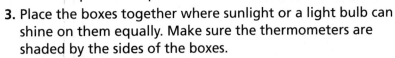

Lab zone Discover **Activity**

What Is the Greenhouse Effect?

1. ✂ Cut two pieces of black construction paper to fit the bottoms of two shoe boxes.
2. 🔧 Place a thermometer in each box. Record the temperatures on the thermometers. Cover one box with plastic wrap.
3. Place the boxes together where sunlight or a light bulb can shine on them equally. Make sure the thermometers are shaded by the sides of the boxes.
4. Wait 15 minutes and read the thermometers again. Record the temperatures.

Think It Over
Inferring How can you explain any temperature difference between the two boxes?

If you live in one area for several years, you get to know the area's climate. But in some years, the weather is so unusual that you might think the climate has changed. That's what happened in several different parts of the world during 1997–1998. Droughts occurred in parts of Africa, Asia, and Australia. Heavy rains struck parts of South America. In the United States, very heavy rains swept across California and the South.

What produced these global changes? During the droughts and floods of 1998, parts of the Pacific Ocean were much warmer than usual. Even the ocean's winds and currents changed. Scientists have evidence that these changes in the Pacific Ocean led to wild weather in other parts of the world.

◀ In 1998, mudslides from heavy rains caused severe damage in California.

▲ In **normal years**, water in the eastern Pacific is kept relatively cool by currents along the coast of North and South America.

▲ When **El Niño** occurs, warm surface water from the western Pacific moves east toward the coast of South America.

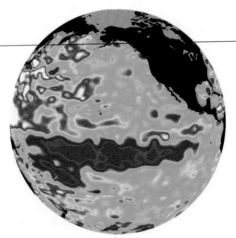

▲ **La Niña** occurs when surface waters in the eastern Pacific Ocean are colder than normal.

FIGURE 21
El Niño and La Niña
In these satellite images, warmer water is red and white. Cooler water is blue and purple.

Short-Term Climate Change

Changes in ocean currents and winds can greatly affect climate. **El Niño and La Niña are short-term changes in the tropical Pacific Ocean caused by changes in ocean surface currents and prevailing winds.** El Niño and La Niña both influence weather patterns all over the world.

El Niño The warm-water event known as **El Niño** begins when an unusual pattern of winds forms over the western Pacific. This causes a vast sheet of warm water to move eastward toward the South American coast, as shown in Figure 21. El Niño causes the surface of the ocean in the eastern Pacific to be unusually warm. El Niño typically occurs every two to seven years.

The arrival of El Niño's warm surface water disrupts the cold ocean currents along the western coast of South America and changes weather patterns there. El Niño also affects weather patterns around the world, often bringing severe conditions such as heavy rains or droughts. El Niño conditions can last for one to two years before normal winds and currents return.

La Niña When surface waters in the eastern Pacific are colder than normal, a climate event known as **La Niña** occurs. A La Niña event is the opposite of an El Niño event. La Niña events typically bring colder than normal winters and greater precipitation to the Pacific Northwest and the north central United States. Another major effect of La Niña is greater hurricane activity in the western Atlantic.

 Reading Checkpoint **How often does El Niño typically occur?**

Global Warming

Most changes in world climates are caused by natural factors. But recently scientists have observed climate changes that could be the result of human activities. For example, over the last 120 years, the average temperature of the troposphere has risen by about 0.7 Celsius degree. This gradual increase in the temperature of Earth's atmosphere is called **global warming.**

The Greenhouse Hypothesis Recall that gases in Earth's atmosphere hold in heat from the sun, keeping the atmosphere at a comfortable temperature for living things. The process by which gases in Earth's atmosphere trap this energy is called the greenhouse effect. Look at the greenhouse in Figure 22. Notice that sunlight does not heat the air in the greenhouse directly. Instead, sunlight first heats the soil, benches, and pots. Then infrared radiation from these surfaces heats the air in the greenhouse. The greenhouse effect in Earth's atmosphere is similar in some ways.

Gases in the atmosphere that trap energy are called **greenhouse gases.** Carbon dioxide, water vapor, and methane are some of the greenhouse gases. **Many scientists have hypothesized that human activities that add greenhouse gases to the atmosphere may be warming Earth's atmosphere.**

FIGURE 22
Greenhouse Effect
Sunlight enters a greenhouse and is absorbed. The interior of the greenhouse radiates back energy in the form of infrared radiation, or heat. Much of the heat is trapped and held inside the greenhouse, warming it.
Applying Concepts *What gases in Earth's atmosphere can trap heat like a greenhouse?*

Infrared radiation cannot pass through the greenhouse roof.

Sunlight

Key

Sunlight

Infrared radiation

Changing Levels of Carbon Dioxide Scientists think that an increase in carbon dioxide is a major factor in global warming. Until the late 1800s, the level of carbon dioxide in the atmosphere remained about the same. How did scientists determine this? They measured the amount of carbon dioxide in air bubbles trapped in Antarctic ice. They obtained these samples of ancient air from ice cores, as shown in Figure 23. The glacier that covers Antarctica formed over millions of years. Gas bubbles in the ice cores provide samples of air from the time the ice formed.

Is global warming caused by human activities, or does it have a natural cause? Scientists have done a great deal of research to try to answer this question.

Since the late 1800s, the level of carbon dioxide in the atmosphere has increased steadily, as shown in Figure 23. Most scientists think that this change is a result of increased human activities. For example, the burning of wood, coal, oil, and natural gas adds carbon dioxide to the air. During the last 100 years, these activities have increased greatly in many different countries. Some scientists predict that the level of carbon dioxide could double by the year 2100. If that happens, then global temperature could rise by several Celsius degrees.

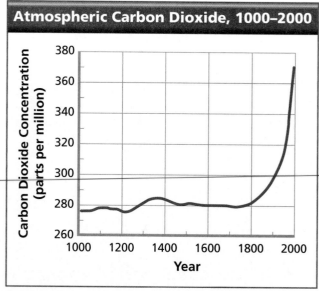

FIGURE 23
Carbon Dioxide Levels
These scientists are taking an ice core from the glacier that covers Antarctica (left). Gas bubbles in the ice provide samples of the atmosphere at the time the ice formed. Data from ice cores enables scientists to graph changing levels of carbon dioxide (above).

1960

1990

Climate Variation Hypothesis Not all scientists agree about the causes of global warming. Some scientists think that the 0.7 Celsius degree rise in global temperatures over the past 120 years may be due in part to natural variations in climate.

Satellite measurements have shown that the amount of energy the sun produces increases and decreases from year to year. Even such small changes in solar energy could be causing periods of warmer and cooler climates. Climate change could be a result of changes in both carbon dioxide levels and the amount of solar energy.

Possible Effects Global warming could have some positive effects. Farmers in some areas that are now cool could plant two crops a year instead of one. Places that are too cold for farming today could become farmland. However, many effects of global warming are likely to be less positive. Higher temperatures would cause water to evaporate from exposed soil, such as plowed farmland. Dry soil blows away easily. Thus, some fertile fields might become "dust bowls."

A rise in temperatures of even a few degrees could warm up water in the oceans. Some scientists think warmer ocean water could increase the strength of hurricanes.

As the water warmed, it would expand, raising sea level around the world. The melting of glaciers and polar ice caps could also increase sea level. Sea level has already risen by 10 to 20 centimeters over the last 100 years, and could rise another 25 to 80 centimeters by the year 2100. Even such a small rise in sea level would flood low-lying coastal areas.

 **Reading Checkpoint** What are three possible effects of global warming?

FIGURE 24
Melting Glaciers
The photos show the Burroughs glacier in Alaska. The photo on the left was taken in 1960. The photo on the right was taken in 1990, and shows the large amount of melting that has taken place.

Go Online
PLANET DIARY

For: More on the greenhouse effect
Visit: PHSchool.com
Web Code: cfd-4044

It's Your Skin!

Compare how well sunscreens block out ultraviolet rays.

1. Close the blinds or curtains in the room. Place one square of sun-sensitive paper inside each of three plastic sandwich bags.

2. Place three drops of one sunscreen on the outside of one bag. Spread the sunscreen as evenly as possible. Label this bag with the SPF number of the sunscreen.

3. On another bag, repeat Step 2 using a sunscreen with a different SPF. Wash your hands after spreading the sunscreen. Leave the third bag untreated as a control.

4. Place the bags outside in direct sunlight. Bring them back inside after 3 minutes or after one of the squares turns completely white.

Drawing Conclusions Did both of the sunscreens block ultraviolet radiation? Was one better than the other? Explain.

Ozone Depletion

Another global change in the atmosphere involves the ozone layer. Ozone in the stratosphere filters out much of the harmful ultraviolet radiation from the sun, as shown in Figure 25.

In the 1970s, scientists noticed that the ozone layer over Antarctica was growing thinner each spring. A large area of reduced ozone, or ozone hole, was being created. In 2000, the ozone hole reached a record size of more than 28.5 million km^2—almost the size of Africa. By 2004, the maximum size of the ozone hole decreased to about 20 million km^2. What created the ozone hole? **Chemicals produced by humans have been damaging the ozone layer.**

Chlorofluorocarbons A major cause of ozone depletion is a group of compounds called **chlorofluorocarbons,** or CFCs. CFCs were used in air conditioners and refrigerators, as cleaners for electronic parts, and in aerosol sprays, such as deodorants.

Most chemical compounds released into the air eventually break down. CFCs, however, can last for decades and rise all the way to the stratosphere. In the stratosphere, ultraviolet radiation breaks down the CFC molecules into atoms, including chlorine. The chlorine atoms then break ozone down into oxygen atoms.

Results of Ozone Depletion Because ozone blocks ultraviolet radiation, a decrease in ozone means an increase in the amount of ultraviolet radiation that reaches Earth's surface. Ultraviolet radiation can cause eye damage and several kinds of skin cancer.

In the late 1970s, the United States and many other countries banned most uses of CFCs in aerosol sprays. In 1990, many nations agreed to phase out the production and use of CFCs. Because ozone depletion affects the whole world, such agreements must be international to be effective. Worldwide production of the chemicals has greatly decreased. In the United States, at the current rate it will take until 2010 to completely eliminate the use of CFCs. The size of the ozone hole is expected to gradually shrink over time as these agreements take effect.

 **What are CFCs?**

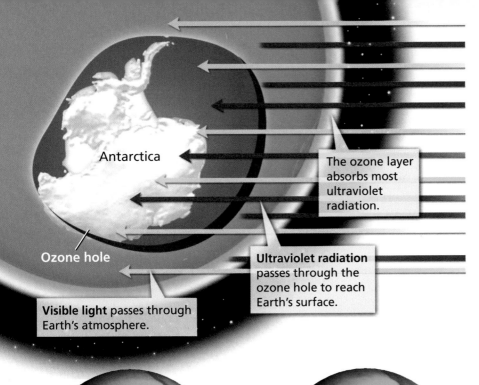

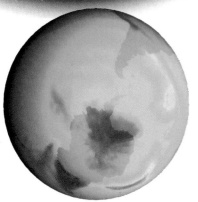
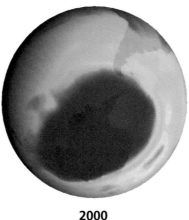
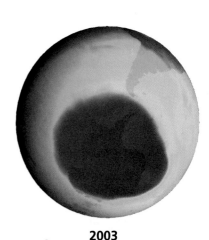

FIGURE 25
The Ozone Hole
The ozone layer blocks much of the ultraviolet radiation (purple) coming from the sun. Visible light (yellow) can pass through the ozone layer. The satellite images below show the concentration of ozone over the South Pole for three years. The dark area shows where the ozone layer is thinnest. **Observing** *How has the size of the ozone layer changed over time?*

Antarctica

The ozone layer absorbs most ultraviolet radiation.

Ozone hole

Ultraviolet radiation passes through the ozone hole to reach Earth's surface.

Visible light passes through Earth's atmosphere.

| 1979 | 2000 | 2003 |

Section 4 Assessment

Target Reading Skill

Asking Questions Use the answers to your *what* and *how* questions to help you answer the questions below.

Reviewing Key Concepts

1. **a. Listing** What are two events that can cause short-term climate change?
   b. Describing Describe the changes that occur in the Pacific Ocean and the atmosphere above it during El Niño.
   c. Relating Cause and Effect What effects does El Niño have on weather and climate?
2. **a. Defining** What is global warming?
   b. Relating Cause and Effect How do scientists think that increased carbon dioxide levels contributed to global warming?

3. **a. Reviewing** What effect have human activities had on the ozone layer?
   b. Summarizing Summarize the cause of ozone depletion and the steps taken to reverse it.

Lab zone At-Home **Activity**

Sun Protection Visit a drugstore with your family. Compare the SPF (sun protection factor) of the various sunscreens for sale. Explain why it is important to protect your skin from ultraviolet radiation. Ask your family members to determine the best value for the money in terms of SPF rating and price.

The **BIG** Idea

Earth's Many Climates The major factors that influence a region's climate are latitude, distance from large bodies of water, ocean currents, prevailing winds, the presence of mountains, and seasonal winds.

① What Causes Climate?

Key Concepts

- The main factors that influence temperature are latitude, altitude, distance from large bodies of water, and ocean currents.

- The main factors that influence precipitation are prevailing winds, the presence of mountains, and seasonal winds.

- The seasons are caused by the tilt of Earth's axis as Earth travels around the sun.

Key Terms

- climate • microclimate • tropical zone
- polar zone • temperate zone
- marine climate • continental climate
- windward • leeward • monsoon

② Climate Regions

Key Concepts

- Scientists classify climates according to two major factors: temperature and precipitation.

- There are six main climate regions: tropical rainy, dry, temperate marine, temperate continental, polar, and highlands.

- The tropics have two types of rainy climates: tropical wet and tropical wet-and-dry.

- Dry climates can be arid and semiarid climates.

- There are three kinds of temperate marine climates: marine west coast, humid subtropical, and Mediterranean.

- Temperate continental climates are only found on continents in the Northern Hemisphere, and include humid continental and subarctic.

- The polar climate is the coldest climate region, and includes the ice cap and tundra climates.

- Temperature falls as altitude increases, so highland regions are colder than regions that surround them.

Key Terms

rain forest
savanna
desert
steppe
humid subtropical
subarctic
tundra
permafrost

③ Long-Term Changes in Climate

Key Concepts

- In studying ancient climates, scientists follow an important principle: If plants or animals today need certain conditions to live, then similar plants and animals in the past also required those conditions.

- During each ice age, huge sheets of ice called glaciers covered large parts of Earth's surface.

- Possible explanations for major climate changes include variations in the position of Earth relative to the sun, changes in the sun's energy output, major volcanic eruptions, and the movement of continents.

Key Terms

ice age   sunspot

④ Global Changes in the Atmosphere

Key Concepts

- El Niño and La Niña are short-term changes in the tropical Pacific Ocean caused by changes in ocean surface currents and prevailing winds.

- Human activities that add greenhouse gases to the atmosphere may be warming Earth's atmosphere.

- Chemicals produced by humans have been damaging the ozone layer.

Key Terms

- El Niño • La Niña • global warming
- greenhouse gas • chlorofluorocarbon

Review and Assessment

Go Online
PHSchool.com

For: Self-Assessment
Visit: PHSchool.com
Web Code: cfa-4040

Organizing Information

Concept Mapping Copy the graphic organizer about climate onto a separate sheet of paper. Then complete it and add a title. (For more on Concept Mapping, see the Skills Handbook.)

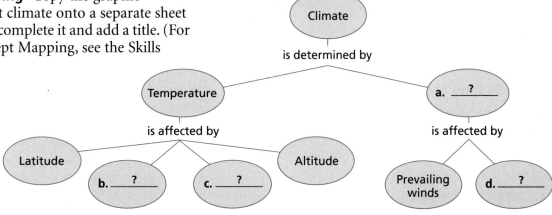

Reviewing Key Terms

Choose the letter of the best answer.

1. The average conditions of temperature, precipitation, wind, and clouds in an area over a period of years make up its
   a. weather. **b.** latitude.
   c. climate. **d.** season.

2. Temperatures range from warm or hot in summer to cool or cold in winter in
   a. polar zones.
   b. tropical zone.
   c. tundra climates.
   d. temperate zones.

3. A wet, warm climate zone on the edge of the tropics is
   a. humid subtropical.
   b. tundra.
   c. subarctic.
   d. continental climate.

4. A tropical grassland with scattered clumps of trees is a
   a. steppe. **b.** desert.
   c. savanna. **d.** rain forest.

5. The main cause of ozone depletion is
   a. global warming.
   b. chlorofluorocarbons.
   c. greenhouse gases.
   d. sunspots.

If the statement is true, write *true*. If it is false, change the underlined word or words to make the statement true.

6. The climate conditions that exist in a small area are its <u>microclimate</u>.

7. Rain or snow usually falls on the <u>leeward</u> side of a mountain range.

8. Permanently frozen soil is called <u>tundra</u>.

9. During <u>ice ages</u> large parts of Earth's surface are covered by glaciers.

10. Carbon dioxide is a <u>chlorofluorocarbon</u> that traps energy in the atmosphere.

Writing in Science

Expedition Plan Suppose that you are preparing to take a trip back in time to the last ice age. Write a list of the equipment you will need to bring with you and describe what the climate will be like.

Discovery CHANNEL SCHOOL™

Climate and Climate Change
Video Preview
Video Field Trip
▶ Video Assessment

Checking Concepts

11. Explain how distance from large bodies of water can affect the temperature of nearby land areas.

12. What are monsoons, and how do they affect climate in the regions where they occur?

13. What causes Earth's seasons?

14. How are "dry" climates defined? How do the two types of dry climate differ?

15. How does the movement of continents explain major changes in climate over time?

16. To be effective, why must agreements aimed at preventing or reducing ozone depletion be international?

Thinking Critically

17. **Relating Cause and Effect** Describe three ways in which water influences climate.

18. **Relating Cause and Effect** Why do parts of the United States have a semiarid climate while neighboring areas have a humid continental climate?

19. **Reading Graphs** Which month shown on the graph has the warmest average temperature? Which month is the wettest? What type of climate is indicated by the graph?

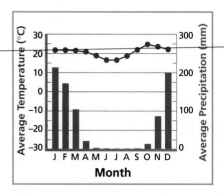

20. **Inferring** How is Earth's climate affected by major volcanic eruptions?

21. **Comparing and Contrasting** How is global warming different from earlier changes in Earth's climate?

Math Practice

22. **Percentage** Suppose a city receives an average of 35 cm of precipitation in November. If an average of 140 cm of precipitation falls there in a year, what percentage falls in November?

Applying Skills

Use the map of world temperature zones to answer Questions 23–26.

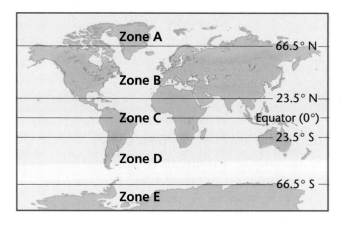

23. **Interpreting Maps** Name each of the five zones shown on the map.

24. **Measuring** What is the name of the temperature zone that includes the equator? How many degrees of latitude does this zone cover?

25. **Interpreting Data** Which of the five zones shown on the map has the greatest amount of land area suitable for people to live?

26. **Drawing Conclusions** Which zone has the highest average temperatures all year round? Explain why.

Lab zone · Chapter **Project**

27. **Performance Assessment** Now share your project with your class. In your presentation, describe the patterns you found in your graphs. Then explain what you think causes different microclimates. After your presentation, think about how you could have improved your investigation.

Standardized Test Prep

Choose the letter of the best answer.

1. Predict what type of climate would be the most likely in an area located in the interior of a large continent, on the east side of a major mountain range. Winds in the area commonly blow from west to east.

  A dry   **B** polar

  C temperate marine   **D** tropical rainy

2. What two major factors are usually used to classify climates?

  F precipitation and altitude

  G temperature and air pressure

  H temperature and precipitation

  J air pressure and humidity

3. What is the major result at Earth's surface of ozone depletion in the stratosphere?

  A an increase in the amount of ultraviolet radiation reaching the surface

  B a decrease in the amount of ultraviolet radiation reaching the surface

  C an increase in global temperatures

  D a decrease in global temperatures

The graphs below show average monthly precipitation for two locations in Arizona. Use the information and your knowledge of science to answer Questions 4–5.

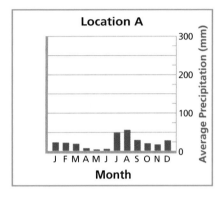

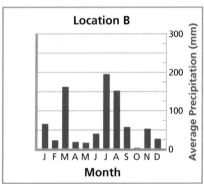

4. During which months do these locations receive the most precipitation?

  F January through March

  G April through June

  H July through September

  J October through December

5. Although they are only a few kilometers apart, Location B receives nearly three times as much precipitation as Location A. What is the best explanation for this fact?

  A Location B is in a rain shadow.

  B Location B is near a mountain top.

  C Location A is dried by prevailing winds.

  D Location A is much colder than Location B.

Constructed Response

6. Ice ages have occurred at several times during Earth's history. What is an ice age, and how does an ice age affect the land surface and the oceans?

Antarctica

On July 21, 1983, the temperature at the Russian research station Vostok dropped to a world record low of −89°C. Welcome to Antarctica!

Amundsen-Scott Station
This is one of the United States stations at the South Pole.

Because Antarctica is in the Southern Hemisphere, July is midwinter there. But the temperature isn't very warm in summer, either. The average summer temperature at Vostok is −33°C. Antarctica's climate is unusual in other ways. It's the windiest continent as well as the coldest. Even though Antarctica is covered with snow and ice, it's also the driest continent—a snowy desert. Less than five centimeters of precipitation falls in the interior in a year. Antarctic blizzards are terrifying, but they don't bring much new snow. They just blow drifts from one place to another.

Many countries have set up research stations in Antarctica to study climate, temperature, and the atmosphere. Scientists in Antarctica also research wildlife and geology.

Antarctica
The map shows major research stations established in Antarctica by countries around the world.

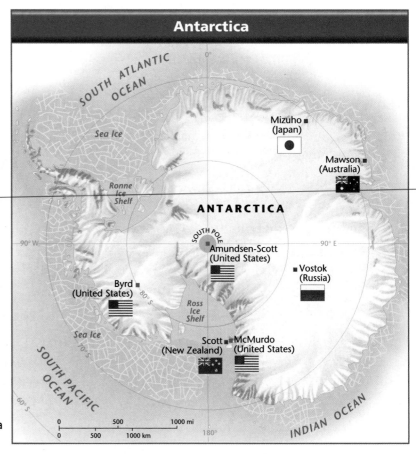

1912
Robert Falcon Scott (below center) and his men reached the South Pole, but lost the race.

Race to the South Pole

Would you brave the darkness and cold of Antarctica? In the early 1900s, several famous explorers began a "race to the pole." Their attempts to reach the South Pole produced stories of heroism—and tragedy.

In October 1911, the British explorer Robert Scott traveled to the South Pole. He started overland with dog teams, motorized sleds, and ponies. He and four other explorers reached the South Pole in January 1912—only to find that a Norwegian expedition led by Roald Amundsen had beaten them there by a month! Scott's team had lost the race!

Soon after, Scott and his crew started back. But all of them died in a blizzard. Searchers later found their tent, Scott's diary, and photographs. Scott's team had been only 18 kilometers from a supply camp.

In 1914, Sir Ernest Shackleton was the hero of an incredible Antarctic survival story. On the way to the South Pole, ice trapped and crushed his ship. He and his men escaped to an island. Shackleton and a few others sailed in a small whaleboat to find help. Amazingly, everyone was rescued.

Other expeditions followed. In 1929, American explorer Richard E. Byrd led the first flight over the South Pole. More recently, in 2001, Ann Bancroft and Liv Arnesen became the first women to cross Antarctica.

Antarctic Crossing
Bancroft (United States) and Arnesen (Norway) ski across Antarctica.

Social Studies Activity

Create a timeline of important events in Antarctica. Find photos or draw sketches to illustrate the events. Include the following events:

- early expeditions
- "race to the pole" in the early 1900s
- International Geophysical Year
- Antarctic Treaty
- new research stations

Why did it take courage and endurance to try to reach the South Pole in the early 1900s?

Continent of Extremes

Why is Antarctica so cold? Its high latitude and months of darkness are important reasons. In addition, the broad expanses of white snow and icy glaciers reflect back sunlight before much heat is absorbed.

As on every continent, climates vary from place to place. Warmer parts of Antarctica are at lower elevations, at lower latitudes, or near the coast. Coastal areas are warmer because the nearby ocean moderates temperatures. These areas also have bare land, which absorbs heat.

Summer weather patterns in Antarctica are different from winter patterns. The short summer warm-up starts in October. The warmest temperatures are from mid-December to mid-January. Then temperatures drop suddenly. So by mid-March, the beginning of winter, the temperature has fallen to winter levels. Over the next six months Antarctica remains very cold—and dark.

Science Activity

Staying warm is essential for life in the Antarctic. Set up an experiment to test how well different materials keep heat from escaping. Use socks made of nylon, silk, cotton, and wool. You will need a jar for each material plus one jar as a control.

- Fill jars with equal amounts of very hot water. The water in each jar should be the same temperature.
- Record the temperature of each jar and screw each cap on.
- Place each jar, except the control, inside a sock. Refrigerate all the jars for 30 minutes.
- Remove the jars and record the water temperature of each.

Which jar cooled fastest? Which materials retained the heat best?

Cold-Weather Clothing

The secret to staying warm is to wear layers of clothing that keep body heat from escaping.

Inner Layer
An inner layer of long underwear carries moisture away from the skin.

Insulating Layer
A fluffy insulating layer, such as fleece or down, traps pockets of air that are warmed by body heat.

Outer Layer
The outer shell layer protects against wind and water. An insulated hood and a face mask protect against wind. Boots and gloves are layered, too. Fleece in boots may be sealed in by a waterproof rubber layer.

Protective Gear
Goggles, or sunglasses worn by this man in Antarctica, reduce the glare of sunlight and protect eyes from freezing.

Sky Watch

It's March 21—the beginning of winter—and you're watching the sun set very, very slowly. It takes 30 hours—more than a day—for the sun to disappear below the horizon. Once it's gone, you won't see sunshine again until September! April and early May aren't completely dark, but there is hardly enough light to cast a shadow. Then it's dark for two months. In August, light begins again. The sky brightens quickly until the polar sunrise.

The tilt of Earth on its axis affects the hours of daylight and darkness from season to season. At the poles, midsummer brings the "midnight sun," which circles around the sky but does not set. Midwinter brings almost total darkness.

Anvers Island in Antarctica

Math Activity

The table (right) shows hours of daylight on the 15th of each month. It shows readings at two different Antarctic locations—the Amundsen-Scott station and Japan's Mizuho station.

Use the table to make a graph that shows hours of daylight for the Mizuho station and the Amundsen-Scott station.

- On the horizontal axis of the graph, list the months.

- On the vertical axis, mark off spaces for 0 to 24 hours.

- Choose a different color marker for each latitude. Above the month for each location, place a colored dot at the correct hour mark. Connect the dots to show changes in daylight at each place during a year.

- How are the changes in darkness and daylight in Antarctica like those you see at home? How are they different?

Hours of Daylight in Antarctica*

Month	Mizuho Station 70° S	Amundsen-Scott Station 90° S
January	24	24
February	18	24
March	14	24
April	9	0
May	3	0
June	0	0
July	0	0
August	7	0
September	11	0
October	16	24
November	22	24
December	24	24

*Sunrise to sunset, rounded to nearest hour

Alone in Antarctica

Admiral Richard Byrd worked in the Antarctic for nearly 30 years after his flight over the South Pole. He led several expeditions and set up research stations at Little America. Byrd's book *Alone* is based on the journal he kept while spending the winter of 1934 alone at a weather station outpost. During his four-and-a-half-month stay, Byrd nearly gave up mentally and physically. He endured, however, and kept up his weather research until help arrived in August.

In this memoir of his days in early April, 1934, Byrd describes some of the problems of working in the intense cold.

Admiral Byrd
In his small shack at Little America, Byrd tries to keep warm.

At times I felt as if I were the last survivor of an Ice Age, striving to hold on with the flimsy tools bequeathed by an easy-going, temperate world. Cold does queer things. At 50° Fahrenheit below zero a flashlight dies out in your hand. At −55° Fahrenheit kerosene will freeze, and the flame will dry up on the wick.

At −60° Fahrenheit rubber turns brittle. One day, I remember, the antenna wire snapped in my hands when I tried to bend it to make a new connection. Below −60° Fahrenheit cold will find the last microscopic touch of oil in an instrument and stop it dead. If there is the slightest breeze, you can hear your breath freeze as it floats away, making a sound like that of Chinese firecrackers.... And if you work too hard and breathe too deeply, your lungs will sometimes feel as if they were on fire.

Cold—even April's relatively moderate cold—gave me plenty to think about.... Two cases of tomato juice shattered their bottles. Whenever I brought canned food inside the shack I had to let it stand all day near the stove to thaw.... Frost was forever collecting on the electrical contact points of the wind vane and wind cups. Some days I climbed the twelve-foot anemometer pole two and three times to clean them. It was a bitter job, especially on blustery nights. With my legs twined around the slender pole, my arms flung over the cleats, and my free hands trying to scrape the contact point clean with a knife and at the same time hold a flashlight to see, I qualified for the world's coldest flagpole sitter. I seldom came down from that pole without a frozen finger, toe, nose, or cheek.

The shack was always freezingly cold in the morning. I slept with the door open [for ventilation]. When I arose the inside temperature (depending upon the surface weather) might be anywhere from 10° to 40° Fahrenheit below zero. Frost coated the sleeping bag where my breath had condensed during the night; my socks and boots, when I picked them up, were so stiff with frozen sweat that I first had to work them between my hands. A pair of silk gloves hung from a nail over the bunk, where I could grab them the first thing. Yet, even with their protection, my fingers would sting and burn from the touch of the lamp and stove as I lighted them.

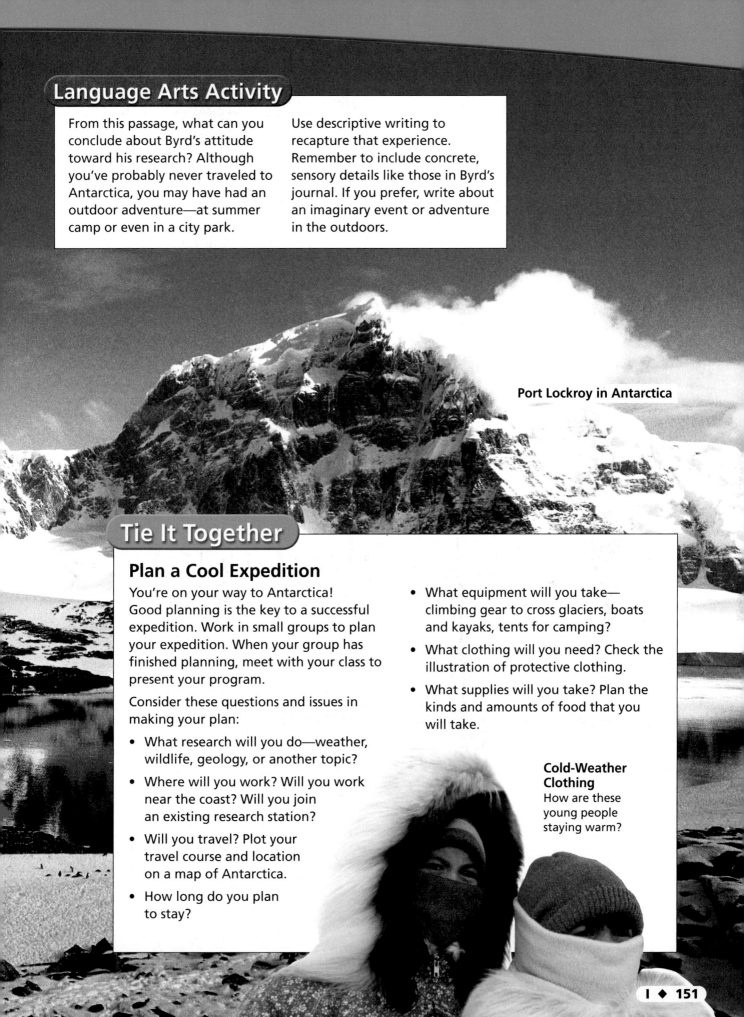

Language Arts Activity

From this passage, what can you conclude about Byrd's attitude toward his research? Although you've probably never traveled to Antarctica, you may have had an outdoor adventure—at summer camp or even in a city park.

Use descriptive writing to recapture that experience. Remember to include concrete, sensory details like those in Byrd's journal. If you prefer, write about an imaginary event or adventure in the outdoors.

Port Lockroy in Antarctica

Tie It Together

Plan a Cool Expedition

You're on your way to Antarctica! Good planning is the key to a successful expedition. Work in small groups to plan your expedition. When your group has finished planning, meet with your class to present your program.

Consider these questions and issues in making your plan:

- What research will you do—weather, wildlife, geology, or another topic?

- Where will you work? Will you work near the coast? Will you join an existing research station?

- Will you travel? Plot your travel course and location on a map of Antarctica.

- How long do you plan to stay?

- What equipment will you take— climbing gear to cross glaciers, boats and kayaks, tents for camping?

- What clothing will you need? Check the illustration of protective clothing.

- What supplies will you take? Plan the kinds and amounts of food that you will take.

Cold-Weather Clothing
How are these young people staying warm?

Think Like a Scientist

Scientists have a particular way of looking at the world, or scientific habits of mind. Whenever you ask a question and explore possible answers, you use many of the same skills that scientists do. Some of these skills are described on this page.

Observing

When you use one or more of your five senses to gather information about the world, you are **observing.** Hearing a dog bark, counting twelve green seeds, and smelling smoke are all observations. To increase the power of their senses, scientists sometimes use microscopes, telescopes, or other instruments that help them make more detailed observations.

An observation must be an accurate report of what your senses detect. It is important to keep careful records of your observations in science class by writing or drawing in a notebook. The information collected through observations is called evidence, or data.

Inferring

When you interpret an observation, you are **inferring,** or making an inference. For example, if you hear your dog barking, you may infer that someone is at your front door. To make this inference, you combine the evidence— the barking dog—and your experience or knowledge—you know that your dog barks when strangers approach—to reach a logical conclusion.

Notice that an inference is not a fact; it is only one of many possible interpretations for an observation. For example, your dog may be barking because it wants to go for a walk. An inference may turn out to be incorrect even if it is based on accurate observations and logical reasoning. The only way to find out if an inference is correct is to investigate further.

Predicting

When you listen to the weather forecast, you hear many predictions about the next day's weather—what the temperature will be, whether it will rain, and how windy it will be. Weather forecasters use observations and knowledge of weather patterns to predict the weather. The skill of **predicting** involves making an inference about a future event based on current evidence or past experience.

Because a prediction is an inference, it may prove to be false. In science class, you can test some of your predictions by doing experiments. For example, suppose you predict that larger paper airplanes can fly farther than smaller airplanes. How could you test your prediction?

Activity

Use the photograph to answer the questions below.

Observing Look closely at the photograph. List at least three observations.

Inferring Use your observations to make an inference about what has happened. What experience or knowledge did you use to make the inference?

Predicting Predict what will happen next. On what evidence or experience do you base your prediction?

Classifying

Could you imagine searching for a book in the library if the books were shelved in no particular order? Your trip to the library would be an all-day event! Luckily, librarians group together books on similar topics or by the same author. Grouping together items that are alike in some way is called **classifying.** You can classify items in many ways: by size, by shape, by use, and by other important characteristics.

Like librarians, scientists use the skill of classifying to organize information and objects. When things are sorted into groups, the relationships among them become easier to understand.

> **Activity**
>
> **Classify the objects in the photograph into two groups based on any characteristic you choose. Then use another characteristic to classify the objects into three groups.**

> **Activity**
>
> **This student is using a model to demonstrate what causes day and night on Earth. What do the flashlight and the tennis ball in the model represent?**

Making Models

Have you ever drawn a picture to help someone understand what you were saying? Such a drawing is one type of model. A model is a picture, diagram, computer image, or other representation of a complex object or process. **Making models** helps people understand things that they cannot observe directly.

Scientists often use models to represent things that are either very large or very small, such as the planets in the solar system, or the parts of a cell. Such models are physical models—drawings or three-dimensional structures that look like the real thing. Other models are mental models—mathematical equations or words that describe how something works.

Communicating

Whenever you talk on the phone, write a report, or listen to your teacher at school, you are communicating. **Communicating** is the process of sharing ideas and information with other people. Communicating effectively requires many skills, including writing, reading, speaking, listening, and making models.

Scientists communicate to share results, information, and opinions. Scientists often communicate about their work in journals, over the telephone, in letters, and on the Internet.

They also attend scientific meetings where they share their ideas with one another in person.

> **Activity**
>
> **On a sheet of paper, write out clear, detailed directions for tying your shoe. Then exchange directions with a partner. Follow your partner's directions exactly. How successful were you at tying your shoe? How could your partner have communicated more clearly?**

Making Measurements

By measuring, scientists can express their observations more precisely and communicate more information about what they observe.

Measuring in SI

The standard system of measurement used by scientists around the world is known as the International System of Units, which is abbreviated as SI (**Système International d'Unités,** in French). SI units are easy to use because they are based on powers of 10. Each unit is ten times larger than the next smallest unit and one tenth the size of the next largest unit. The table lists the prefixes used to name the most common SI units.

Common SI Prefixes		
Prefix	Symbol	Meaning
kilo-	k	1,000
hecto-	h	100
deka-	da	10
deci-	d	0.1 (one tenth)
centi-	c	0.01 (one hundredth)
milli-	m	0.001 (one thousandth)

Length To measure length, or the distance between two points, the unit of measure is the **meter (m).** The distance from the floor to a doorknob is approximately one meter. Long distances, such as the distance between two cities, are measured in kilometers (km). Small lengths are measured in centimeters (cm) or millimeters (mm). Scientists use metric rulers and meter sticks to measure length.

Common Conversions	
1 km	= 1,000 m
1 m	= 100 cm
1 m	= 1,000 mm
1 cm	= 10 mm

Liquid Volume To measure the volume of a liquid, or the amount of space it takes up, you will use a unit of measure known as the **liter (L).** One liter is the approximate volume of a medium-size carton of milk. Smaller volumes are measured in milliliters (mL). Scientists use graduated cylinders to measure liquid volume.

Activity

The larger lines on the metric ruler in the picture show centimeter divisions, while the smaller, unnumbered lines show millimeter divisions. How many centimeters long is the shell? How many millimeters long is it?

Activity

The graduated cylinder in the picture is marked in milliliter divisions. Notice that the water in the cylinder has a curved surface. This curved surface is called the *meniscus*. To measure the volume, you must read the level at the lowest point of the meniscus. What is the volume of water in this graduated cylinder?

Common Conversion
1 L = 1,000 mL

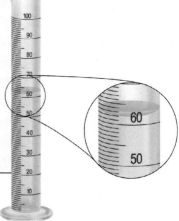

Mass To measure mass, or the amount of matter in an object, you will use a unit of measure known as the **gram (g).** One gram is approximately the mass of a paper clip. Larger masses are measured in kilograms (kg). Scientists use a balance to find the mass of an object.

Common Conversion

1 kg = 1,000 g

Activity

The mass of the potato in the picture is measured in kilograms. What is the mass of the potato? Suppose a recipe for potato salad called for one kilogram of potatoes. About how many potatoes would you need?

0.25 KG

Temperature To measure the temperature of a substance, you will use the **Celsius scale.** Temperature is measured in degrees Celsius (°C) using a Celsius thermometer. Water freezes at 0°C and boils at 100°C.

Time The unit scientists use to measure time is the **second (s).**

Activity

What is the temperature of the liquid in degrees Celsius?

Converting SI Units

To use the SI system, you must know how to convert between units. Converting from one unit to another involves the skill of **calculating,** or using mathematical operations. Converting between SI units is similar to converting between dollars and dimes because both systems are based on powers of ten.

Suppose you want to convert a length of 80 centimeters to meters. Follow these steps to convert between units.

1. Begin by writing down the measurement you want to convert—in this example, 80 centimeters.

2. Write a conversion factor that represents the relationship between the two units you are converting. In this example, the relationship is 1 meter = 100 centimeters. Write this conversion factor as a fraction, making sure to place the units you are converting from (centimeters, in this example) in the denominator.

3. Multiply the measurement you want to convert by the fraction. When you do this, the units in the first measurement will cancel out with the units in the denominator. Your answer will be in the units you are converting to (meters, in this example).

Example

80 centimeters = ■ meters

$$80 \text{ centimeters} \times \frac{1 \text{ meter}}{100 \text{ centimeters}} = \frac{80 \text{ meters}}{100}$$

$$= 0.8 \text{ meters}$$

Activity

Convert between the following units.

1. 600 millimeters = ■ meters
2. 0.35 liters = ■ milliliters
3. 1,050 grams = ■ kilograms

Conducting a Scientific Investigation

In some ways, scientists are like detectives, piecing together clues to learn about a process or event. One way that scientists gather clues is by carrying out experiments. An experiment tests an idea in a careful, orderly manner. Although experiments do not all follow the same steps in the same order, many follow a pattern similar to the one described here.

Posing Questions

Experiments begin by asking a scientific question. A scientific question is one that can be answered by gathering evidence. For example, the question "Which freezes faster—fresh water or salt water?" is a scientific question because you can carry out an investigation and gather information to answer the question.

Developing a Hypothesis

The next step is to form a hypothesis. A **hypothesis** is a possible explanation for a set of observations or answer to a scientific question. In science, a hypothesis must be something that can be tested. A hypothesis can be worded as an *If . . . then . . .* statement. For example, a hypothesis might be *"If I add table salt to fresh water, then the water will freeze at a lower temperature."* A hypothesis worded this way serves as a rough outline of the experiment you should perform.

Designing an Experiment

Next you need to plan a way to test your hypothesis. Your plan should be written out as a step-by-step procedure and should describe the observations or measurements you will make.

Two important steps involved in designing an experiment are controlling variables and forming operational definitions.

Controlling Variables In a well-designed experiment, you need to keep all variables the same except for one. A **variable** is any factor that can change in an experiment. The factor that you change is called the **manipulated variable**. In this experiment, the manipulated variable is the amount of table salt added to the water. Other factors, such as the amount of water or the starting temperature, are kept constant.

The factor that changes as a result of the manipulated variable is called the **responding variable**. The responding variable is what you measure or observe to obtain your results. In this experiment, the responding variable is the temperature at which the water freezes.

An experiment in which all factors except one are kept constant is called a **controlled experiment**. Most controlled experiments include a test called the control. In this experiment, Container 3 is the control. Because no salt is added to Container 3, you can compare the results from the other containers to it. Any difference in results must be due to the addition of salt alone.

Forming Operational Definitions Another important aspect of a well-designed experiment is having clear operational definitions. An **operational definition** is a statement that describes how a particular variable is to be measured or how a term is to be defined. For example, in this experiment, how will you determine if the water has frozen? You might decide to insert a stick in each container at the start of the experiment. Your operational definition of "frozen" would be the time at which the stick can no longer move.

Experimental Procedure
1. Fill 3 containers with 300 milliliters of cold tap water.
2. Add 10 grams of salt to Container 1; stir. Add 20 grams of salt to Container 2; stir. Add no salt to Container 3.
3. Place the 3 containers in a freezer.
4. Check the containers every 15 minutes. Record your observations.

Interpreting Data

The observations and measurements you make in an experiment are called **data.** At the end of an experiment, you need to analyze the data to look for any patterns or trends. Patterns often become clear if you organize your data in a data table or graph. Then think through what the data reveal. Do they support your hypothesis? Do they point out a flaw in your experiment? Do you need to collect more data?

Drawing Conclusions

A **conclusion** is a statement that sums up what you have learned from an experiment. When you draw a conclusion, you need to decide whether the data you collected support your hypothesis or not. You may need to repeat an experiment several times before you can draw any conclusions from it. Conclusions often lead you to pose new questions and plan new experiments to answer them.

Activity

Is a ball's bounce affected by the height from which it is dropped? Using the steps just described, plan a controlled experiment to investigate this problem.

Technology Design Skills

Engineers are people who use scientific and technological knowledge to solve practical problems. To design new products, engineers usually follow the process described here, even though they may not follow these steps in the exact order. As you read the steps, think about how you might apply them in technology labs.

Identify a Need

Before engineers begin designing a new product, they must first identify the need they are trying to meet. For example, suppose you are a member of a design team in a company that makes toys. Your team has identified a need: a toy boat that is inexpensive and easy to assemble.

Research the Problem

Engineers often begin by gathering information that will help them with their new design. This research may include finding articles in books, magazines, or on the Internet. It may also include talking to other engineers who have solved similar problems. Engineers often perform experiments related to the product they want to design.

For your toy boat, you could look at toys that are similar to the one you want to design. You might do research on the Internet. You could also test some materials to see whether they will work well in a toy boat.

Drawing for a boat design ▼

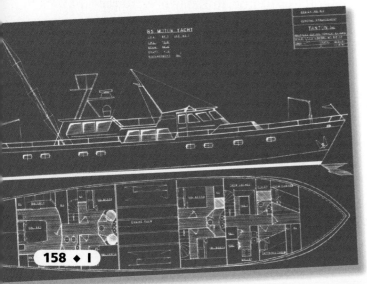

Design a Solution

Research gives engineers information that helps them design a product. When engineers design new products, they usually work in teams.

Generating Ideas Often design teams hold brainstorming meetings in which any team member can contribute ideas. **Brainstorming** is a creative process in which one team member's suggestions often spark ideas in other group members. Brainstorming can lead to new approaches to solving a design problem.

Evaluating Constraints During brainstorming, a design team will often come up with several possible designs. The team must then evaluate each one.

As part of their evaluation, engineers consider constraints. **Constraints** are factors that limit or restrict a product design. Physical characteristics, such as the properties of materials used to make your toy boat, are constraints. Money and time are also constraints. If the materials in a product cost a lot, or if the product takes a long time to make, the design may be impractical.

Making Trade-offs Design teams usually need to make trade-offs. In a **trade-off,** engineers give up one benefit of a proposed design in order to obtain another. In designing your toy boat, you will have to make trade-offs. For example, suppose one material is sturdy but not fully waterproof. Another material is more waterproof, but breakable. You may decide to give up the benefit of sturdiness in order to obtain the benefit of waterproofing.

Build and Evaluate a Prototype

Once the team has chosen a design plan, the engineers build a prototype of the product. A **prototype** is a working model used to test a design. Engineers evaluate the prototype to see whether it works well, is easy to operate, is safe to use, and holds up to repeated use.

Think of your toy boat. What would the prototype be like? Of what materials would it be made? How would you test it?

Troubleshoot and Redesign

Few prototypes work perfectly, which is why they need to be tested. Once a design team has tested a prototype, the members analyze the results and identify any problems. The team then tries to **troubleshoot,** or fix the design problems. For example, if your toy boat leaks or wobbles, the boat should be redesigned to eliminate those problems.

Communicate the Solution

A team needs to communicate the final design to the people who will manufacture and use the product. To do this, teams may use sketches, detailed drawings, computer simulations, and word descriptions.

Activity

You can use the technology design process to design and build a toy boat.

Research and Investigate

1. Visit the library or go online to research toy boats.

2. Investigate how a toy boat can be powered, including wind, rubber bands, or baking soda and vinegar.

3. Brainstorm materials, shapes, and steering for your boat.

Design and Build

4. Based on your research, design a toy boat that
   • is made of readily available materials
   • is no larger than 15 cm long and 10 cm wide
   • includes a power system, a rudder, and an area for cargo
   • travels 2 meters in a straight line carrying a load of 20 pennies

5. Sketch your design and write a step-by-step plan for building your boat. After your teacher approves your plan, build your boat.

Evaluate and Redesign

6. Test your boat, evaluate the results, and troubleshoot any problems.

7. Based on your evaluation, redesign your toy boat so it performs better.

Creating Data Tables and Graphs

**How can you make sense of the data in a science experiment?
The first step is to organize the data to help you understand them.
Data tables and graphs are helpful tools for organizing data.**

Data Tables

You have gathered your materials and set up your experiment. But before you start, you need to plan a way to record what happens during the experiment. By creating a data table, you can record your observations and measurements in an orderly way.

Suppose, for example, that a scientist conducted an experiment to find out how many Calories people of different body masses burn while doing various activities. The data table shows the results.

Notice in this data table that the manipulated variable (body mass) is the heading of one column. The responding variable (for

Calories Burned in 30 Minutes			
Body Mass	Experiment 1: Bicycling	Experiment 2: Playing Basketball	Experiment 3: Watching Television
30 kg	60 Calories	120 Calories	21 Calories
40 kg	77 Calories	164 Calories	27 Calories
50 kg	95 Calories	206 Calories	33 Calories
60 kg	114 Calories	248 Calories	38 Calories

Experiment 1, the number of Calories burned while bicycling) is the heading of the next column. Additional columns were added for related experiments.

Bar Graphs

To compare how many Calories a person burns doing various activities, you could create a bar graph. A bar graph is used to display data in a number of separate, or distinct, categories. In this example, bicycling, playing basketball, and watching television are the three categories.

To create a bar graph, follow these steps.

1. On graph paper, draw a horizontal, or *x*-, axis and a vertical, or *y*-, axis.

2. Write the names of the categories to be graphed along the horizontal axis. Include an overall label for the axis as well.

3. Label the vertical axis with the name of the responding variable. Include units of measurement. Then create a scale along the axis by marking off equally spaced numbers that cover the range of the data collected.

4. For each category, draw a solid bar using the scale on the vertical axis to determine the height. Make all the bars the same width.

5. Add a title that describes the graph.

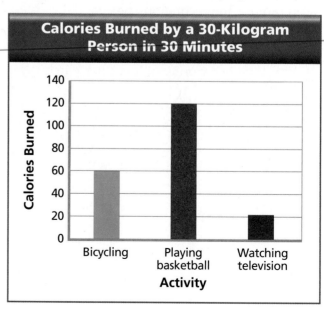

Line Graphs

To see whether a relationship exists between body mass and the number of Calories burned while bicycling, you could create a line graph. A line graph is used to display data that show how one variable (the responding variable) changes in response to another variable (the manipulated variable). You can use a line graph when your manipulated variable is **continuous,** that is, when there are other points between the ones that you tested. In this example, body mass is a continuous variable because there are other body masses between 30 and 40 kilograms (for example, 31 kilograms). Time is another example of a continuous variable.

Line graphs are powerful tools because they allow you to estimate values for conditions that you did not test in the experiment. For example, you can use the line graph to estimate that a 35-kilogram person would burn 68 Calories while bicycling.

To create a line graph, follow these steps.

1. On graph paper, draw a horizontal, or *x*-, axis and a vertical, or *y*-, axis.

2. Label the horizontal axis with the name of the manipulated variable. Label the vertical axis with the name of the responding variable. Include units of measurement.

3. Create a scale on each axis by marking off equally spaced numbers that cover the range of the data collected.

4. Plot a point on the graph for each piece of data. In the line graph above, the dotted lines show how to plot the first data point (30 kilograms and 60 Calories). Follow an imaginary vertical line extending up from the horizontal axis at the 30-kilogram mark. Then follow an imaginary horizontal line extending across from the vertical axis at the 60-Calorie mark. Plot the point where the two lines intersect.

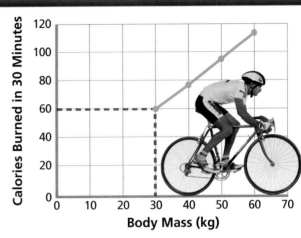

Effect of Body Mass on Calories Burned While Bicycling

5. Connect the plotted points with a solid line. (In some cases, it may be more appropriate to draw a line that shows the general trend of the plotted points. In those cases, some of the points may fall above or below the line. Also, not all graphs are linear. It may be more appropriate to draw a curve to connect the points.)

6. Add a title that identifies the variables or relationship in the graph.

Activity

Create line graphs to display the data from Experiment 2 and Experiment 3 in the data table.

Activity

You read in the newspaper that a total of 4 centimeters of rain fell in your area in June, 2.5 centimeters fell in July, and 1.5 centimeters fell in August. What type of graph would you use to display these data? Use graph paper to create the graph.

Circle Graphs

Like bar graphs, circle graphs can be used to display data in a number of separate categories. Unlike bar graphs, however, circle graphs can only be used when you have data for *all* the categories that make up a given topic. A circle graph is sometimes called a pie chart. The pie represents the entire topic, while the slices represent the individual categories. The size of a slice indicates what percentage of the whole a particular category makes up.

The data table below shows the results of a survey in which 24 teenagers were asked to identify their favorite sport. The data were then used to create the circle graph at the right.

Favorite Sports	
Sport	Students
Soccer	8
Basketball	6
Bicycling	6
Swimming	4

To create a circle graph, follow these steps.

1. Use a compass to draw a circle. Mark the center with a point. Then draw a line from the center point to the top of the circle.

2. Determine the size of each "slice" by setting up a proportion where x equals the number of degrees in a slice. (*Note:* A circle contains 360 degrees.) For example, to find the number of degrees in the "soccer" slice, set up the following proportion:

$$\frac{\text{Students who prefer soccer}}{\text{Total number of students}} = \frac{x}{\text{Total number of degrees in a circle}}$$

$$\frac{8}{24} = \frac{x}{360}$$

Cross-multiply and solve for x.

$$24x = 8 \times 360$$
$$x = 120$$

The "soccer" slice should contain 120 degrees.

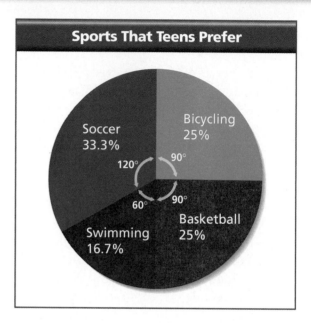

Sports That Teens Prefer

Soccer 33.3%
Bicycling 25%
Basketball 25%
Swimming 16.7%
120° 90° 60° 90°

3. Use a protractor to measure the angle of the first slice, using the line you drew to the top of the circle as the 0° line. Draw a line from the center of the circle to the edge for the angle you measured.

4. Continue around the circle by measuring the size of each slice with the protractor. Start measuring from the edge of the previous slice so the wedges do not overlap. When you are done, the entire circle should be filled in.

5. Determine the percentage of the whole circle that each slice represents. To do this, divide the number of degrees in a slice by the total number of degrees in a circle (360), and multiply by 100%. For the "soccer" slice, you can find the percentage as follows:

$$\frac{120}{360} \times 100\% = 33.3\%$$

6. Use a different color for each slice. Label each slice with the category and with the percentage of the whole it represents.

7. Add a title to the circle graph.

Activity

In a class of 28 students, 12 students take the bus to school, 10 students walk, and 6 students ride their bicycles. Create a circle graph to display these data.

Math Review

Scientists use math to organize, analyze, and present data. This appendix will help you review some basic math skills.

Mean, Median, and Mode

The **mean** is the average, or the sum of the data divided by the number of data items. The middle number in a set of ordered data is called the **median.** The **mode** is the number that appears most often in a set of data.

> **Example**
>
> A scientist counted the number of distinct songs sung by seven different male birds and collected the data shown below.
>
> | Male Bird Songs | | | | | | | |
> |---|---|---|---|---|---|---|---|
> | Bird | A | B | C | D | E | F | G |
> | Number of Songs | 36 | 29 | 40 | 35 | 28 | 36 | 27 |
>
> To determine the mean number of songs, add the total number of songs and divide by the number of data items—in this case, the number of male birds.
>
> $$\text{Mean} = \frac{231}{7} = 33 \text{ songs}$$
>
> To find the median number of songs, arrange the data in numerical order and find the number in the middle of the series.
>
> **27 28 29 35 36 36 40**
>
> The number in the middle is 35, so the median number of songs is 35.
>
> The mode is the value that appears most frequently. In the data, 36 appears twice, while each other item appears only once. Therefore, 36 songs is the mode.

> **Practice**
>
> Find out how many minutes it takes each student in your class to get to school. Then find the mean, median, and mode for the data.

Probability

Probability is the chance that an event will occur. Probability can be expressed as a ratio, a fraction, or a percentage. For example, when you flip a coin, the probability that the coin will land heads up is 1 in 2, or $\frac{1}{2}$, or 50 percent.

The probability that an event will happen can be expressed in the following formula.

$$P(\text{event}) = \frac{\text{Number of times the event can occur}}{\text{Total number of possible events}}$$

> **Example**
>
> A paper bag contains 25 blue marbles, 5 green marbles, 5 orange marbles, and 15 yellow marbles. If you close your eyes and pick a marble from the bag, what is the probability that it will be yellow?
>
> $$P(\text{yellow marbles}) = \frac{15 \text{ yellow marbles}}{50 \text{ marbles total}}$$
>
> $$P = \frac{15}{50}, \text{ or } \frac{3}{10}, \text{ or } 30\%$$

> **Practice**
>
> Each side of a cube has a letter on it. Two sides have *A*, three sides have *B*, and one side has *C*. If you roll the cube, what is the probability that *A* will land on top?

Area

The **area** of a surface is the number of square units that cover it. The front cover of your textbook has an area of about 600 cm².

Area of a Rectangle and a Square To find the area of a rectangle, multiply its length times its width. The formula for the area of a rectangle is

$$A = \ell \times w, \text{ or } A = \ell w$$

Since all four sides of a square have the same length, the area of a square is the length of one side multiplied by itself, or squared.

$$A = s \times s, \text{ or } A = s^2$$

Example

A scientist is studying the plants in a field that measures 75 m × 45 m. What is the area of the field?

$$A = \ell \times w$$
$$A = 75 \text{ m} \times 45 \text{ m}$$
$$A = 3{,}375 \text{ m}^2$$

Area of a Circle The formula for the area of a circle is

$$A = \pi \times r \times r, \text{ or } A = \pi r^2$$

The length of the radius is represented by r, and the value of π is approximately $\frac{22}{7}$.

Example

Find the area of a circle with a radius of 14 cm.

$$A = \pi r^2$$
$$A = 14 \times 14 \times \frac{22}{7}$$
$$A = 616 \text{ cm}^2$$

Practice

Find the area of a circle that has a radius of 21 m.

Circumference

The distance around a circle is called the circumference. The formula for finding the circumference of a circle is

$$C = 2 \times \pi \times r, \text{ or } C = 2\pi r$$

Example

The radius of a circle is 35 cm. What is its circumference?

$$C = 2\pi r$$
$$C = 2 \times 35 \times \frac{22}{7}$$
$$C = 220 \text{ cm}$$

Practice

What is the circumference of a circle with a radius of 28 m?

Volume

The volume of an object is the number of cubic units it contains. The volume of a wastebasket, for example, might be about 26,000 cm³.

Volume of a Rectangular Object To find the volume of a rectangular object, multiply the object's length times its width times its height.

$$V = \ell \times w \times h, \text{ or } V = \ell w h$$

Example

Find the volume of a box with length 24 cm, width 12 cm, and height 9 cm.

$$V = \ell w h$$
$$V = 24 \text{ cm} \times 12 \text{ cm} \times 9 \text{ cm}$$
$$V = 2{,}592 \text{ cm}^3$$

Practice

What is the volume of a rectangular object with length 17 cm, width 11 cm, and height 6 cm?

Fractions

A **fraction** is a way to express a part of a whole. In the fraction $\frac{4}{7}$, 4 is the numerator and 7 is the denominator.

Adding and Subtracting Fractions

To add or subtract two or more fractions that have a common denominator, first add or subtract the numerators. Then write the sum or difference over the common denominator.

To find the sum or difference of fractions with different denominators, first find the least common multiple of the denominators. This is known as the least common denominator. Then convert each fraction to equivalent fractions with the least common denominator. Add or subtract the numerators. Then write the sum or difference over the common denominator.

Example

$$\frac{5}{6} - \frac{3}{4} = \frac{10}{12} - \frac{9}{12} = \frac{10 - 9}{12} = \frac{1}{12}$$

Multiplying Fractions

To multiply two fractions, first multiply the two numerators, then multiply the two denominators.

Example

$$\frac{5}{6} \times \frac{2}{3} = \frac{5 \times 2}{6 \times 3} = \frac{10}{18} = \frac{5}{9}$$

Dividing Fractions

Dividing by a fraction is the same as multiplying by its reciprocal. Reciprocals are numbers whose numerators and denominators have been switched. To divide one fraction by another, first invert the fraction you are dividing by—in other words, turn it upside down. Then multiply the two fractions.

Example

$$\frac{2}{5} \div \frac{7}{8} = \frac{2}{5} \times \frac{8}{7} = \frac{2 \times 8}{5 \times 7} = \frac{16}{35}$$

Practice

Solve the following: $\frac{3}{7} \div \frac{4}{5}$.

Decimals

Fractions whose denominators are 10, 100, or some other power of 10 are often expressed as decimals. For example, the fraction $\frac{9}{10}$ can be expressed as the decimal 0.9, and the fraction $\frac{7}{100}$ can be written as 0.07.

Adding and Subtracting With Decimals

To add or subtract decimals, line up the decimal points before you carry out the operation.

Example

$$\begin{array}{r} 27.4 \\ + \ 6.19 \\ \hline 33.59 \end{array} \qquad \begin{array}{r} 278.635 \\ - \ 191.4 \\ \hline 87.235 \end{array}$$

Multiplying With Decimals

When you multiply two numbers with decimals, the number of decimal places in the product is equal to the total number of decimal places in each number being multiplied.

Example

$$\begin{array}{r} 46.2 \ \text{(one decimal place)} \\ \times \ 2.37 \ \text{(two decimal places)} \\ \hline 109.494 \ \text{(three decimal places)} \end{array}$$

Dividing With Decimals

To divide a decimal by a whole number, put the decimal point in the quotient above the decimal point in the dividend.

Example

$$15.5 \div 5$$
$$\begin{array}{r} 3.1 \\ 5\overline{)15.5} \end{array}$$

To divide a decimal by a decimal, you need to rewrite the divisor as a whole number. Do this by multiplying both the divisor and dividend by the same multiple of 10.

Example

$$1.68 \div 4.2 = 16.8 \div 42$$
$$\begin{array}{r} 0.4 \\ 42\overline{)16.8} \end{array}$$

Practice

Multiply 6.21 by 8.5.

Ratio and Proportion

A **ratio** compares two numbers by division. For example, suppose a scientist counts 800 wolves and 1,200 moose on an island. The ratio of wolves to moose can be written as a fraction, $\frac{800}{1,200}$, which can be reduced to $\frac{2}{3}$. The same ratio can also be expressed as 2 to 3 or 2 : 3.

A **proportion** is a mathematical sentence saying that two ratios are equivalent. For example, a proportion could state that $\frac{800 \text{ wolves}}{1,200 \text{ moose}} = \frac{2 \text{ wolves}}{3 \text{ moose}}$. You can sometimes set up a proportion to determine or estimate an unknown quantity. For example, suppose a scientist counts 25 beetles in an area of 10 square meters. The scientist wants to estimate the number of beetles in 100 square meters.

Example

1. Express the relationship between beetles and area as a ratio: $\frac{25}{10}$, simplified to $\frac{5}{2}$.

2. Set up a proportion, with x representing the number of beetles. The proportion can be stated as $\frac{5}{2} = \frac{x}{100}$.

3. Begin by cross-multiplying. In other words, multiply each fraction's numerator by the other fraction's denominator.

   $5 \times 100 = 2 \times x$, or $500 = 2x$

4. To find the value of x, divide both sides by 2. The result is 250, or 250 beetles in 100 square meters.

Practice

Find the value of x in the following proportion: $\frac{6}{7} = \frac{x}{49}$.

Percentage

A **percentage** is a ratio that compares a number to 100. For example, there are 37 granite rocks in a collection that consists of 100 rocks. The ratio $\frac{37}{100}$ can be written as 37%. Granite rocks make up 37% of the rock collection.

You can calculate percentages of numbers other than 100 by setting up a proportion.

Example

Rain falls on 9 days out of 30 in June. What percentage of the days in June were rainy?

$$\frac{9 \text{ days}}{30 \text{ days}} = \frac{d\%}{100\%}$$

To find the value of d, begin by cross-multiplying, as for any proportion:

$9 \times 100 = 30 \times d \qquad d = \frac{900}{30} \qquad d = 30$

Practice

There are 300 marbles in a jar, and 42 of those marbles are blue. What percentage of the marbles are blue?

Significant Figures

The **precision** of a measurement depends on the instrument you use to take the measurement. For example, if the smallest unit on the ruler is millimeters, then the most precise measurement you can make will be in millimeters.

The sum or difference of measurements can only be as precise as the least precise measurement being added or subtracted. Round your answer so that it has the same number of digits after the decimal as the least precise measurement. Round up if the last digit is 5 or more, and round down if the last digit is 4 or less.

Example

Subtract a temperature of 5.2°C from the temperature 75.46°C.

75.46 − 5.2 = 70.26

5.2 has the fewest digits after the decimal, so it is the least precise measurement. Since the last digit of the answer is 6, round up to 3. The most precise difference between the measurements is 70.3°C.

Practice

Add 26.4 m to 8.37 m. Round your answer according to the precision of the measurements.

Significant figures are the number of nonzero digits in a measurement. Zeroes between nonzero digits are also significant. For example, the measurements 12,500 L, 0.125 cm, and 2.05 kg all have three significant figures. When you multiply and divide measurements, the one with the fewest significant figures determines the number of significant figures in your answer.

Example

Multiply 110 g by 5.75 g.

110 × 5.75 = 632.5

Because 110 has only two significant figures, round the answer to 630 g.

Scientific Notation

A **factor** is a number that divides into another number with no remainder. In the example, the number 3 is used as a factor four times.

An **exponent** tells how many times a number is used as a factor. For example, $3 \times 3 \times 3 \times 3$ can be written as 3^4. The exponent ^{4} indicates that the number 3 is used as a factor four times. Another way of expressing this is to say that 81 is equal to 3 to the fourth power.

Example

$$3^4 = 3 \times 3 \times 3 \times 3 = 81$$

Scientific notation uses exponents and powers of ten to write very large or very small numbers in shorter form. When you write a number in scientific notation, you write the number as two factors. The first factor is any number between 1 and 10. The second factor is a power of 10, such as 10^3 or 10^6.

Example

The average distance between the planet Mercury and the sun is 58,000,000 km. To write the first factor in scientific notation, insert a decimal point in the original number so that you have a number between 1 and 10. In the case of 58,000,000, the number is 5.8.

To determine the power of 10, count the number of places that the decimal point moved. In this case, it moved 7 places.

$$58,000,000 \text{ km} = 5.8 \times 10^7 \text{ km}$$

Practice

Express 6,590,000 in scientific notation.

Reading Comprehension Skills

Each section in your textbook introduces a Target Reading Skill. You will improve your reading comprehension by using the Target Reading Skills described below.

Using Prior Knowledge

Your prior knowledge is what you already know before you begin to read about a topic. Building on what you already know gives you a head start on learning new information. Before you begin a new assignment, think about what you know. You might look at the headings and the visuals to spark your memory. You can list what you know. Then, as you read, consider questions like these.

- How does what you learn relate to what you know?
- How did something you already know help you learn something new?
- Did your original ideas agree with what you have just learned?

Asking Questions

Asking yourself questions is an excellent way to focus on and remember new information in your textbook. For example, you can turn the text headings into questions. Then your questions can guide you to identify the important information as you read. Look at these examples:

Heading: Using Seismographic Data

Question: How are seismographic data used?

Heading: Kinds of Faults

Question: What are the kinds of faults?

You do not have to limit your questions to text headings. Ask questions about anything that you need to clarify or that will help you understand the content. *What* and *how* are probably the most common question words, but you may also ask *why, who, when,* or *where* questions.

Previewing Visuals

Visuals are photographs, graphs, tables, diagrams, and illustrations. Visuals contain important information. Before you read, look at visuals and their labels and captions. This preview will help you prepare for what you will be reading.

Often you will be asked what you want to learn about a visual. For example, after you look at the normal fault diagram below, you might ask: What is the movement along a normal fault? Questions about visuals give you a purpose for reading—to answer your questions.

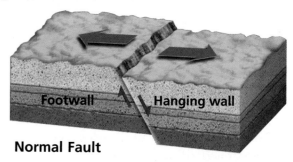

Footwall   Hanging wall

Normal Fault

Outlining

An outline shows the relationship between main ideas and supporting ideas. An outline has a formal structure. You write the main ideas, called topics, next to Roman numerals. The supporting ideas, called subtopics, are written under the main ideas and labeled A, B, C, and so on. An outline looks like this:

Technology and Society
I. Technology through history
II. The impact of technology on society
A.
B.

Identifying Main Ideas

When you are reading science material, it is important to try to understand the ideas and concepts that are in a passage. Each paragraph has a lot of information and detail. Good readers try to identify the most important—or biggest—idea in every paragraph or section. That's the main idea. The other information in the paragraph supports or further explains the main idea.

Sometimes main ideas are stated directly. In this book, some main ideas are identified for you as key concepts. These are printed in bold-face type. However, you must identify other main ideas yourself. In order to do this, you must identify all the ideas within a paragraph or section. Then ask yourself which idea is big enough to include all the other ideas.

Comparing and Contrasting

When you compare and contrast, you examine the similarities and differences between things. You can compare and contrast in a Venn diagram or in a table.

Venn Diagram A Venn diagram consists of two overlapping circles. In the space where the circles overlap, you write the characteristics that the two items have in common. In one of the circles outside the area of overlap, you write the differing features or characteristics of one of the items. In the other circle outside the area of overlap, you write the differing characteristics of the other item.

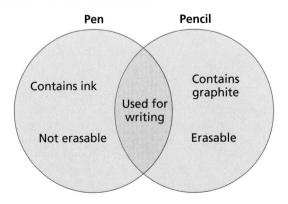

Pen   Pencil

Contains ink   Contains graphite
        Used for
        writing
Not erasable   Erasable

Table In a compare/contrast table, you list the characteristics or features to be compared across the top of the table. Then list the items to be compared in the left column. Complete the table by filling in information about each characteristic or feature.

Blood Vessel	Function	Structure of Wall
Artery	Carries blood away from heart	
Capillary		
Vein		

Identifying Supporting Evidence

A hypothesis is a possible explanation for observations made by scientists or an answer to a scientific question. Scientists must carry out investigations and gather evidence that either supports or disproves the hypothesis.

Identifying the supporting evidence for a hypothesis or theory can help you understand the hypothesis or theory. Evidence consists of facts—information whose accuracy can be confirmed by testing or observation.

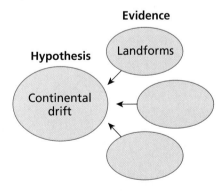

Evidence

Hypothesis   Landforms

Continental
drift

Sequencing

A sequence is the order in which a series of events occurs. A flowchart or a cycle diagram can help you visualize a sequence.

Flowchart To make a flowchart, write a brief description of each step or event in a box. Place the boxes in order, with the first event at the top of the chart. Then draw an arrow to connect each step or event to the next.

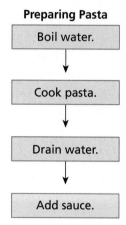

Preparing Pasta

Boil water.
↓
Cook pasta.
↓
Drain water.
↓
Add sauce.

Cycle Diagram A cycle diagram shows a sequence that is continuous, or cyclical. A continuous sequence does not have an end because when the final event is over, the first event begins again. To create a cycle diagram, write the starting event in a box placed at the top of a page in the center. Then, moving in a clockwise direction, write each event in a box in its proper sequence. Draw arrows that connect each event to the one that occurs next.

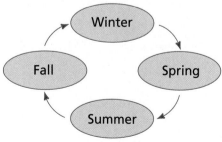

Seasons of the Year

Winter → Spring → Summer → Fall → Winter

Relating Cause and Effect

Science involves many cause-and-effect relationships. A cause makes something happen. An effect is what happens. When you recognize that one event causes another, you are relating cause and effect.

Words like *cause, because, effect, affect,* and *result* often signal a cause or an effect. Sometimes an effect can have more than one cause, or a cause can produce several effects.

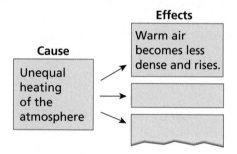

Cause

Unequal heating of the atmosphere

Effects

Warm air becomes less dense and rises.

Concept Mapping

Concept maps are useful tools for organizing information on any topic. A concept map begins with a main idea or core concept and shows how the idea can be subdivided into related subconcepts or smaller ideas.

You construct a concept map by placing concepts (usually nouns) in ovals and connecting them with linking words (usually verbs). The biggest concept or idea is placed in an oval at the top of the map. Related concepts are arranged in ovals below the big idea. The linking words connect the ovals.

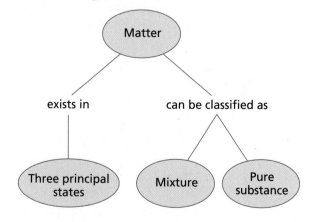

Matter
— exists in → Three principal states
— can be classified as → Mixture, Pure substance

Building Vocabulary

Knowing the meaning of these prefixes, suffixes, and roots will help you understand the meaning of words you do not recognize.

Word Origins Many science words come to English from other languages, such as Greek and Latin. By learning the meaning of a few common Greek and Latin roots, you can determine the meaning of unfamiliar science words.

Prefixes A prefix is a word part that is added at the beginning of a root or base word to change its meaning.

Suffixes A suffix is a word part that is added at the end of a root word to change the meaning.

Greek and Latin Roots		
Greek Roots	**Meaning**	**Example**
ast-	star	astronaut
geo-	Earth	geology
metron-	measure	kilometer
opt-	eye	optician
photo-	light	photograph
scop-	see	microscope
therm-	heat	thermostat
Latin Roots	**Meaning**	**Example**
aqua-	water	aquarium
aud-	hear	auditorium
duc-, duct-	lead	conduct
flect-	bend	reflect
fract-, frag-	break	fracture
ject-	throw	reject
luc-	light	lucid
spec-	see	inspect

Prefixes and Suffixes		
Prefix	**Meaning**	**Example**
com-, con-	with	communicate, concert
de-	from; down	decay
di-	two	divide
ex-, exo-	out	exhaust
in-, im-	in, into; not	inject, impossible
re-	again; back	reflect, recall
trans-	across	transfer
Suffix	**Meaning**	**Example**
-al	relating to	natural
-er, -or	one who	teacher, doctor
-ist	one who practices	scientist
-ity	state of	equality
-ology	study of	biology
-tion, -sion	state or quality of	reaction, tension

Safety Symbols

These symbols warn of possible dangers in the laboratory and remind you to work carefully.

 Safety Goggles Wear safety goggles to protect your eyes in any activity involving chemicals, flames or heating, or glassware.

 Lab Apron Wear a laboratory apron to protect your skin and clothing from damage.

 Breakage Handle breakable materials, such as glassware, with care. Do not touch broken glassware.

 Heat-Resistant Gloves Use an oven mitt or other hand protection when handling hot materials such as hot plates or hot glassware.

 Plastic Gloves Wear disposable plastic gloves when working with harmful chemicals and organisms. Keep your hands away from your face, and dispose of the gloves according to your teacher's instructions.

 Heating Use a clamp or tongs to pick up hot glassware. Do not touch hot objects with your bare hands.

 Flames Before you work with flames, tie back loose hair and clothing. Follow instructions from your teacher about lighting and extinguishing flames.

 No Flames When using flammable materials, make sure there are no flames, sparks, or other exposed heat sources present.

 Corrosive Chemical Avoid getting acid or other corrosive chemicals on your skin or clothing or in your eyes. Do not inhale the vapors. Wash your hands after the activity.

 Poison Do not let any poisonous chemical come into contact with your skin, and do not inhale its vapors. Wash your hands when you are finished with the activity.

 Fumes Work in a ventilated area when harmful vapors may be involved. Avoid inhaling vapors directly. Only test an odor when directed to do so by your teacher, and use a wafting motion to direct the vapor toward your nose.

 Sharp Object Scissors, scalpels, knives, needles, pins, and tacks can cut your skin. Always direct a sharp edge or point away from yourself and others.

 Animal Safety Treat live or preserved animals or animal parts with care to avoid harming the animals or yourself. Wash your hands when you are finished with the activity.

 Plant Safety Handle plants only as directed by your teacher. If you are allergic to certain plants, tell your teacher; do not do an activity involving those plants. Avoid touching harmful plants such as poison ivy. Wash your hands when you are finished with the activity.

 Electric Shock To avoid electric shock, never use electrical equipment around water, or when the equipment is wet or your hands are wet. Be sure cords are untangled and cannot trip anyone. Unplug equipment not in use.

 Physical Safety When an experiment involves physical activity, avoid injuring yourself or others. Alert your teacher if there is any reason you should not participate.

 Disposal Dispose of chemicals and other laboratory materials safely. Follow the instructions from your teacher.

 Hand Washing Wash your hands thoroughly when finished with the activity. Use soap and warm water. Rinse well.

 General Safety Awareness When this symbol appears, follow the instructions provided. When you are asked to develop your own procedure in a lab, have your teacher approve your plan before you go further.

Science Safety Rules

General Precautions

Follow all instructions. Never perform activities without the approval and supervision of your teacher. Do not engage in horseplay. Never eat or drink in the laboratory. Keep work areas clean and uncluttered.

Dress Code

Wear safety goggles whenever you work with chemicals, glassware, heat sources such as burners, or any substance that might get into your eyes. If you wear contact lenses, notify your teacher.

Wear a lab apron or coat whenever you work with corrosive chemicals or substances that can stain. Wear disposable plastic gloves when working with organisms and harmful chemicals. Tie back long hair. Remove or tie back any article of clothing or jewelry that can hang down and touch chemicals, flames, or equipment. Roll up long sleeves. Never wear open shoes or sandals.

First Aid

Report all accidents, injuries, or fires to your teacher, no matter how minor. Be aware of the location of the first-aid kit, emergency equipment such as the fire extinguisher and fire blanket, and the nearest telephone. Know whom to contact in an emergency.

Heating and Fire Safety

Keep all combustible materials away from flames. When heating a substance in a test tube, make sure that the mouth of the tube is not pointed at you or anyone else. Never heat a liquid in a closed container. Use an oven mitt to pick up a container that has been heated.

Using Chemicals Safely

Never put your face near the mouth of a container that holds chemicals. Never touch, taste, or smell a chemical unless your teacher tells you to.

Use only those chemicals needed in the activity. Keep all containers closed when chemicals are not being used. Pour all chemicals over the sink or a container, not over your work surface. Dispose of excess chemicals as instructed by your teacher.

Be extra careful when working with acids or bases. When mixing an acid and water, always pour the water into the container first and then add the acid to the water. Never pour water into an acid. Wash chemical spills and splashes immediately with plenty of water.

Using Glassware Safely

If glassware is broken or chipped, notify your teacher immediately. Never handle broken or chipped glass with your bare hands.

Never force glass tubing or thermometers into a rubber stopper or rubber tubing. Have your teacher insert the glass tubing or thermometer if required for an activity.

Using Sharp Instruments

Handle sharp instruments with extreme care. Never cut material toward you; cut away from you.

Animal and Plant Safety

Never perform experiments that cause pain, discomfort, or harm to animals. Only handle animals if absolutely necessary. If you know that you are allergic to certain plants, molds, or animals, tell your teacher before doing an activity in which these are used. Wash your hands thoroughly after any activity involving animals, animal parts, plants, plant parts, or soil.

During field work, wear long pants, long sleeves, socks, and closed shoes. Avoid poisonous plants and fungi as well as plants with thorns.

End-of-Experiment Rules

Unplug all electrical equipment. Clean up your work area. Dispose of waste materials as instructed by your teacher. Wash your hands after every experiment.

English and Spanish Glossary

A

acid rain Rain that contains more acid than normal. (p. 24)
lluvia ácida Lluvia que contiene más acidez de la normal.

air mass A huge body of air that has similar temperature, humidity, and air pressure at any given height.
masa de aire Gran volumen de aire que tiene temperatura, humedad y presión similares en todos sus puntos. (p. 72)

air pressure The pressure caused by the weight of a column of air pushing down on an area. (p. 11)
presión de aire Presión causada por el peso de una columna de aire que empuja hacia abajo en una área.

altitude Elevation above sea level. (p. 13)
altitud Elevación sobre el nivel del mar.

anemometer An instrument used to measure wind speed. (p. 47)
anemómetro Instrumento que se usa para medir la velocidad del viento.

aneroid barometer An instrument that measures changes in air pressure without using a liquid. (p. 12)
barómetro aneroide Instrumento que mide los cambios en la presión del aire sin usar líquido.

anticyclone A high-pressure center of dry air. (p. 78)
anticiclón Centro de aire seco de alta presión.

atmosphere The envelope of gases that surrounds Earth. (p. 6)
atmósfera Capa de gases que rodea la Tierra.

B

barometer An instrument used to measure changes in air pressure. (p. 12)
barómetro Instrumento que se usa para medir cambios en la presión del aire.

C

chlorofluorocarbons Chlorine compounds that are the main cause of ozone depletion. (p. 140)
clorofluorocarbonos Compuestos de cloro que son la causa principal de la destrucción del ozono.

cirrus Wispy, feathery clouds made of ice crystals that form at high levels. (p. 58)
cirros Nubes parecidas a plumas o pinceladas blancas formadas principalmente por cristales de hielo que se crean a grandes altitudes.

climate The average, year-after-year conditions of temperature, precipitation, winds, and clouds in an area. (p. 108)
clima Promedio, año a año, de las condiciones de temperatura, precipitación, viento y nubes en una área.

condensation The process by which molecules of water vapor in the air become liquid water. (p. 57)
condensación Proceso por el cual las moléculas de vapor de agua en el aire se convierten en agua líquida.

conduction The direct transfer of thermal energy from one substance to another that it is touching.
conducción Transferencia directa de energía térmica de una sustancia a otra que la toca. (p. 44)

continental (air mass) A dry air mass that forms over land. (p. 73)
masa de aire continental Masa de aire seco que se forma sobre la tierra.

continental climate The climate of the centers of continents, with cold winters and warm or hot summers. (p. 110)
clima continental Clima del centro de los continentes, con inviernos fríos y veranos templados o calurosos.

convection The transfer of thermal energy by the movement of a fluid. (p. 44)
convección Transferencia de energía térmica por el movimiento de un líquido.

convection currents The circulation of a fluid as it alternately heats up and cools down. (p. 44)
corrientes de convección Circulación de un líquido a medida que se calienta y se enfría alternadamente.

Coriolis effect The change that Earth's rotation causes in the motion of objects and that explains how winds curve. (p. 49)
efecto de Coriolis Cambio que causa la rotación de la Tierra en el movimiento de objetos y que explica cómo se curvan los vientos.

cumulus Fluffy, white clouds, usually with flat bottoms, that look like rounded piles of cotton.
cúmulos Nubes blancas, que normalmente tienen la parte inferior plana, que parecen grandes masas de algodón esponjosas y redondas. (p. 58)

cyclone A swirling center of low air pressure. (p. 78)
ciclón Centro de un remolino de aire de baja presión.

density The amount of mass of a substance in a given volume. (p. 11)
densidad Cantidad de masa de una sustancia en un volumen dado.

desert An arid region that on average receives less than 25 centimeters of rain per year. (p. 122)
desierto Región árida que, como promedio, recibe menos de 25 centímetros de lluvia al año.

dew point The temperature at which condensation begins. (p. 57)
punto de rocío Temperatura a la que comienza la condensación.

droughts Long periods of low precipitation. (p. 65)
sequía Largos períodos de poca precipitación.

El Niño A climate event in the Pacific Ocean during which winds shift and push warm water toward the coast of South America. (p. 136)
El Niño Fenómeno climático en el océano Pacífico durante el cual los vientos se desvían y empujan la superficie más templada del agua hacia la costa de América del Sur.

electromagnetic waves Waves that transfer electric and magnetic energy through the vacuum of space.
ondas electromagnéticas Ondas que transfieren energía eléctrica y magnética a través del vacío.(p. 36)

evaporation The process by which water molecules in liquid water escape into the air as water vapor.
evaporación Proceso por el cual las moléculas de agua líquida son liberadas al aire como vapor de agua. (p. 54)

exosphere The outer layer of the thermosphere.
exosfera Capa externa de la termosfera. (p. 21)

front The boundary where unlike air masses meet but do not mix. (p. 75)
frente Límite en donde se encuentran masas de aire diferentes, pero no se mezclan.

global warming A gradual increase in the average temperature of Earth's atmosphere. (p. 137)
calentamiento global Aumento gradual en la temperatura promedio de la atmósfera terrestre.

global winds Winds that blow steadily from specific directions over long distances. (p. 49)
vientos globales Vientos que soplan constantemente desde direcciones específicas por largas distancias.

greenhouse effect The process by which heat is trapped in the atmosphere by gases that form a "blanket" around Earth. (p. 39)
efecto invernadero Proceso por el cual el calor queda atrapado en la atmósfera por gases que forman una "manta" alrededor de la Tierra.

greenhouse gases Gases in the atmosphere that trap energy. (p. 137)
gases de invernadero Gases de la atmósfera que atrapan la energía.

heat The transfer of thermal energy from one object to another because of a difference in temperature.
calor Transferencia de energía térmica de un objeto a otro debido a una diferencia de temperatura. (p. 44)

humid subtropical A wet and warm climate found on the edges of the tropics. (p. 124)
subtropical húmedo Clima húmedo y templado que se encuentra en los límites de los trópicos.

humidity The amount of water vapor in a given volume of air. (p. 55)
humedad Cantidad de vapor de agua en un volumen de aire definido.

hurricane A tropical storm that has winds of about 119 kilometers per hour or higher. (p. 86)
huracán Tormenta tropical que tiene vientos de cerca de 119 kilómetros por hora o más.

ice ages Cold periods in Earth's history during which glaciers covered large parts of the surface. (p. 132)
glaciaciones Períodos fríos en la historia de la Tierra durante los cuales los glaciares cubrieron grandes partes de la superficie.

infrared radiation Electromagnetic waves with wavelengths that are longer than visible light but shorter than microwaves. (p. 37)
radiación infrarroja Ondas electromagnéticas con longitudes de onda más largas que la luz visible, pero más cortas que las microondas.

ionosphere The lower part of the thermosphere.
ionosfera Parte inferior de la termosfera. (p. 21)

isobar A line on a weather map that joins places that have the same air pressure. (p. 96)
isobara Línea en un mapa del tiempo que une lugares que tienen la misma presión de aire.

isotherm A line on a weather map that joins places that have the same temperature. (p. 96)
isoterma Línea en un mapa del tiempo que une lugares que tienen la misma temperatura.

jet streams Bands of high-speed winds about 10 kilometers above Earth's surface. (p. 52)
corriente de chorro Bandas de vientos de alta velocidad a unos 10 kilómetros sobre la superficie de la Tierra.

La Niña A climate event in the eastern Pacific Ocean in which surface waters are colder than normal.
La Niña Fenómeno climático que ocurre en la parte este del océano Pacífico, en el cual las aguas superficiales están más frías que lo normal. (p. 136)

land breeze The flow of air from land to a body of water. (p. 48)
brisa terrestre Flujo de aire desde la tierra a una masa de agua.

leeward The side of a mountain range that faces away from the oncoming wind. (p. 112)
sotavento Lado de una cadena montañosa que está resguardado del viento.

lightning A sudden spark, or energy discharge, caused when electrical charges jump between parts of a cloud, between nearby clouds, or between a cloud and the ground. (p. 81)
rayo Chispa repentina o descarga de energía causada por cargas eléctricas que saltan entre partes de una nube, entre nubes cercanas o entre una nube y la tierra.

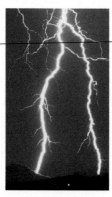

local winds Winds that blow over short distances.
vientos locales Vientos que soplan por distancias cortas. (p. 48)

marine climate The climate of some coastal regions, with relatively warm winters and cool summers.
clima marino Clima de algunas regiones costeras, con inviernos relativamente templados y veranos fríos. (p. 110)

maritime (air mass) A humid air mass that forms over oceans. (p. 73)
masa de aire marítima Masa de aire húmedo que se forma sobre los océanos.

mercury barometer An instrument that measures changes in air pressure, consisting of a glass tube partially filled with mercury, with its open end resting in a dish of mercury. (p. 12)
barómetro de mercurio Instrumento que mide los cambios en la presión del aire; consiste de un tubo de vidrio parcialmente lleno de mercurio con su extremo abierto posado en un recipiente con mercurio.

mesosphere The layer of Earth's atmosphere immediately above the stratosphere. (p. 20)
mesosfera Capa de la atmósfera de la Tierra inmediatamente sobre la estratosfera.

meteorologists Scientists who study the causes of weather and try to predict it. (p. 93)
meteorólogos Científicos que estudian las causas del tiempo e intentan predecirlo.

microclimate Climate conditions within a small area that differ from those in the surrounding area.(p. 108)
microclima Condiciones climáticas en una área pequeña que son diferentes del clima de las áreas de alrededor.

monsoon Sea or land breeze over a large region that changes direction with the seasons. (p. 113)
monzón Vientos marinos o terrestres que soplan sobre una extensa región y cambian de dirección según las estaciones.

occluded Cut off, as in a front where a warm air mass is caught between two cooler air masses. (p. 77)
ocluido Aislado o cerrado, como cuando la masa de aire cálido queda atrapada entre dos masas de aire más frío.

ozone A form of oxygen that has three oxygen atoms in each molecule instead of the usual two. (p. 7)
ozono Forma de oxígeno que tiene tres átomos de oxígeno en cada molécula en vez de las dos normales.

P

permafrost Permanently frozen soil found in the tundra climate region. (p. 126)
permagélido Suelo permanentemente helado que se encuentra en la región climática de la tundra.

photochemical smog A brownish haze that is a mixture of ozone and other chemicals, formed when pollutants react with each other in the presence of sunlight. (p. 24)
neblina tóxica fotoquímica Densa bruma pardusca que es una mezcla de ozono y otras sustancias químicas, que se forma cuando los contaminantes reaccionan entre ellos en presencia de luz solar.

polar (air mass) A cold air mass that forms north of 50° north latitude or south of 50° south latitude and has high air pressure. (p. 73)
masa de aire polar Masa de aire frío que se forma al norte de los 50° de latitud norte o al sur de los 50° de latitud sur y que tiene presión alta.

polar zones The areas near both poles, from about 66.5° to 90° north and 66.5° to 90° south latitudes.
zona polar Áreas cercanas a los polos, desde unos 66.5° a 90° de latitud norte y 66.5° a 90° de latitud sur. (p. 109)

pollutants Harmful substances in air, water, or soil.
contaminantes Sustancias dañinas en el aire, agua o suelo. (p. 23)

precipitation Any form of water that falls from clouds and reaches Earth's surface. (p. 61)
precipitación Cualquier forma de agua que cae desde las nubes y llega a la superficie de la Tierra.

pressure The amount of force pushing on an area.
presión Cantidad de fuerza de empuje en una área. (p. 11)

psychrometer An instrument used to measure relative humidity. (p. 56)
psicrómetro Instrumento que se usa para medir la humedad relativa.

R

radiation The direct transfer of energy by electromagnetic waves. (p. 36)
radiación Transferencia directa de energía por ondas electromagnéticas.

rain forest A forest in the tropical wet climate zone.
bosque tropical Selva ubicada dentro de la zona de clima tropical húmedo. (p. 119)

rain gauge An instrument used to measure precipitation. (p. 64)
pluviómetro Instrumento que se usa para medir la precipitación.

relative humidity The percentage of water vapor in the air compared to the maximum amount of water vapor that air can contain at a particular temperature. (p. 55)
humedad relativa Porcentaje de vapor de agua en el aire comparado con la cantidad máxima de vapor de agua que puede contener el aire a una temperatura particular.

S

savanna A tropical grassland with clumps of trees. (p. 119)
sabana Pradera tropical con grupos de árboles.

scattering Reflection of light in all directions. (p. 38)
dispersión Reflexión de la luz en todas las direcciones.

sea breeze The flow of cooler air from over an ocean or lake toward land. (p. 48)
brisa marina Flujo de aire más frío desde un océano o lago hacia la costa.

steppe A prairie or grassland found in semiarid regions.
estepa Pradera o pastizal que se encuentra en las regiones semiáridas. (p. 122)

storm A violent disturbance in the atmosphere. (p. 80)
tormenta Alteración violenta en la atmósfera.

storm surge A "dome" of water that sweeps across the coast where a hurricane lands. (p. 87)
marejadas "Cúpula" de agua que se desplaza a lo largo de la costa donde aterriza un huracán.

stratosphere The second-lowest layer of Earth's atmosphere. (p. 19)
estratosfera Segunda capa inferior de la atmósfera de la Tierra.

stratus Clouds that form in flat layers and often cover much of the sky. (p. 58)
estratos Nubes que forman capas planas y que a menudo cubren gran parte del cielo.

subarctic A climate zone that lies north of the humid continental climates. (p. 125)
subártico Zona climática que se encuentra al norte de los climas continentales húmedos.

sunspots Relatively dark, cool regions on the surface of the sun. (p. 133)
manchas solares Regiones relativamente frías y oscuras en la superficie del Sol.

 T

temperate zones The areas between the tropical and the polar zones. (p. 109)
áreas templadas Áreas entre las zonas tropical y polar.

temperature A measure of how hot or cold an object is compared to a reference point. (p. 43)
temperatura Medida de lo caliente o frío que está un objeto comparado con un punto de referencia.

thermal energy The total energy of motion in the particles of a substance. (p. 43)
energía térmica Energía de movimiento total en las partículas de una sustancia.

thermometer An instrument used to measure temperature. (p. 43)
termómetro Instrumento que se usa para medir la temperatura.

thermosphere The outermost layer of Earth's atmosphere. (p. 20)
termosfera Capa exterior de la atmósfera de la Tierra.

thunderstorm A small storm often accompanied by heavy precipitation and frequent thunder and lightning.
tronada Pequeña tormenta acompañada de fuerte precipitación y frecuentes rayos y truenos. (p. 81)

tornado A rapidly whirling, funnel-shaped cloud that reaches down to touch Earth's surface. (p. 83)
tornado Nube con forma de embudo que gira rápidamente y que desciende hasta la superficie terrestre.

tropical (air mass) A warm air mass that forms in the tropics and has low air pressure. (p. 73)
masa de aire tropical Masa de aire templado que se forma en los trópicos y tiene presión baja.

tropical zone The area near the equator, between about 23.5° north latitude and 23.5° south latitude.
zona tropical Área cercana al ecuador, entre aproximadamente los 23.5° de latitud norte y los 23.5° de latitud sur. (p. 109)

troposphere The lowest layer of Earth's atmosphere.
troposfera Capa más inferior de la atmósfera de la Tierra. (p. 18)

tundra A polar climate region, with short, cool summers and bitterly cold winters. (p. 126)
tundra Región climática polar que tiene veranos cortos y fríos, e inviernos extremadamente fríos.

 U

ultraviolet radiation Electromagnetic waves with wavelengths that are shorter than visible light but longer than X-rays. (p. 37)
radiación ultravioleta Ondas electromagnéticas con longitudes de onda más cortas que la luz visible, pero más largas que los rayos X.

 W

water cycle The continual movement of water among Earth's atmosphere, oceans, and land surface through evaporation, condensation, and precipitation. (p. 54)
ciclo del agua Movimiento continuo de agua entre la atmósfera, los océanos y la superficie de la Tierra mediante la evaporación, condensación y precipitación.

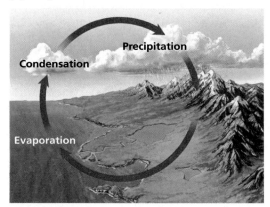

Precipitation

Condensation

Evaporation

water vapor Water in the form of a gas. (p. 8)
vapor de agua Agua en forma de gas.

weather The condition of Earth's atmosphere at a particular time and place. (p. 6)
tiempo meteorológico Condición de la atmósfera de la Tierra en un tiempo y lugar determinados.

wind The horizontal movement of air from an area of high pressure to an area of lower pressure. (p. 47)
viento Movimiento horizontal de aire de una área de alta presión a una área de menor presión.

wind-chill factor A measure of cooling combining temperature and wind speed. (p. 47)
factor de sensación térmica Medida de enfriamiento que combina la temperatura y la velocidad del viento.

windward The side of a mountain range that faces the oncoming wind. (p. 112)
barlovento Lado de una cadena montañosa donde pega el viento de frente.

A

acid rain *24*
air masses **72–77**, 112
air pollution **22–25**
    acid rain and *24*
    cars and 25, 28–29
air pressure 10, *11,* 12–13, 49, 78–79, 96
    altitude and *13*
    falling 93
    winds caused by differences in 47
air quality **22–25**
altitude *13,* 127
    air pressure and 13
    climates and 110
    density and 14
altocumulus clouds 60
altostratus clouds 60
anemometer 47
aneroid barometers **12,** *13*
Antarctica 146–151
anticyclones *78,* 79
area 164
arid climate 122
atmosphere **6–9.** *See also* **air pressure**
    composition of 7–8
    energy in 38
    global changes in 135–141
    layers of 16–21
    properties of air 11
    water vapor in 8, 54–60
aurora borealis 21
automated weather stations 95

B

barometer *12–13,* 18
brainstorming 158
"butterfly effect" 97

C

calculating, skill of 155
carbon dioxide 8, 138
cars, air pollution and 25, 28–29
Celsius scale 43, **155**
chaparral 124
chlorofluorocarbons (CFCs) 140
cirrocumulus clouds 58
cirrus clouds 58, *59,* 93
classifying, skill of 153

climate **108–115**
    altitude and 110
    continental **110**
    marine **110,** 111
    precipitation and 112–113
    temperature and 109–111
climate change
    causes of 133–134
    ice ages *132,* 133
    long-term 130–134
    short-term 135, 136
climate graphs *119*
climate regions 108, **118–127**
    dry 122
    highlands 127
    polar 126
    temperate continental 125
    temperate marine 123–124
    tropical rainy 119
clouds 8. *See also* **storms**
    cyclones and *78*
    formation of 57
    precipitation and **61,** 62
    storms and 81, 83
    types of 58, *59,* 60
cloud seeding *64*
cold fronts 76
communicating, skill of 153
conclusion 157
condensation 57
conduction 42, **44,** *45*
constraint 158
continental air masses 73
continental climates **110,** 125
continents, climate changes due to movement of 134
controlled experiment 157
convection **44,** *45*
convection currents **44**
    global 49
    winds and **47**
Coriolis effect *49,* 50, 52, 78
cumulonimbus clouds 58, 93
    hail formed inside 63
    thunderheads 81
    tornadoes formed in *83*
cumulus clouds 58, *59,* 93
cyclones *78,* 79, 86–87

D

data 157
density 11
    altitude and 14

deserts *122*
dew 57
dew point **57,** 76
doldrums 50
Doppler radar 100–101
downdrafts 81
drizzle 62
droughts **64,** 130, 135
    El Niño and *136*
dry climates 122
"dust bowls" 139

E

Earth
    atmosphere of. *See* **atmosphere**
    energy at surface of 39
    position relative to sun, climate changes and 133
    tilted axis of 114, 133
electromagnetic waves 36
El Niño *136*
energy
    in atmosphere 38
    at Earth's surface 39
    from the sun 36–39, 133, 139
    thermal **43**
Environmental Protection Agency (EPA) 25
evacuate 87
evaporation 54
exosphere 21, 94
exponent 167
eye of hurricane 86
eyewall 86

F

factor 167
Fahrenheit scale 43
flash flood 82
floods 82, 135, 136
fog 60
forests 119, 123–125, 127
fossil fuels, burning of 23–25, 28–29, 137–139
fossils 131, 132
fraction 165
freezing rain 62
fronts *75–77*
frost 57
fulgurite 80

Index

Page numbers for key terms are printed in **boldface** type.
Page numbers for illustrations, maps, and charts are printed in *italics*.

G

gases
in Earth's atmosphere 6, 7–8
greenhouse **137**
glaciers 132
global warming and melting of 139
global warming **137**–139
global winds **49**, 50–52
gram (g) **155**
grassland 122
greenhouse effect **39**, 137
greenhouse gases **137**
Gulf Stream 111

H

hail 63, 81
heat **44**
heat transfer *42–45*
highlands 127
high-pressure centers 78, *79*
horse latitudes 50
humid continental climate 125
humidity **55**–56, 73–74
humid subtropical climate 124
hurricanes *86*–87
"hurricane warning" 87
"hurricane watch" 87
hydrocarbons 23
hypothesis **156**

I

ice ages *132*, 133
ice cap climates 126
inches of mercury 13
inferring, skill of 152
infrared radiation *37*–39, 44
ionosphere 21
isobars 96
isotherms 96

J

jet streams *52,* 75

K

Köppen, Wladimir 118

L

laboratory safety 172–173
lake breeze 48
lake-effect snow 88
land breeze **48**, 113
La Niña *136*
latitude **50**, 109
layers of atmosphere 16–21
leeward side of mountains 112
lightning **81**, 82
liter (L) **154**
local winds *48*
London-type smog 24
low-pressure area 78, *79*, 86, 93

M

mackerel sky 58
making models, skill of 153
manipulated variable **157**
marine climates 110, 111
marine west coast climate 123
maritime air masses **73,** 74
mass of air 11
mean **163**
median **163**
Mediterranean climate 124
mercury barometers *12*
mesosphere *17*, **20**
meteoroids 20
meteorologists x–3, *93*
technology used by 94–95, 97
meter (m) **154**
microclimate **108**
millibars 13
mist 62
mode **163**
monsoons *113*
mountain ranges 110, 112

N

National Weather Service 13, 93, 95, 96
newspaper weather maps 97, *98*
nimbostratus clouds 58
nitrogen oxides 24
Northern Lights 21

O

observing, skill of 152
occluded fronts 77

ocean currents 111, 136
oceans, temperature and 110
operational definition **157**
oxygen in atmosphere 7, 9
ozone **7**, 19, 24, 38, 140
ozone hole 140, 141
ozone layer 19, 38, 140, *141*

P

Pangaea 134
particles
in atmosphere 8
cloud formation and 57
percentage **166**
permafrost **126**
photochemical smog 24
polar air masses **73,** 74
polar easterlies 52
polar front 52
polar zones *109,* 111
pollen, as evidence of climate change 131
pollutants **22**, 23–25. *See also* air pollution
prairie 122
precipitation **61**
climate regions classified by 118, 120–121
factors affecting 112–113
measuring 64–65
modifying 64
types of 62–63
precision **167**
predicting, skill of 152
prevailing westerlies 50, 75
prevailing winds 75, 112
probability **163**
proportion **166**
prototype 159
psychrometer *56*
public transportation 25

R

radar, Doppler 100–101
radiation **36**, *37*
heat transfer by 44, *45*
infrared *37*, 38, 39, 44
ultraviolet 19, *37*, 38, 140
visible light 37, 38
radio waves 21
rain 24, 61, 62, 81, 82
rain forests *119*

rain gauge 64, **65**
rain shadow 112, 123
ratio 166
relative humidity **55**
   measuring 56
responding variable **157**

S

safety
   hurricane 87
   in the laboratory 172–173
   snowstorm 89
   thunderstorm 82
   tornado 85
satellites, weather 94
saturated air 55
savannas 119
scattering 38
scientific notation 167
sea breeze 48
seasons 114, *115*
second (time) 155
semiarid climate 122
significant figures 167
SI units of measurement 154
sleet 62
smog 24
snow 63
   lake-effect 88
   snowfall measurement 64
snowstorms 88–89
solar energy 36–39, 139
   climate changes and 133
stationary fronts 77
steppe 122
storms 80–89
storm surge 87
stratosphere *17*, **19**
   ozone in 19, 38, 140
stratus clouds 58, *59*, 62
subarctic climates *125*
subtropical climate, humid
   124
sulfur oxides 24
sun, energy from 36–39, 133,
   139
sunspots 133

T

technology, weather 94–95, 97
temperate climates 123–125
temperate zones *109*

temperature 18–21, **43**, 55, 73
   air masses classified by
      73–74
   climate and 109–111
   climate regions classified by
      118, *120–121*
   factors affecting 109–111
   global warming and
      137–139
   greenhouse effect and **39**
   layers of atmosphere
      classified by changes in
      16–21
   measuring 43
temperature scales 43
Terra satellite 19, 94
thermal energy **43**
thermometer **43**, 56
thermosphere *17*, **20**–21
thunder 81
thunderheads 81
thunderstorms *81*–83
TIROS-1 (satellite) 19, 94
"tornado alley" 84
tornadoes *83*–85
"tornado warning" 85
"tornado watch" 85
trade-off 158
trade winds 50, 87
tree rings, climate change
   indicated by 131
tropical air masses 73, 74
tropical climates 119
tropical zone *109*
troposphere *17*, **18**, 24, 44
troubleshooting 159
tundra climate *126*
typhoons 86

U

ultraviolet radiation *37*, 38
   ozone layer and protection
      from 19, 140
updrafts 81

V

variable 157
visible light 37
   scattered 38
volcanic activity, climate
   changes and 133

W

warm fronts 77
water, climate and distance
   from large bodies of 110
water cycle **54**, *55*
waterspout 83
water vapor *8*
   in atmosphere 8, 54–60
   cloud formation from
      condensation of **57**
   humidity as measure of
      55–56
   in prevailing winds 112
weather **6**. *See also* **air masses**
   anticyclones and **78**, *79*
   climate versus **108**
   cyclones and **78**, *79*
   predicting 92–98
   types of fronts and 76–77
weather balloons 94
weather forecasting 93
   Doppler radar and 100–101
   limits of forecasts 98
   reading weather maps
      96–97, *98*
   technology for 94–95
weather maps 96–101
wind-chill factor 47
winds 46, **47**–52, 112, 113, 136
   air masses moved by 75, 112
   cause of 47
   global **49**, 50–52
   hurricane 86
   local **48**
   measuring 47
   prevailing 50, 75, 112
   seasonal 113
   in tornadoes **83**
wind vane 47
windward side of mountains
   112

Acknowledgments

Grateful acknowledgment is made to the following for copyrighted material:

Acknowledgement for page 150: Excerpt from *Alone* by Richard E. Byrd. Copyright © 1938 by Richard E. Byrd, copyright © renewed 1966 by Marie A. Byrd. Reprinted by permission of Island Press.

Note: Every effort has been made to locate the copyright owner of material reproduced in this component. Omissions brought to our attention will be corrected in subsequent editions.

Staff Credits

Diane Alimena, Michele Angelucci, Scott Andrews, Jennifer Angel, Laura Baselice, Carolyn Belanger, Barbara A. Bertell, Suzanne Biron, Peggy Bliss, Stephanie Bradley, James Brady, Anne M. Bray, Sarah M. Carroll, Kerry Cashman, Jonathan Cheney, Joshua D. Clapper, Lisa J. Clark, Bob Craton, Patricia Cully, Patricia M. Dambry, Kathy Dempsey, Leanne Esterly, Emily Ellen, Thomas Ferreira, Jonathan Fisher, Patricia Fromkin, Paul Gagnon, Kathy Gavilanes, Holly Gordon, Robert Graham, Ellen Granter, Diane Grossman, Barbara Hollingdale, Linda Johnson, Anne Jones, John Judge, Kevin Keane, Kelly Kelliher, Toby Klang, Sue Langan, Russ Lappa, Carolyn Lock, Rebecca Loveys, Constance J. McCarty, Carolyn B. McGuire, Ranida Touranont McKneally, Anne McLaughlin, Eve Melnechuk, Natania Mlawer, Janet Morris, Karyl Murray, Francine Neumann, Baljit Nijjar, Marie Opera, Jill Ort, Kim Ortell, Joan Paley, Dorothy Preston, Maureen Raymond, Laura Ross, Rashid Ross, Siri Schwartzman, Melissa Shustyk, Laurel Smith, Emily Soltanoff, Jennifer A. Teece, Elizabeth Torjussen, Amanda M. Watters, Merce Wilczek, Amy Winchester, Char Lyn Yeakley. **Additional Credits:** Tara Alamilla, Louise Gachet, Allen Gold, Andrea Golden, Terence Hegarty, Etta Jacobs, Meg Montgomery, Stephanie Rogers, Kim Schmidt, Adam Teller, Joan Tobin.

Illustration

Morgan Cain & Associates: 12, 13t, 15, 43, 45t, 51, 61; **Kerry Cashman:** 92, 134; **John Edwards and Associates:** 76, 77, 104l, 114, 115, 142; **GeoSystems Global Corporation:** 88, 90, 96t, 120, 121, 132r; **Andrea Golden:** 2; **Martucci Design:** 96, 97b; **Steve McEntee:** 17, 33, 37, 38, 39, 57, 58, 59, 73, 78, 100, 112, 113, 137; **Richard McMahon:** 53, 65, 83; **Ortelius Design Inc.:** 104r, 109, 113l; **Matthew Pippin:** 11, 30, 68; **Brucie Rosch:** 45b; **Walter Stuart:** 132l; **XNR Productions:** 49, 52, 74, 83b, 86, 111, 140, 141. **All charts and graphs by Matt Mayerchak.**

Photography

Photo Research Paula Wehde
Cover Image top, John Beatty/Getty Images, Inc.; **bottom,** Alamy Images.
Page vi, Jeremy Horner/Corbis; **vii,** Richard Haynes; **viii,** Steve Vidler/SuperStock; **x both,** NASA; **1,** William Wantland/Tom Stack & Associates; **1 inset,** NASA; **2 both,** NASA; **3,** NASA.

Chapter 1
Pages 4–5, Steve Neidorf Photography/Getty Images, Inc.; **5r,** Richard Haynes; **6t,** Russ Lappa; **6b,** NASA/Photo Researchers, Inc.; **7,** Steve Mason/Getty Images, Inc.; **8t,** Tom Bean/DRK Photo; **8b,** Karl H. Switak/Photo Researchers, Inc.; **9l,** Michael Fogden/DRK Photo; **9r,** Gail Shumway/Getty Images, Inc.; **10t,** Russ Lappa; **10b,** Eric A. Kessler; **13t,** Ivan Bucher/Photo Researchers, Inc.; **13b,** Zandria Muench Beraldo/Muench Photography; **14,** Zandria Muench Beraldo/Muench Photography; **16t,** Russ Lappa; **16b,** Steve Vidler/SuperStock; **18l,** The Granger Collection, NY; **18m,** The Granger Collection, NY; **18r,** Bettmann/Corbis; **19l,** Corbis; **19m,** NASA; **19r,** NASA; **21,** Photographer's Choice/Getty Images, Inc.; **22t,** Russ Lappa; **22b,** Liba Taylor/Corbis; **23,** Aaron Haupt/Photo Researchers, Inc.; **24,** Will McIntyre/Photo Researchers, Inc.; **25,** AP/Wide World Photos; **26,** Eric Horan/Getty Images, Inc.; **27,** Richard Haynes; **28l,** Ford Motor Co./AP/Wide World Photos; **28–29,** Rob Francis/Robert Harding World Imagery; **30,** Steve Vidler/SuperStock.

Chapter 2
Pages 34–35, Roy Morsch/Corbis; **35r,** Richard Haynes; **37,** David Lawrence/Panoramic Images; **41,** Richard Haynes; **42t,** Russ Lappa; **42b,** Yang Liu/Corbis; **43,** Russ Lappa; **46t,** Richard Haynes; **46b,** Anna Zieminski/AFP/Getty Images, Inc.; **47,** SPL/Photo Researchers, Inc.; **48 both,** James Schwabel/Panoramic Images; **50,** Austin Brown/Getty Images, Inc.; **54t,** Russ Lappa; **54–55b,** Jeremy Horner/Corbis; **56,** Barry Runk/Grant Heilman/Photography; **57,** Bruce Coleman, Inc.; **58t,** Scott Nielsen/Bruce Coleman, Inc.; **58m,** John Shaw/Bruce Coleman, Inc.; **58b,** Claudia Parks/Corbis; **60,** Ed Pritchard/Getty Images, Inc.; **61,** Richard Haynes; **62t,** Bill Marchel; **62b,** William Johnson/Stock Boston; **63t,** Gerben Oppermans/Getty Images, Inc.; **63m,** Nuridsany et Perennou/Photo Researchers, Inc.; **63b,** Phil Degginger/Bruce Coleman, Inc.; **64,** Jim Brandenburg/Minden Pictures; **66,** Scott Nielsen/Bruce Coleman, Inc.

Chapter 3
Pages 70–71, TSADO/NCDA/NOAA/Tom Stack & Associates; **71r,** Richard Haynes; **72t,** Russ Lappa; **72–73b,** Benjamin Lowy/Corbis; **75,** Gene Rhoden/Peter Arnold, Inc.; **79t,** Accuweather; **79bl,** Mike Chew/Corbis; **79br,** Getty Images Inc.; **80t,** Richard Haynes; **80b,** Peter Menzel; **82,** Warren Faidley/DRK Photo; **84 all,** The Granger Collection, NY; **85t,** North Wind Picture Archives; **85bl,** Roger de la Harpe/Dorling Kindersley; **85br,** Corbis; **87t,** NASA; **87b,** AP Photo/Ben Sklar; **88,** Reuters/Corbis; **89,** Reuters; **90,** Brownie Harris/Corbis; **92–93b,** Photo Researchers, Inc.; **93t,** Bob Daemmrich/Stock Boston; **94l,** European Space Agency/Science Photo Library/Photo Researchers, Inc.; **94r,** NASA/Goddard Space Flight Center; **100–101 background,** A. & J. Verkik/Corbis; **101 both,** ©UCAR; **102,** Richard Haynes.

Chapter 4
Pages 106–107, J. Bennett-Peter Arnold, Inc.; **107r,** Richard Haynes; **108t,** Richard Haynes; **108b,** David Muench Photography; **110,** David Madison/Bruce Coleman, Inc.; **113,** Steve McCurry/Magnum Photos; **114 both,** Bruce Coleman, Inc.; **116,** Richard Haynes; **118t,** Russ Lappa; **118–119b,** Royalty-Free/Corbis; **119t,** Getty Images, Inc.; **120l,** Bruce Forster/Getty Images Inc.; **120m,** Jess Stock/Getty Images, Inc.; **120r,** David Muench Photography; **121l,** Tom Till/DRK Photo; **121m,** Ragnar Th. Sigurdsson/Artic-Images; **121r,** David Muench Photography; **122l,** J. Cancalosi/DRK Photo; **122r,** Jeff Hunter/Getty Images, Inc.; **123,** Tom Bean/DRK Photo; **124,** Charlie Waite/Getty Images, Inc.; **125l,** Liz Hymans/Corbis; **125r,** DRK Photo; **126,** Bryan & Cherry Alexander/Artic-Images; **127,** Adam Jones/Photo Researchers, Inc.; **130,** George H.H. Huey; **131,** Tony Craddock/SPL/Photo Researchers, Inc.; **131 inset,** George Godfrey/Animals Animals/Earth Scenes; **135t,** Richard Haynes; **135b,** A. Ramey/PhotoEdit; **136 all,** NOAA; **138,** Anne Howard/Artic Images; **139l,** Larry Taylor; **139r,** Kent Syverson; **141 all,** TOMS; **142,** J. Cancalosi/DRK Photo.

Page 146, Bryan & Cherry Alexander/Artic Images; **147t,** The Granger Collection, NY; **147b,** AP/Wide World Photos; **148,** Ragnur Th. Sigurdsson/Artic-Images; **149,** Corbis; **150t,** Bettmann/Corbis; **150b,** Dorling Kindersley/New York Museum of Natural History; **150–151 background,** Masterfile; **151b,** Alaska Stock; **152,** Tony Freeman/PhotoEdit; **153t,** Russ Lappa; **153m,** Richard Haynes; **153b,** Russ Lappa; **154,** Richard Haynes; **156,** Richard Haynes; **158,** Tanton Yachts; **159,** Richard Haynes; **161t,** Dorling Kindersley; **161b,** Richard Haynes; **163,** Image Stop/Phototake; **166,** Richard Haynes; **173,** Richard Haynes; **175,** NASA; **176,** Warren Faidley/DRK Photo; **177,** William Johnson/Stock Boston.